New Art Writing:

Creating a Culture of Cyber Criticism

Jeanne S. M. Willette

Author of

The Writing of Cubism. The Construction of a Discourse, 1901-1914

Cover and Layout by Anthony Garcia

© AHS Publishing 2013

Introduction: The Field of Knowledge Production

As an alternative to the normal narrowed channels of academic publication, the Web is the great leveler of scholars and writers and academics and scientists. The Internet flattens the field of knowledge production, creating a plain where all offerings are assumed worthy until proven otherwise. In its destruction of traditional hierarchies, in its relentless demolition of authority, the Web is all the predictions of Postmodernism come true.[1] Here is where the metanarrative comes to die. Here is where the surface of pure effects lives. The Internet is the graveyard of control over discourse and the crypt of command over erudition and the tomb of binaries. Old definitions and ancient distinctions that once ruled the world of university life are now as extinct as the lumbering dinosaurs. But, in contrast to the fossilization of academia, the Web is also the birthplace of new ways of reading and writing and learning and dispensing knowledge and disseminating information—all of which escape the controls of those who would guard the intellectual territory and keep the gates of publication and promotion closed to all but the anointed few.[2] The Internet has the capacity to grow organically in a fashion that defies gates—where should one place a gate? And who would be the keepers?—in its conceptual vastness as it expands, like the universe, into the always open cyberspace.

Now, that the meteor of the Internet has fallen upon the preserves of academia and the once clear skies are darkening, the question has become: who will be the survivors and what will be the shape of the world to come? As the post-impact clouds of privilege rise and disperse into the historical air, Cyberspace has become the new site where intellectual content is produced. Under a mode of production that leaps from text to text with giant hyper strides, a new form of free and open discourse, an exchange of knowledge among peers and equals, has emerged. Such imaginative "writerly" leaps from node to node are possible because the "field" of content production has changed its texture, from a mountain top home of those who ruled from on high to a system of knots that link strings which create a net with tantalizing spaces waiting to be filled in, even by those from the flatlands.[3]

Such a landscape is a new-found paradise for all of us who write, who create, and who reach audiences with our thoughts and words by composing the books we wish we could read. For those of us in the arts, the most hidebound and the most exclusionary of intellectual fields, the Internet has created a New Paradigm of production and publication and promises a democratization of knowledge that has the potential to rupture the historical boundaries and rules of the Old Paradigm. The Net is a natural destination for people who believe in the free distribution of intellectual capital and who are dubious of the old-fashioned practice of hoarding symbolic capital.[4] But sadly there is an entire contingent of thinkers in university and college communities who are reluctant to partake of the new freedoms for intellectuals on the Internet.[5] It is as if some of the best minds in the world—especially in the humanities—are not only reluctant to participate in this new field of Internet content production but are also discouraging free thinkers from straying off the reservations of received customs of command and control.[6]

It should be stated at the outset that the Old Paradigm—of Submitting and Waiting for Acceptance, of Subjugation to the Peer Review—in order to Publish intellectual work in print for a small and limited academic audience is a hard and arduous path to take.[7] Such a process, and this is a process that is, if nothing else, is, as they say, "time-honored," demands tremendous patience and a strong psychological constitution. Those who survive and thrive are to be celebrated, if for their ability to endure years of suspense and suffering and rejection in order to publish now and then over a period of many years. However meritorious its original intent—and this so-called merit system is a product of the seventeenth century[8]—the Old Paradigm is flawed at its heart.[9] There is no way to know empirically if the "best" works, books or articles, are published. There is no empirical way of measuring the "quality" of writing either published or unpublished. There is no way to be sure "peer review" is not a system of intellectual nepotism.[10] Many a "war story" can be told of a book not published because this book did not conform to the norm and many tales can be related of reviewers who were incompetent [11] and unknowledgeable of the very subject under consideration.[12] And yet the peer review system limps on because nothing else—it is claimed—has been invented to take the place of the Old Paradigm.[13]

The New Paradigm of open source/open access Web publication has already arrived. The Peer Review is the Internet audience.[14] Unlike the Old Paradigm, where the writer can be protected by the journal and its name and by the one or two reviewers who have read the work, the Web Writer is exposed, not to a small audience of like-minded readers or an audience of producers, but is opened to an infinitely larger group of reviewers—the Internet audience. Whatever the merits or demerits of the New Paradigm, this new system offers an alternative form of publication especially to a younger group of scholars who face an uncertain future in a world of dwindling job prospects in colleges and universities[15] and diminishing opportunities in a faltering publishing business.[16] Those who have profited most from the Old Paradigm hesitate to face, not the future, but the living, breathing present.[17] The question is how long can this reluctance to engage with the Net continue within the university community before this group of writers who explore so many fields and who have so much to contribute fall so far out of step that they are no longer relevant?[18] The refusal to engage will be a costly one, stunting disciplines and ossifying entire fields of study and condemning a new generation of scholars publishing for the dusty shelves of libraries where no one browses anymore.

Thanks to an ever-improving technology of information circulation, with a new computer savvy generation of students and scholars and readers, the instinctive first "move" in the game of research and writing is to reach for the search engine of choice. Typing in keywords into a search bar has taken the place of browsing through the card catalogue and perusing the shelves of a library.[19] Indeed, it is possible that the time to change has come and gone, and a valuable opportunity has been lost. The older generation has stubbornly held onto the Old Ways and perhaps it is best that they stay where they feel comfortable because the Web is no place for those who are of an obedient nature and who like to follow rules and obey orders and eschew innovative ways of thinking. And it is equally likely that the Old Ones will be left behind by the younger generation of intellectuals who will engage fully in cyberspace.[20] If this is the case, then how will this new mode of production, Web writing and Web reading, powered by links, change intellectual writing? What will the Internet look like once it becomes the unlikely home of the New Public Intellectual?[21]

Theory and the Web

To suggest that the Internet constitutes a new form of the production and distribution of knowledge is to imply a delivery system that is a new genre of media, a new form of communication, a new way in which discourses evolve and dissolve. And if this conclusion that there is now a new form of knowledge production is correct and empirical evidence of this assertion can be easily obtained by simply logging on, then this new system of discursive formation and content production needs to be theorized. But Cyberspace is inherently resistant to theory. Not only can the Internet not be contained nor corralled nor gated, it is also resistant to theorizing.[22] On one hand, it is possible to perform comparisons based on what can be termed a "morphological affinity," in other words, if there are elements in the Web that seem to resemble the ideas of a particular theorist, then these similarities can be matched up. On the other hand, the exercise is a rather crude one, risking a surface analysis, when a comparison of structures or functionality might be more appropriate. So far academics and traditional intellectuals of the university community have circled around the Internet warily, often falling back upon tried and true ways in which various postmodern theorists are introduced by academics out to "explain" the Web.[23]

The problem for attempting to apply critical theory to the Internet is that the object of study is a phenomenon fundamentally different from modern philosophy and eludes the Metanarrative of the Enlightenment.[24] The Web is just that—a web that conceptually stretches beyond the peripheral vision of the theorist. Modernist and Postmodern theories have always engaged with Western culture and its philosophical heritage from the eighteenth century, but the Internet is as boundless as it is aimless and timeless and its culture and heritage comes from the worlds of science and technology and is based upon sharing, not protecting, knowledge.[25] Enlightenment philosophy emerged out of a shared faith in something called progress, which implies a forward movement towards a desired end. With its purpose constantly mutating and its refusal to consider either teleology or end point, the Web presents an interesting challenge to philosophy and tempts further investigation of possible theoretical study. Perhaps the difficulty of discussing the Internet as anything other than a constantly evolving roiling complex of churning information is the reason why an entire generation of scholars and writers in the humanities have not only turned their backs on the future[26] but are also "forbidding" the younger generation from participating as scholars, researchers, and as writers on the Internet.[27]

One of the more intriguing aspects of Postmodern theory from the sixties and the seventies was the way in which certain theorists foresaw a new "postmodern" or post-Enlightenment culture, open and free for all, rootless, unable to be mapped but available for exploration.[28] And certainly many postmodern theorists seemed very prescient in their insights about the implications of Postmodernism for the future.[29] If postmodern theorists were predictors of a post-postmodern culture that eventually upended postmodern theory itself, then what traces of these once-vaunted theories still remain in the still-twitching body of all things "post?" As the prominent sociologist George Ritzer[30] pointed out at the "Theorizing the Web Conference" of 2011, modern social theory has not been used as a theorizing tool for the Internet and its productions.[31]

Speaking on "Why the Web Needs Postmodern Theory," Ritzer pointed out that postmodern theorists, such as Jean Baudrillard, "anticipated" what is now the virtual reality or the simulacra of the Internet. Ritzer claimed that postmodern social theory was better understood in Europe than in America where, I would add, "theory" was more discussed in seminars than put into activist practice. Baudrillard died in 2007 and lived long enough to witness his predictions of a postmodern dystopian society come to pass. Indeed it is easier for us to read and understand his most important works today than when he wrote them thirty years ago. When published in 1983, *Simulations* and its opening paragraphs sounded like theoretical poetry; in the twenty-first century, the same words read like today's weather report:

> Today abstraction is no longer that of the map, the double, the mirror, or the concept. Simulation is no longer that of a territory, a referential being, or a substance. It is the generation by models of a real without origin or reality: a hyper real. The territory no longer precedes the map, nor does it survive it. It is nevertheless the map that precedes the territory - precession of simulacra - that engenders the territory, and if one must return to the fable, today it is the territory whose shreds slowly rot across the extent of the map. It is the real, and not the map, whose vestiges persist here and there in the deserts that are no longer those of the Empire, but ours. The desert of the real itself.[32]

When Baudrillard remarked that, "We live in a world where there is more and more information, and less and less meaning,"[33] he understood that Marshall McLuhan's famous dictate, "The Medium is the Message"[34] was already outdated. In a footnote to his section on "The Implosion of Meaning in the Media," Baudrillard theorized on the intersection between the computer and information:

> Here we have not spoken of information except in the social register of communication. But it would be enthralling to consider this hypothesis even within the parameters of cybernetic information theory. There also, the fundamental thesis calls for this information to be synonymous with negentropy with the resistance to entropy, with an excess of meaning and organization.[35]

Rather than the foretold implosion feared by Baudrillard, the explosion of information on the Internet has only increased the appetite for "content" which is now more of a place than an entity, a place where the real and the unreal and the non-real collide and careen.[36] Oddly Baudrillard did not immediately take to the Internet where meaning becomes absorbed into simulacra of the hyper real.[37] In a 1996 interview with Claude Thibaut, he stated that he did not like working with computers and commented on the future of the Internet, then in its infancy,

> Certainly, because it is the system of representation that is at issue. The image that he has of himself is virtualized. One is no longer in front of the mirror; one is in the screen, which is entirely different. One finds himself in a problematic universe, one hides in the network, that is, one is no longer anywhere. What is fascinating and exercises such an attraction is perhaps less the search for information or the thirst for knowledge than the desire to disappear, the possibility of dissolving and disappearing into the network.[38]

Baudrillard, like other postmodern theorists, was certainly correct to be concerned about the fate of "reality" caught within the system of representation as inherited from the period of modernism and disinherited by postmodernism.[39] The problem of representation is now most acute in the exploding world of mass media, rapidly leaving traditional print and broadcast media behind in the rear view mirror of blogs and the Twitter-verse. If it is accepted that representation is in and of itself an ideology and not some kind of "reflection" of a "truth," then what happened with mass media on the Web is that representation has lost any connection with a controlling force, whether a government or a corporation, that might manufacture a unified overarching ideology for society. On the Internet, representation (discourse) has been given over to disparate individuals controlled by no one. But this new lack of coherence has allowed some commentators to be propelled by new and multiple viewpoints and ideologies, which have become unmoored from "facts." We exist we are told in a "post-fact society,"[40] possibly that which was foretold in postmodern theory and its presumed "inherent" relativity.[41] But what was unforeseen by the postmodern theorists was the concurrent rise of so-called "fact checkers" and the resulting and unpredictable fascination with searching for the "truth," a sentimental notion that facts should be based soundly in provable and discernible evidence.[42] The point is that for those who imagine the Internet as a place of simulacra and implosion,[43] the Web, as a no-place, has become an open space where an antithesis will immediately rise to counter the thesis and the post-facts will be faced by the facts of the checkers.

For these past decades of the Web, we have been living either in a Baudrillardian nightmare or a Baudrillardian utopia—the philosopher himself could not decide, but he proscribed resistance.[44] But what does "resistance" to the system, as Baudrillard put it, mean in terms of the Internet? Resistance or the antithesis to the dominant system has always assumed a locus of power or a central thesis to combat.[45] In fact, our very language is based upon oppositions and binaries that have conditioned our thinking.[46] But the Web is not a binary system; it is a "web" or a network of contributions (posts), a proliferation of conversations, implying an infinite expansion and infinite connections among discourses. When returning to Baudrillard's appropriation of a scientific term, "negentropy," a process that enables a living organism to perpetuate itself, it is possible to conceptualize the Web as a growing organism, inherently resistant to entropy or death or a finality of means and ends. But the philosopher did not live long enough to pursue significance of negentropy to the Net.

To imagine the Internet as a connective tissue, constantly expanding and creating multiple functions, is to understand that the Web is like Michel Foucault's concept of modern power without the controlling *pouvoir*, only the *voir* and the *savoir*.[47] An entity unto itself, the Internet is the ultimate Panopticon in which the terrifying concept has been inverted: there is no "inspector" or overseer and unlike the Jeremy Bentham's original plan, all the inmates can see each other.[48] Even the most oppressive regimes, those most obsessed with power are hard-pressed in a wired society to control the uncontrollable, growing, writhing Web that twists and turns like a thwarted plant, seeking purchase and light, desiring always to expand. In nations such as China,[49] Iran and Pakistan, people hide, not from each other, but from the government, and instead, seek, sometimes valiantly, to make connections and to share information with each other in the anonymity of Cyberspace.[50]

What all users of the Internet seek is revelation or what visionary architect Jeremy Bentham called a "through light," a tearing down of the imaginary partitions so lovingly detailed by the eighteenth century theorist of architecture of discipline.[51] Based on the stand-off between the hope of the Enlightenment and the pessimism of post-war disillusionment born of the smoking ruins of Hiroshima and Nagasaki, modernist and postmodernist theory is ill-equipped to deal with the Web,[52] which consists of a quilt of autonomous discourses, most of them independent, self-started, self-financed and free-floating.[53] In contrast, "knowledge" has traditionally been assumed to be a locatable body of discourses, organized in a certain fashion for a particular purpose, whether it be in order to construct a national identity or to speculate on the nature of the universe, etc. with each discourse rotating in its separate and easily locatable sphere.[54] Starting with his influential book, *The Archaeology of Knowledge*, Michel Foucault formulated a widely respected concept of "discourse" or a specific body of knowledge built over time on what became over time a particular subject or topic of study. In relation to the Internet and its permeable non-borders, Foucault's early statement on discourse is of special relevance today. As he stated,

> Disciplines constitute a system of control in the production of discourse, fixing its limits through the action of an identity taking the form of a permanent reactivation of the rules. We tend to see, in an author's fertility, in the multiplicity of commentaries and in the development of the discipline so many infinite resources available for the creation of discourse. Perhaps so, but they are nonetheless principles of constraint, and it is probably impossible to appreciate their positive multiplicatory role without first taking into consideration their restrictive, constraining role...it is more a question of determining the conditions under which it may be employed, or imposing a certain number of rules upon those individuals who employ it, thus denying access to everyone else. This amounts to a rarefication among speaking subjects: none may enter into discourse on a specific subject unless he has satisfied certain conditions or if he is not, from the outset, qualified to do so. More exactly, not all areas of discourse are equally open and penetrable; some are forbidden territory...[55]

Foucault repeatedly used words such as "control," "fixing," "rules," "constraint," "restrictive," "constraining," and "forbidden" to explain how discourse are formed—through deliberate limitation of knowledge. What can and cannot be said constitutes the "truth," or something that passes for truth. These published and public texts are/were written by academic or scientific experts, trained and educated through consecrated and legitimate channels, vetted and validated by other experts, and are/were allowed to enter into open circulation only via proscribed institutional portals.[56] Through the collective efforts of institutional control, this intellectual knowledge, shaped for the purposes of maintaining a power structure, became a series of discourses, and, arguably, only a fraction of the aspirants to a given field were/are recognized as being worthy of admitted into the Meta Presence of the controlled terrain of the Meta Narrative.[57]

The Web, in contrast to the traditional methods by which something called "knowledge," is collected and displayed and largely remains free of external forces which might seek to patrol its precincts. Although Internet discourse would seem to be a cacophony of voices, these singular acts of Web-speech tend to coalesce into loose groupings that share similar interests or share the same Google page, if based only upon a single key word or tag or a series of links.[58] One of the central tenets of Foucault's concept of discourse is that the formation of the discourse is in and of itself is a form of "violence" due to the very system of rule and regulation which links power with knowledge.[59] For Foucault, the power-knowledge is inherently and inescapably "transgressive," meaning that the will to truth is a transgression against power-knowledge. If transgression is a pushing against the limits of what can be said on the part of those who may have been silenced speaking of that which the prevailing discourse has forbidden, then, in Foucault's world, there is no real way out of the system. If control breeds transgression, then transgression is the inevitable outcome of repression and cannot escape the bounds of constriction but twists back upon itself. But the Web allows its players to slip through the gates of discourse and to commit the ultimate transgression:[60] freely forming discourses through free gifts of knowledge.[61]

The Internet has been shaped by a simple ethos or ethic, which is that of democratic equality of opportunity and access. The Web is a shared space where Capitalism and Communism, Commodities and Gift-Giving, or what Marcel Mauss called "pure irrational expenditure," coexist in an open and uncontrolled territory.[62] The aspect of the Web that is of most concern for this book is the free exchange of information and the accumulation of new forms of maintaining the circulation of knowledge that eludes all efforts at external control.[63] As Mauss stated, there are certain societies that have a system of gift-giving that entail responsibilities:

> To appreciate fully the institutions of total prestation and the potlatch we must seek to explain two complementary factors. Total prestation not only carries with it the obligation to repay gifts receiver, but it implies two others equally important: the obligation to give presents and the obligation to receive them.[64]

For Mauss, gift giving takes place in a fixed and often ritually based social ceremony.[65] The display of "giving" is part of a social fabric connecting a tribe in a shared exchange that is reciprocity without any necessary obligation. As Mauss wrote,

> ...there is a series of rights and duties about consuming and repaying existing side by side with rights and duties about giving and receiving. The pattern of symmetrical and reciprocal rights is not difficult to understand if we realize that it is first and foremost a pattern of spiritual bonds between things which are to some extent parts of persons, and persons and groups that behave in some measure as if they were things.[66]

In critiquing Mauss seven decades later,[67] Jacques Derrida removed the gift from the system of economic exchange, not only as expenditure but also as intent on the part of the giver—a gift is not a gift unless one expects nothing in return. In fact, Mauss's very use of the term "prestation," which is defined as payment or toll or as a duty, makes Derrida's critique even more interesting. Indeed he argued that if the gift is part of a giving ceremony or a social exchange of something, it must enter into the realm of the economy. If Derrida is correct and that a true gift must be forgotten (by the giver) over time, then the Web is a place where gifts are offered regardless of the fact that there is an absence of any system of exchange.[68] A post on the Internet is an oddly altruistic gesture, a freely executed act perhaps in the Derridian tradition of the gift.[69] That said, traditional critical theory assumes ownership or property rights and rarely discusses the Potlatch economy or a gift-giving culture, except as an intellectual exercise, such as Derrida's critique of the writing of another writer who wrote of long-extinct cultures. But over time, long after critical theory was developed in the decades after the Second World War, the Internet has become a place of potlatch where people expect to be educated and informed[70] through "gifts" of knowledge.

And the gift, left like an abandoned child, exposed on a hill, is picked up by an unknown receiver, who makes the offering his or her own possession. The consumer of information is free to pick and chose and select according to his or her purpose or needs and whereas the reciprocity of this gift-giving society is rarely precisely even, it equals out across a wide spectrum—one "takes" from here but later one "gives" to there.[71] The result is a "conversation" among contributors, most who do not know and will never know with whom they are communicating. The significance of this new kind of "communication" is that a new group of self-designated newly minted "experts" are self-creating and self-identifying themselves and are self-building new sites of knowledge.[72] And if, conceivably, these alternative locales could be the case, then the Foucauldian concept of an Archive naturally comes to mind. When Michel Foucault described his concept of the Archive in *The Archaeology of Knowledge*,[73] he (and he was famous for this) said more about what the Archive was not than what it was.

According to Foucault (leaving out his negatives), the Archive is

> ...the system of discursivity...the enunciative possibilities and impossibilities that it lays down. The archive is the first law of what can be said, the system that governs the appearance of statements as unique events...

In other words, the Archive is not a library or a section in a library or part of an institution; the archive is the *system* that allows statements and therefore can be conceived of as an accumulation of acceptable statements. Foucault continued,

> ...the archive defines a particular level: that of a practice that causes a multiplicity of statements to emerge as so many regular events...It is the *general system of the formation and transformation of statements*. (Italics Foucault's)[74]

The Internet is in and in of itself a new type of archive, in that is both a system and an anti-system. It "governs" what can be said only in terms of requiring that the participants learn the rules of the game or acquire the necessary *habitus*. But beneath Foucault's philosophy, as is true of other postmodern philosophers, there is an assumption of a lurking power, hiding in the wings: "law" "system" and "governs" are words that imply the existence of controlling mechanisms. The role of philosophy has been to define "knowledge" or the epistemology of what constitutes knowledge or knowing, i.e., the ability to judge what knowledge is. However, this historical approach to epistemology or the grounds of knowledge may be too theoretical or too detached from the twenty-first century methods of circulation of productive information, which is commensurate to knowledge. And what precisely would happen to knowledge once it could be placed and found on computers was the task entrusted to Jean-François Lyotard in 1979, long before the birth of the World Wide Web.

Paralogy and the Web

If there is any scholar who produced a coherent and still-viable theory of the web, then it would be the pioneering postmodernist, Jean-François Lyotard, who was arguably the first of the philosophers to theorize the Web. When Lyotard wrote *The Postmodern Condition. A Report on Knowledge* in 1979, his brief was to project or conjecture, without, as he put it, practicing "futurology," the future of knowledge in an increasingly technological society. At the edge of a world that would, in twenty years, be dominated by the widespread use of personal computers, Lyotard could only include computers, as one among many of the factors that were changing knowledge. But he saw clearly that technology would free knowledge from the academic constraints and state controls that had both constrained freedom of thought and contained participation in production to those who were properly legitimated. Indeed, Lyotard, who was writing specifically in reaction to the new kind of "knowledge in computerized societies," said,

> Knowledge is and will be produced in order to be sold; it is and will be consumed in order to be valorized in a new production: in both cases, the goal is exchange.
> Knowledge ceases to be an end in itself; it loses its "use-value."[75]

In such a computerized marketplace, there can be no metanarrative because the goal is not to converge knowledge but to exchange data. It follows that without a metanarrative; there can be no center.[76] Indeed, the Internet lacks center and could be described as Derrida wrote, "...the moment when, in the absence of a center or origin, everything became discourse..."[77] At the time Lyotard wrote of the demise of the metanarrative, most intellectuals had only the dimmest notions of computers were[78] and could also not have imagined the extent to which the philosopher's predictions for how information would be disseminated in the future would come to fruition.[79] Academics interpreted Lyotard within the boundaries of philosophy, specifically epistemology, and the breakdown of the metanarrative was understood as a fragmentation of the *grand récit* and not as the mechanism of distribution, or what became known as the Internet. Writing in 2009, William Martin described the outcome or what he termed the "posthuman condition:"

> In his later lectures on The Inhuman, however, Lyotard recognizes that the growing information network becomes capable of directly socializing subjects to the techno-scientific system, such that the "performativity" of individuals becomes a measure of their adaptation to this new informational environment. Taking into account this change of perspective, I will use the term "posthuman condition" to refer to the state of society in which individuals are directly socialized to the techno-scientific system by means of their performance of operations that not only draw on the resources of the information network but also contribute to its expansion.[80]

Knowledge, under this "inhuman" (as Lyotard expressed it) regime is no longer controlled by institutions but is performed by the speakers and therefore becomes "performative."[81] The players in this new "language game" must possess *savoir-faire* or know how. In other words, one learns how to play this new game or how to perform to its specifications. In addition to his famous opening phrase defining postmodernism as "incredulity towards metanarratives," Lyotard also stated flatly,

> Postmodern knowledge is not simply a tool of the authorities; it refines our sensitivity to differences and reinforces our ability to tolerate the incommensurable. Its principle is not the expert's homology, but the inventor's paralogy.[82]

Remember that Lyotard was referring to belief systems, rather than to any specific narrative. In other words, computerization is that which "performs." We call "paralogy" by another name: "little narratives" or disruptive discourses that interject themselves into the "grand narratives."[83] And little narratives always decenter the universe of scientific (academic) authority, because suddenly the emphasis is on difference, distinction, and deviations.[84] Lyotard borrowed the term "paralogy," which is not necessarily "innovation," from science and equates this local counter narrative to a "move" in a language game. Such "moves" and such "games" are related to consensus and power—or an agreement to play by the rules. As he explained,

> Countless scientists have seen their move ignored or repressed, sometimes for decades, because it too abruptly destabilized the accepted positions not only in the university and scientific hierarchy, but also in the problematic. The stronger the "move" the more likely it is to be denied the minimum consensus, precisely because it changes the rules of the game upon which consensus has been based. But when the institution of knowledge functions in this manner, it is acting like and ordinary power center whose behavior is governed by a principle of homeostasis. Such behavior is terrorist...By terror I mean the efficiency gained by eliminating or threatening to eliminate a player form the language game one shares with him. He is silenced or consensus, not because he has been refuted, but because his ability to participate has been threatened (there are many ways to prevent someone from playing). The decision makers' arrogance, which in principle has no equivalent in the sciences, consists in the exercise of terror. It says: "Adapt your aspirations to our end—or else."

Lyotard ends the remarkable section on paralogy by imagining two ends for "the computerization of society:" "It" and by "it" Lyotard means knowledge disseminated by computers could be "governed exclusively by the performativity principle. In that case it would inevitably involve terror." Or, he suggested,

> "...give the public free access to the memory and data banks. Language games would then be games of perfect information at any given moment...This sketches the outline of a politics that would respect both the desire for justice and the desire for the unknown."[85]

Paralogy, as a term purloined from Lyotard, refuses unity or coherence and in this refusal becomes disruptive to any implied metanarrative. Although he did not live to see the fruition of the Internet (as it currently exists today), Lyotard arrived at the point where he had to consider "the problem of the legitimation of knowledge" when "we no longer have recourse to the grand narratives" and when "the little narrative (*petit récit*) remains the quintessential form of imaginative invention." For the purposes of this book, it is interesting that Lyotard noted that when consensus, which is a dialogue or an agreement, could no longer be obtained, and that if consensus was "an instrument to be used toward achieving the real goal, which is what legitimates the system—power" then a problem emerges. "The problem," Lyotard continued," is therefore to determine whether it is possible to have a form of legitimation based solely on paralogy."[86]

Paralogy—alternative narrative or conflicting stories—is so disruptive that it is fiercely resisted by intellectual authorities, but paralogy is simply a new way of thinking or a different way of taking the old (language) game and searching out its inherent instabilities. To speak of paralogy and the Internet is to describe a breaking away or a breaking out of a restrictive system I think of as the Field of Intellectual Production, where the "production" was deliberately restricted. The paralogy of cyberspace is that explosion of little narratives shattering the globe of the *grand récit*. Because for our purposes, the Web is the site of unrestricted free play, certainly the most important binary to fall by the wayside of hyperlinking should be the highly influential "margin/center" relationship, in an echo of Yeats,[87] the center does not hold.[88] These changes—the innovations of paralogy, which displace a center, reflect the postmodern mash-up of the producer and the consumer into the "prosumer," or as Jay Rosen expressed it, the audience becomes a participant, contributing to media. "The people formerly known as the audience"[89] are talking back, going from scribbling notes in the margins of printed books to writing their own blogs, seizing the means of production of culture, all thanks to the openness of the Web. Technology has redefined "knowledge."

As Lyotard wrote,

> The nature of knowledge cannot survive unchanged within this context of general transformation. It can fit

> into the new channels, and become operational, only if
> learning is translated into quantities of information…"
> Along with the hegemony of computers comes a certain
> kind of logic, and therefore a certain set of prescriptions
> determining which statements are accepted as
> "knowledge" statements. We may thus expect a
> thorough exteriorisation of knowledge with respect to
> the "knower," at whatever point he or she may occupy in
> the knowledge process. The old principle that the
> acquisition of knowledge is indissociable from the
> training (*Bildung*) of minds, or even of individuals, is
> becoming obsolete and will become ever more so. The
> relationships of the suppliers and users of knowledge to
> the knowledge they supply and use is now tending, and
> will increasingly tend, to assume the form already taken
> by the relationship of commodity producers and
> consumers to the commodities they produce and
> consume – that is, the form of value. Knowledge is and
> will be produced in order to be sold, it is and will be
> consumed in order to be valorised in a new production:
> in both cases, the goal is exchange.[90]

When knowledge becomes what Lyotard called "an informational commodity," the issue that results from these changes in knowledge production is that of legitimation. Indeed in his Introduction to *The Postmodern Condition*, Lyotard defined Postmodern as "incredulity towards metanarratives." This "crisis" of metanarratives is also a crisis for the universities, which have relied upon these metanarratives, and when these institutions are confronted with Lyotards's paralogy."[91] The fall back position is resistance. And so paralogy is the position of the academic on the Web, the situation of the scholar on the Internet, an escapee from institutional "silencing." The Cyber writer is someone who changes the rules of the game, or to be more precise, has elected to opt out of the game as it is currently (and anachronistically) being played and has made another "move" swerving away from discourse as usual. As Ian Angus pointed out in *The Critical Turn: Rhetoric and Philosophy in Postmodern Discourse*,

> Lyotard proposes a local form of criticism that he terms
> "paralogy"…Whereas innovation is a move within the
> language game as constituted—or a continuing of the
> conversation in Rorty's sense—paralogy is the proposal
> of new norms for understanding, an utterance that shifts
> the rules whereby new utterances are produced. The

> production of paralogy is always in response to a local situation and disturbs existing consensus...[92]

In retrospect, Lyotard becomes a figure, somewhat like Baudrillard, who is better understood in the present than in the past, now that we have arrived at the future they wrote of but could not experience. Lyotard understood knowledge to be a form of "know-how" or competence, which in the postmodern era is performative knowledge. Although the commentators on Lyotard, to this day, rarely[93] discuss the link between postmodernism, knowledge, and computers, Lyotard, himself, ends his book by connecting computers with language games. In 1979 with remarkable perceptiveness he wrote,

> We are finally in a position to understand how the computerization of a society affects this problematic. It could become the "dream" instrument for controlling and regulating the market system, extended to include knowledge itself and governed exclusively by the performativity principle. In that case, it would inevitably involve the use of terror. But it could also aid groups discussing metaprescriptives by supplying them with the information they usually lack for making knowledge decisions. The line to follow for computerization to take the second of these two paths is, in principle, quite simple: give the public free access to the memory and data banks. Language games would then be games of perfect information at any given moment. But they would also be zero-sum games, and by virtue of that fact discussion would never risk fixating in a position of minimax equilibrium because it had exhausted its stakes. For the stakes would be knowledge (or information, if you will), and the reserve of knowledge—language's reserve of possible utterances—is in exhaustible. This sketches the outline of a politics hat would respect both the desire for justice and the desire for the unknown.[94]

The production of a newly defined knowledge also raises Lyotard's question as to whether or not the traditional educator could survive the computerized system of dissemination. As Lyotard noted,

> The process of delegitimation and the predominance of the performance criterion are sounding the knell of the age of the Professor: a professor is no more competent than memory bank networks in transmitting established

knowledge, nor more competent than interdisciplinary teams in imagining new moves or new games.[95]

Once again, Lyotard foresaw the logical consequences of what is essentially a more efficient delivery system: the professor can never be as fulsome as the computer which is always a creature of surplus and excess. Today, we are eye-witnesses to his prediction coming true and will live to see the demise of the college professor, except perhaps at the graduate level or in studios or labs.[96] As primitive as Massive Open On-Line Courses are at this moment,[97] they are the future of education, both higher and lower. There will be a debate between those who think of "education" as being about interacting people—students and teachers—and those who think that education is only about "knowledge" no matter how or who distributes it. Thanks to computerized education, students of MOOCs are able to talk across cultures to each other, and it is their conversations that become part of the course in question, contributing spontaneously to "knowledge." In this new Internet model "conversations" among a multiple of participants create and become "knowledge."

Conversations, Artifacts and the Web

In America, the Internet has become a site of "conversations" where all participants are entitled to speak.[98] Of special interest here are those public conversations, which are serious speech utterances and the sheer willingness to enter into the digital public square and stand on the speaker's soapbox give some level of credence to the speaker. What is different about Web "speaking" is that fact that there are few if any gatekeepers controlling the discourse.[99] There are judges and judgments, yes, but the desire to contribute overcomes, for most writers, the fear of criticism and scorn. The human need to socialize and to communicate and to contribute can be fully expressed on the Internet.[100]

I will return to the trope of conversations later, but first it is necessary to investigate the epistemology of the Internet. If we think of the Internet as a gigantic ever-expanding bulletin board, then anything from homegrown pornography to directions on how to apply make-up to PDFs of books by famous scholars can be pinned and posted to the spaceless corkboard of cyberspace.[101] And this outpouring of democratization on the Web and its torrential discourses were not precisely predicted by postmodern theory and are entirely new, being out of the scope and out of the reach of twentieth century concepts.[102] Rather than think of the digital universe as a means of representation or as yet another skirmish between power groups, it might be more satisfying to reconsider the Internet as a new form of knowledge, beginning with how this "knowledge," or form of knowing, thinking and archiving information, comes into being.[103]

In the past, such consensus on the nature of "knowledge" would be the result of "conversations" that would be held among academic professionals with credentials, such as philosophers, but postmodern philosophy left behind the old-fashioned Socratic method and shifted to an exchange among equals, similar to what is taking place on the Internet. Traditional philosophy, from Socrates to Plato to Aristotle to Kant to Marx,[104] centered upon questions of epistemology, or the grounds of knowledge. But in the twenty-first century, while the Kantian position that the mind structures incoming data into understandable thoughts has been largely accepted, epistemological questions can be shifted from the grounds of human reason to the foundation of "knowledge" in a more literal fashion: how, in the twenty-first century, is knowledge identified, accumulated, assembled and distributed? Or to be more precise, how, in the twenty-first century, is knowledge defined?

In a very influential 2000 essay, John Willinsky explained the way knowledge was/would be produced and named through Web productivity in his "Knowledge Exchange Model:"

> The Knowledge Exchange Model (KEM) presented here is designed to return the emphasis of scholarly publishing to its original exchange economy. It employs peer-to-peer communication at the institutional level of the research library—with its paramount concern for the organization and conservation of this knowledge—while retaining those publishing services that improve the quality of the research. This exchange would be managed through a global system of research libraries and learned societies. Economically, this model seeks to demonstrate that redirecting a substantial portion of the research library's current serial acquisitions budget to building and sustaining this, or a variation on this, exchange model will not only improve the scholarly quality of this research knowledge but will, at very little extra cost, afford free universal access to what is, after all, claimed to be a public good. This is, then, a model for fostering scholarly exchange and public education.[105]

It is interesting that Willinsky uses the idea of "exchange" as opposed to the notion that the old-fashioned peer review system was also a "marketplace of ideas."[106] More and more, certain scholars who have realized that time and technology have changed the game of how ideas are marketed are coming forward and restating the question of what is knowledge and how is information to be properly disseminated? Today, for all practical purposes, information is considered to be knowledge and vice versa. On the Internet, knowledge is produced, constantly, through information systems or through systems in which information is exchanged and shared and augmented and distributed and over the course of the process is transformed into consensus, which then acquires the status of "knowledge."[107]

The knowledge system of the Web is distinct from the model of the university philosopher, whose task it is to delve into theories of knowledge, and is more practical and less bounded by a disciplinary framework because the cyber networks of information are communal and open. The Internet has reframed and redefined knowledge but, decades ago, philosophy intuited the concept that knowledge/information would become a system or what Brian Whitworth and Rob Friedman call Knowledge Exchange Systems,[108] which are defined as

> ...any dynamic system, print or electronic that innovates, discriminates and disseminates knowledge. The overall goal is to contribute to knowledge growth, so a knowledge exchange system can be likened to an orchard whose "fruit" is research...Dissemination in turn results in creating both more new ideas and new critical challenges to correctness...the academic publishing system today is focused not on growth but on selection, which has reduced its creative and educational roles. This outdated "gatekeeper" model, based partly on traditional print culture, as produced a system "under siege" from an increasing number of applicants seeking its benefits. Academics are finding themselves knowledge gatekeepers using rigor to defend elite knowledge castles, rather than what we believe they should be: *knowledge gardeners.*[109]

The phrase "knowledge gardeners" brings to mind the Garden of Eden where the Tree of Knowledge bloomed untouched until the transgressive humans brazenly plucked its fruits.[110] The Bible implies that those humans, Adam and Eve, took it upon themselves to produce knowledge, stealing the power of God to speak, and to create discourses. These post-Fall antediluvian discourses certainly began as a series of "conversations" between the damned couple who have consumed knowledge (the fruit) and who have become the vintners of knowledge. These errant sinners escaped Omnipotent control by slipping past the Gates of the Garden and *nouveau* gatekeepers have been re-erecting barriers ever since. Whitworth and Friedman[111] have tempted us to reconsider the intersection between the sin of absconding with (forbidden) knowledge and the freedom of thought at the site of Knowledge Exchange.

It is at this precise point of consumers of knowledge or information becoming producers of knowledge or information that traditional theories of media break down. The received wisdom on these theories was based upon audiences being constructed by the hyper-real of mass media, which created a collective consciousness. In contrast to the passive audience, as media critic Mark Poster asserted, the Internet is "underdetermined."[112] The "under-determination" Poster discussed implies that the Internet as a pure machine and its users as independent entities are both displaced from the mechanisms of history, while at the same time are being determined by the capabilities of technology. The author, writing in 2001, correctly warned that anything written about the Web was bound to change and in the past twelve years that Cyber audience has only become more active, more focused and more out of control.[113] The real question, rarely addressed in academia, is that of the breakdown of authority, as the audiences become agents rather than being acted upon or "over-determined" What happens next?

The answer, as with Lyotard, lies in the predictive past, with the concept of "conversations" as philosophy put forward by Richard Rorty in 1979, a year that saw the publications of *The Postmodern Condition* and *Philosophy as the Mirror of Nature*. If, as seems the case, it is the audience who is creating/constructing its own Collective Consciousness, then the perspective on the Internet should be shifted away from the grounds of the "simulacra" or the "hyper real" and should be moved towards the notion of the Web as an "archive" consisting of "continuing conversations." As philosopher Richard Rorty put it,

> To see keeping a conversation going as a sufficient aim of philosophy, to see wisdom as consisting in the ability to sustain a conversation, is to see human beings as generators of new descriptions rather than beings one hopes to be able to describe accurately...The point is always the same—to perform the social function which Dewey called "breaking the crust of convention," preventing man from deluding himself with the notion that he knows himself, or anything else, except under optional descriptions.[114]

Rorty was the heir to American pragmatism and moved away from philosophy as epistemology or philosophy as a form of "knowing" to an acknowledgement of what he called "abnormal discourse" or discourse which does not conform to the expected scientific or philosophical norms. Towards the end of *Philosophy and the Mirror of Nature,* Rorty wrote, "...we are well on the way to seeing conversation as the ultimate context within which knowledge is to be understood."[115] The goal of postmodern philosophy is not only a rereading of modernist philosophy but also a denial of its truth claims and this "deconstruction" of philosophy ultimately decenters authority and empowers the utterances of outsiders.[116]

Calling on the ideas of Richard Rorty, sociologist George Ritzer proposed that the Web is one endless conversation, which is continuously being added to. Rorty's 1979[117] proposal in *Philosophy and the Mirror of Nature* is to "edify" philosophy,[118] that is, to cease the epistemological search for the truth and to simply create a conversation in which one puts forward one's ideas about philosophy, or, "carrying on a conversation."[119] These conversations, which consist of discussions that are never completed and are that open constitute a new philosophy of non-finality.[120] Those who produce the "conversations," the philosophers, are also those who use the conversations, which are always in process, always being added to—much like how discourse on the Web grows. An important example of the endless conversations now possible on the Web would be what media specialist Axel Bruns[121] calls the "artifact," a discussion which is always in process, never completed, forms of textual conversations among a mash up of what Bruns named "produsage" or producers and users, an idea borrowed from Lyotard[122] who made no distinction between the user who was also the producer of knowledge.[123]

As Bruns stated, "The process of Produsage must necessarily remain continually unfinished and infinitely continuing...an iterative, evolutionary process aimed at the gradual improvement of the community's shared content."[124] The unexpected hyperlink from Rorty to Bruns actually underscores the realization that such on-going and continuing "conversations" are destructive to enclosed and bounded systems. From Rorty who considered philosophy to be a series of ongoing conversations to Bruns and his mash-up of produsage, these positions or two "conversations" taking place in different sites and different times, spell out and describe the crumbling of academic consensus. The consensus of control over such discussions, enforced by Lyotardian "terror," continues in the ivy-covered halls of academic institutions, which are, as Brian Whitworth and Rob Freidman pointed out, "under siege." In fact, as Bruns pointed out, *trendwatching.com* predicted something called "casual collapse," defined as "the ongoing demise of many beliefs, rituals, formal requirements and laws that societies have held dear, which continue to collapse without causing the apocalyptic aftermath often predicted." The Website was talking about powerful social changes that move at a "glacial pace"[125] and these changes, such as the move away from traditional institutions, are alive and well in the intellectual works as American academics contemplate a more "French" position in society that of becoming a "public intellectual," located on the Internet.[126]

Due to the enclosure of philosophy in the confines of the university system, philosophers such as Rorty were unwitting prisoners, who, while guarding the gates, wrote of escape from tradition. But their ideas, as has been pointed out, laid the foundation for ways to think about the Web. For example, if we take Rorty's idea of conversations, even those of "abnormal discourse" as the ongoing goal of philosophy, then the Internet might be the new place for these exchanges. Such moves, taken individually, one by one, over time, will have the effect of eroding positions of authority in the traditional fields of cultural production. Traditional modes of creating knowledge are "collapsing" "casually" while vested interests tend to their own concerns as the foundation of their (outmoded) worlds crumble beneath their unheeding feet. The guardians of access to publication of scholarly works rely upon the vestiges of prestige to keep their charges in line and on the academic reservation.[127] If Ritzer and Bruns are correct, and anyone who visits the Internet can see that there is much to be said for their perspectives, then as Ritzer insisted, the Web also ends the grand narrative, a demise predicted by Jean-François Lyotard in 1979. The result is an array of "little narratives," sprouting up everywhere in the fields of knowledge.

In the de-centered dis-organized un-bordered uncontrolled World Wide Web, if the postmodern paradise has come true and with the upending of authority, then perhaps postmodern theory has entered into the precincts of history and transitioned out of the realm of the now.[128] At this point it seems clear that one can continue *ad nauseam* with comparisons between the Internet and critical theory and postmodern theory, from Foucault's archive to Deleuze and Guattari's rhizome;[129] and, indeed, the footnotes for this book are busily spreading beneath this text blooming like mushrooms. However, to continue such a journey is to plunge into a very deep and ultimately unrewarding rabbit hole, and it is preferable to follow another "trail" or click on another hyperlink in the spirit of the Internet and reestablish the proper ground for Web writing and what it means—in the Cyberspace itself.

From Memex to Hyptertext

Cyberspace is characterized by a lack of a center and a lack of organizational control by any government or corporation or institution. The Web is controlled by the activated users, who are the creators and inventors and fabricators of a sprawling rhizomatic discourse[130] in a territory that resembles the Wild West before the schoolmistresses and lawyers arrived. Always haunting postmodern discourse, like a ghost, always present, is the specter of a controlling force, without which, critical theory cannot function.[131] The goal of critical theory is to produce a critique of an object of analysis; the goal of postmodern theory is to re-read modern theories; the task of postmodernism is to deconstruct the writings of modernism, thus reducing philosophy to mere texts rather than transcendent truths. But what can be said when the crowd, the mob, the great unwashed and unvarnished dare to speak?[132] What theoretical framework can be constructed to contain or explain a deluge of outpourings that spew out by the second from all possible Web orifices? In the face of the raw resistance to intellectual constructs, an entirely new territory is endlessly unfolding, undulating outward as far as the mind can reach.[133]

At this liminal point in time, we are forever crossing over from modernism into postmodernism from the twentieth into the twenty-first century, where we are living and existing and working dually, caught uneasily and uncomfortably between an old-fashioned modern world, which is wedded to hierarchies and centers of prestige and clinging to mechanisms of power through exclusion and the new postmodern world of the exciting possibilities of a post modern world imagined by Roland Barthes where all text is "writerly" and everything is "hyper."[134] But "hypertext" as a concept predates Barthes and is connected back to him only anachronistically.[135] Hypertext is, and in fact always was, a computer term from its very inception. The concept originated from a remarkable article written in 1945 by the atomic scientist Vannevar Bush after the Second World War. Contemplating the remarkable advances in technology made during the war, Bush wondered, "What are the scientists to do next?"

After reminding the readers of *The Atlantic* magazine of the mismatch between twentieth century advances and current needs, the scientist understood that the current systems of accumulating data were not in concert with the way the human mind, which actually

> ...operates by association. With one item in its grasp, it snaps instantly to the next that is suggested by the

> association of thoughts, in accordance with some
> intricate web of trails carried by the cells of the brain.

Bush vividly imagined something he called the "memex" and elaborated upon a system of associative memory "trails" that could be somehow be noted and mechanized.[136] Bush never thought of literature, the domain of Barthes, but of a technological replication of the way in which humans thought—through association—as an aid for research or "information retrieval." For the first time the word "hypertext" was coined, and it was in relation to technology, not memory based, but founded in a system of typed "links."[137] Bush, brooding over the terrible war that brought about the innovations and inventions that fueled his vision of the future, wrote of human achievements and the certain dangers, a month before the dropping of the atomic bomb on Hiroshima:

> He has built a civilization so complex that he needs to mechanize his records more fully if he is to push his experiment to its logical conclusion and not merely become bogged down part way there by overtaxing his limited memory. His excursions may be more enjoyable if he can reacquire the privilege of forgetting the manifold things he does not need to have immediately at hand, with some assurance that he can find them again if they prove important. The applications of science have built man a well-supplied house, and are teaching him to live healthily therein. They have enabled him to throw masses of people against one another with cruel weapons. They may yet allow him truly to encompass the great record and to grow in the wisdom of race experience. He may perish in conflict before he learns to wield that record for his true good. Yet, in the application of science to the needs and desires of man, it would seem to be a singularly unfortunate stage at which to terminate the process, or to lose hope as to the outcome.[138]

Who would have predicted that a big idea from the 1940s, atomic power, would never come to pass except as a threat of mass terror, and that a tiny inspiration, the link, would create a new mode of human communication? Vannevar Bush's intuitions would become lost over time and the memex as hypertext would resurface under a new name, intertextuality, in another institutional site: departments of literature and philosophy in European universities.

The difference between "association" and "links" is crucial to pointing to the difference between the idea of "intertextuality"[139] as conceived by Julia Kristeva or Roland Barthes or Jacques Derrida and the concept of "hypertext" as developed by Theodor P. Nelson in 1962, years before the theorists. Julia Kristeva did not originate the idea of intertextuality but; crucially, she introduced the theories of the Russian linguistic scholar Mikhail Bakhtin to Paris in her 1966 presentation, "Word, Dialogue, and Novel."[140] Whether or not one is discussing Barthes' *S/Z*[141] or Derrida's *Of Grammatology,* intertextuality in postmodern theory is confined to the practice of reading within texts, of a play with the knowledge a reader possesses. To "read" under these conditions is to know the references used overtly or covertly by the writer. To read is also to "write" by finding the feints employed by the text by reading against the grain. The act of "writerly" reading or active reading is always confined within a literary circle. In other words, when Jacques Derrida said, "...there is nothing outside the text..." he meant that writers inscribe "textuality in the text."[142]

And here is where the Internet and its technological hypertext as imagined by Theodor Nelson in 1965 are very different from the literary concept of intertextuality. As Nelson stated,

> "Hypertext" means forms of writing, which branch or perform on request; they are best presented on computer display screens. In ordinary writing the author may break sequence for footnotes or insets, but the use of print on paper makes some basic sequence essential. The computer display screen, however, permits footnotes on footnotes on footnotes, and pathways of any structure the author wants to create. Discrete, or chunk style, hypertexts consist of separate pieces of text connected by links. Ordinary prose appears on the screen and may be moved forward and back by throttle. An asterisk or other key in the text means, not an ordinary footnote, but a jump—to an entirely new presentation on the screen. Such jumpable interconnections become part of the writing, entering into the prose medium itself as a new way to provide explanations and details to the seeker. These links may be artfully arranged according to meanings or relations in the subject, and possible tangents in the reader's mind.[143]

The key terms are "jump" and "an entirely new presentation," a set of actions, which are alien to postmodern or literary intertextuality, which is always concerned with the relationship, for example, between *Jane Eyre* and *Wide Sargasso Sea*.[144] The distinctions between intertextuality and hypertext have become apparent only in the twenty-first century as postmodern theory recedes further and further into the distance, and the Internet and its hyperlinks increasingly shape our lives. Today in a world of Web knowledge, which has the potential to live up to its hyperbolic name "World Wide," the elitism inherent of postmodernity is now apparent or as Theodor Nelson said,

> Knowledge is power and so it tends to be hoarded.
> Experts in any field rarely want people to understand
> what they do, and generally enjoy putting people down.

Just as Nelson published his own book to irritate the computer "priesthood," he imagined, in true post-sixties fashion, a world "liberated" because everyone could "...see the choice of dreams."[145]

Released from the constraints of the singular printed book or fixed published article, Paralogy and Hypertext are intimately related and yet unbounded and freely floating in Cyberspace. There is a consequent *fini* to the conceit that any author is an author/ity or that any book is an author/itarian source on any topic. This restricted and controlled approach that reduces knowledge to doxa is literally un/thinkable on the Internet. The Internet is an inter/section of sections that make up the always-expanding "net." The Cyber "reader" seeks, not completeness, but continuance, and the acts of reading are really acts of mental writing now defined as an accumulation of the endlessly delayed. The linear act of reading within an enclosed space gives way to hypertexts, which are always fragments or "textons" or small semiotic or conceptual units that might cohere, under closer scrutiny, into larger segments.[146] As Claire Brossard and Barnard Reber pointed out,

> The role allotted to the reader in hypertext is more
> important than in the classical book. It is his/her personal
> journey, which, by taking a set of information and
> propositions, contribute to construct meaning. Not only,
> as in traditional reading, by a purely intellectual activity
> but through an interaction with the system that updates
> the units of reading and raises statements. Two readers
> never read the same hypertext, not because their
> readings differ but because what they were given to read
> is different. This production of meaning is sometimes
> problematic because the reader can get lost in the
> hypertext. His/her interaction with the system assumes
> that every time he/she chooses, depending on his/her

route and moods, to click on a particular link the reader does not have an overview of what is proposed. To remedy this disorientation or cognitive system of the user interacts with the state of the hypertexual system to determine the route to take. Only this interaction is likely to build knowledge that the reader did not expect, or was not essential. It represents what is sometimes called serendipity or the art of finding the right information accidentally.[147]

Compared to intertextuality, the way in which hypertextuality functions produces a different method of reading. For example, a typical academic article or book is an exercise in intertextuality, from frequent references to authorities to the obligatory endnotes and the ending bibliography, all elements leading to a linear project with a beginning, middle and end. It is the nature of the "book" that it has a structure that must lead to "the end." But hypertexting is an activity that would probably be neither rhizomatic nor growing outward from a single tree.[148] Indeed, as Reber and Brossard point out, the hypertext is but one step on a journey during which the reader can lose track of the origin, but then an origin is a convenience, not a real place. If one follows the term "hypertext"[149] from its origins, that is, from computers, the dislocation from the mind to the machine becomes clear. If, as has been shown, the past decades have been a journey from Postmodern theory to Internet practice, what is the significance of that shift in the scholarly world, where all practice is theory?

The Magical Thinking of the Academic Belief System

Traditional academic writing in the humanities, whether critique or scholarship, has become a strange and stranded anachronism, increasingly isolated from a parallel Web landscape, where knowledge has been redefined as smaller and smaller units of digital information freely strewn by public intellectuals across the Web like bread crumbs to be followed, picked up, and consumed by interested Internet users, who know no barricades. In such a forest of sign/posts, the presentation of a published work in print as "completed" is both egotistical—because something that is inherently unfinished is masquerading as "finished"—and thus an idea of writing as finality is ultimately unsatisfying to the new reader habituated to reading and riding the waves of text and hypertext. Theodor Nelson dreamed of the Internet as being a place of liberation, but in the moribund world of academia, there is still a power base, a center, aging and sagging, well ossified and beyond rigor mortis, but operational, if only as a reanimated corpse which gestures with a bony hand, beckoning through the creaking door of publish or perish.[150] The publish-or-perish model[151] resembles the sacralized ritual of selecting the Pope: the crowd waits breathlessly outside the walls of the Vatican, anxiously scanning the sky for the telltale puff of smoke coming from the Apostolic Palace.

The process of peer review as every bit as secretive and as political and as non-disclosed as the mysterious maneuverings behind the tall walls of the Palace. All those outside the gates can do is decode the smoke signals. Black smoke means the article rejected; the book sent back.[152] Black smoke signifies a job lost, a promotion delayed; a career derailed. White smoke means not just the publication of an article but also a career made and saved. Few of those who enjoy the affirmation of white smoke think of those not affirmed and do not realize academia is indeed a zero-sum game—their victory comes at the expense of someone else, another person's life and career.[153] This loss, signaled by the metaphorical black smoke, is not a small one. People who are self-defined and self-proclaimed scholars must commit themselves to a long period of apprenticeship in graduate school that could, depending upon the field, last up to ten or fifteen years.[154] Most academics, then, begin their careers as mature men and women who have sacrificed a great deal, personal and financial lives, voluntarily taking themselves out of the job market during the same years—the late twenties and early thirties—when a lawyer, for example, is climbing up a career ladder.[155] The scholar or intellectual, who has a sense of vocation or a devotion to learning, has invested much, has trained for little else, and who stands to lose everything—the entire investment—is at the mercy of a covert system that does not value his or her dedication.[156] So that the chosen few can flourish; academia choses to not avail itself of the talents and contributions of literally thousands of highly trained professionals. The waste of human capital is incalculable.[157]

In writing of the medieval nature of academia, New Zealand professor, Brian Whitworth, commented that "academics are the keepers of guarded channels of knowledge, who protect high quality knowledge as soldiers guard a castle."[158] It should be stressed that there is a split in what I have been calling "academia" between the sciences and the humanities. The conditions for research and writing and publishing are very different in the well-granted and government funded sciences and the relatively impoverished humanities, where the gatekeepers are more and the resources are less. The second point I want to emphasize is that although the intellectual talent and capacity to produce knowledge is equal between the sciences and the humanities, due to the lack of economic resources, the barriers to publication in the humanities is higher. The reasons why the humanities are less well supported than the sciences rests almost solely upon the fact that for complex social and political reasons why history, philosophy, sociology, anthropology and so on are less valued than the so-called hard sciences. In academia, publishing is a strictly un-economic activity, shaped by insufficient funding or financial support for scholarly books that few read, and the actual lack of public interest in arcane scholarship, which wears what French philosopher Pierre Bourdieu called a "court cloak" of privilege.[159] However, the real explanation for the comparative difficulty of creating a career in a college or university as a professor in the humanities—less support, less access to opportunity—is strangely shrouded in complicit silence and veiled through an invisible selection process steeped in a mystery that allows some people to avail themselves of the limited resources—the privilege of publishing.

What is guarded in the humanities is a supposedly scarce resource: a place in the printed pages of certain "prestigious" publications and publishers. The traditional world of academic or critical publication has always been based upon the model of scarcity: limitations on the number of pages and a lack of funds resulting on material restrictions on who and what could be printed.[160] Despite the very real economic and material justifications for restriction in publishing, this literal scarcity has been traditionally equated with an indefinable sense of something called "quality" of scholarship. Supposedly, according to the capitalist model, there is great demand (among aspirants) for recognition (publication) but the existing supply (number of "approved" publication sites that "count") cannot satisfy the demand. However, in the metanarrative of "quality in scholarship" rejections come about not because there are not enough publications but because the candidates were inferior. In other words, because the opportunities were severely limited, they had to be carefully protected and parsimoniously doled out on emotional or subjective, not material and objective grounds. The sociological Field of Cultural Production as imagined by Pierre Bourdieu was one embedded in a strange version of inverted capitalism[161] or the capitalist model of lack, and his entire analysis of the "field" was based on a Marxist/Foucauldian analysis of the sociology of how fields were territorialized and patrolled by gatekeepers who protected supposed scarce resources from the supposed unworthy.

Pierre Bourdieu wrote of the humanities, where, in a field lacking real money, all capital must be virtual. The Field of Cultural Production is based, not on financial capital, but upon purely symbolic capital. However, symbolism notwithstanding, real power is still at stake and the real power in The Field of Cultural Production is actual, even if the capital is not. With symbolic capital comes genuine controlling power, which shapes the growth and developments of "the field" or the discipline where the candidate seeks to find his or her psychological (not financial) reward by being made visible (but only in this universe of faith and print, but also to his or her peers). As Pierre Bourdieu stated, the way in which academics are controlled is by a belief system,

> There are surely few social worlds where power depends so strongly on belief, which it is true that, in the words of Hobbes, "Reputation is power." Thus we cannot entirely understand the phenomena of the concentration of academic power without also taking into consideration the contribution made by the claimants, by way of the strategies, which lead them towards the most powerful protectors. These are strategies of the habitus, therefore more unconscious than conscious...It is another example of the way in which capital breeds capital. We can verify in fact that there exists a close relation between the capital of academic power possessed by the different "heads" and their number and status (measured in terms of academic capital) of their clients—who represent a dimension and a display of their symbolic capital.[162]

And indeed, in post-war American academia, we now have what the Europeans have long preserved, an *ancien régime*, a class system[163] of academics that is jealously guarded by privileged gatekeepers, who reserve the right to declare who and who should not be allowed to be published, and who should have privileges which leads to job retention and/or promotion and who decide exactly what knowledge is deemed worthy of being presented. The goal of these gatekeepers is to preserve and protect their existing power[164] over people and over the discourse. Unlike the sciences, the humanities have no incentive to allow in dissident opinions or new perspectives.

The world of Pierre Bourdieu, of *Homo Academicus,* was in crisis when he wrote his book on academics in France. The French university system was the *raison d'être* of the "days of May 1968" when the students rebelled against a restrictive system of command and control by the government. Twenty years later Bourdieu wrote of the impact of this loss of faith in authority and in a fair society[165] and today his words are again sadly pertinent. According to Bourdieu, those who attempt to enter The Field of Cultural Production do so with the future goal of becoming a gatekeeper, thus perpetuating the counterintuitive system of artificially restricting knowledge. The value of what Bourdieu did was to reveal the socio-economic underpinnings of a supposedly disinterested production of academic knowledge in a university culture ruled by strong interests that desire power and control. Bourdieu wrote frequently of the "inversion" of capitalism that operates in the small and exclusive fields of academia and the arts. Today, there is another crisis: the freedom promised by the Internet and the formation of a global academia and an international university life threatens to change academic culture and its restrictive gatekeeping of its local terrains. The fact that academic writing is assessable to only a few makes it so much more valuable, like a large diamond sparkling in a Tiffany window.

But diamonds are not scarce. There are many diamonds in the world diamonds and have existed for centuries and will be mined for centuries to come. The supposed scarcity of diamonds is an illusion created by the cartels, which control the supply, forcing people who have come to believe that the diamond is the superior stone to pay enormous sums of money for an item that is relatively common.[166] Like diamonds, knowledge and the intellectual ability to produce it is not in scarce supply. Many smart people in academic life, trained from their college years, are instilled with the belief that their sole reward, rather than a living wage, should be the recognition and esteem from their peer group and that this reward, if it will ever be bestowed, will be rare.[167] To create a reason to remain in a profession with low pay and intermittent rewards, a strong incentive system must be created, and it takes years of discipline for the aspiring professionals to be shaped to the needs of a system that gives out symbolic rewards only rarely and only to the chosen few. While it has been a point of concern among those outside of academia that less than half of those who start on such a road finish the journey, given the possibility of spending a lifetime chasing after such a scarce good–the diamond of publication–it is remarkable that anyone continues to be a professor.[168]

Academia is sustained by a form of "magical thinking:" the participant is part of an exclusive group of higher beings who accept the myth of scarcity as the price of admission to hallowed ground. But the reality is that the scarcity is maintained through exclusion. As Pierre Bourdieu wrote,

> The educational institution, operating as pleasure principle and reality principle, stimulates the *libido sciendi,* and the *libido dominandi* which conceals, and which is fuelled by competition, but it also assigns them limits, causing the agents to internalize frontiers between what is legitimate to obtain, even in the field of knowledge, and what is legitimate to hope for, to desire, to like...Such are the paths through which, in a phase of equilibrium, the institution manages, more or less well, to persuade all the agents to stake their investments in the games and objectives which it proposes, so that the frustrations which it inevitably provokes in some people

> are not transformed into revolt against the principle of investment, that is, against the game itself...the institution manages to exclude in those it excludes the very idea of contesting the principle of exclusion.[169]

The creation of an insider language that is accessible to those in the discipline but incomprehensible and irritating to those outside the field is part of the strategy of exclusion used to erect gates. In some fields, the use of technical language is a necessity, but in the humanities, the deployment of a set of words and phrases and concepts appear, to the outsider, to be an array of repellents arranged to discourage all interlopers.[170] This odd practice is another inversion, one upon which Bourdieu did not elaborate—the withholding of information. In theory, academic writers write to communicate and publish to spread the knowledge they have acquired and to share their insights. In practice, the texts are coded for colleagues (not for students), not inclusively for any individual who might be working in the field, but exclusively for those who are in a tight circle in a small space. The result is the creation and use of a darkened and opaque language, which is an inversion of the "through light" of the Enlightenment.

The art historian James Elkins wrote an entire book on how art history has become, if nothing else, simply "bad writing." As Elkins wrote,

> In the end, art history is a kind of writing. It has its blindnesses and moments of control just like any other writing, and it expresses the lives and thoughts of its writers just as much as any fiction. Normally art historians don't think about the writing as writing, because it seems more important to convey the facts of the past that are being recovered and displayed for the present. Yet there is no way around it: what we write as art historians—as academics of any sort—expresses who we are. By not thinking too much about the expressive dimension of our writing, we end up writing poorly. Form a writer's point of view, the writing in a typical art history journal might well seem beautiful, but it probably also sounds dry and emotionally distant. In other words—to put it as directly as I an—to an outsider art history will often seem like bad writing, concocted by someone uninterested in the writer's self, and unaware of the writer's voice.[171]

The simple point that Elkins is making is an important one. From an economic point of view, a great deal of money is being spent on salaries of academics, who are engaged in a closed circuit conversation, which uses a deliberately erudite language setting a high barrier to entry. A great deal of money is spent to publish the work of those scholars for the same limited audience of producers, making the publishers dependent upon the libraries to purchase journals and books that have almost no appeal or sales outside of the field. The irony of the situation is that, to the outsider, it appears that the small circle of academic insiders is creating a "discourse" and not pure knowledge.[172] If there is knowledge to be gleaned, in far too many academic publications, any information is obscured by a blanket of terminology and the obligatory genuflection through clusters of references to other writers (the masters).[173] As long as there is no alternative to the traditional academic model of privileged elites in the Ivory Tower, this mode of knowledge production will dominate and hold its privileged space. But, this exclusionary and exclusive practice ironically dedicated to education is founded on the increasingly unstable platform of academic publishing.[174]

To sum up, academic publishers cannot operate on a capitalist economic model, that is, they cannot make a profit. Academic books have a small group of purchasers, mostly college and university libraries, and some books, such as art history books, are especially expensive to produce.[175] In good times universities are able to support academic publishers, some of which are connected to a particular institution; but in bad times, an inevitable contraction of publishing will occur. A limited audience means a limited and restricted production of printed materials.[176] If financial resources are limited because there is so little support for scholarly activity, then only some people will be able to or allowed to publish. Those people are exceptional and deserve the honor. The fact that, beyond university and college libraries and beyond dedicated readers in the particular field, most academic publishing has a very small audience.[177] The chances of success (being published) are slim, and the rejections and refusals are blamed on the producer rather than on the lack of capital available for university scholars.[178]

In a 2005 study of academic publishing, a system upon which lives and careers and futures and fortunes are based, John B. Thompson described the strange psychological nature of "publish or perish" among scholars, otherwise intelligent people who blindly accept a strangely punitive situation. As Thompson explained as,

> The academic field...is governed largely by a symbolic logic of peer recognition and acclaim. What matters in the academic field, above all, is the esteem accorded by one's peers for the work that one produces—esteem

> that is rendered concrete in a multitude of forms, from the acceptance of an article in a peer-reviewed journal to the reviews of a published book, from the number of times an article is cited to the winning of a prize. These and countless other *indices of scholarly esteem* become the credentials that enable individuals to advance their careers within the academic field, to secure tenure or promotion within an institution or to move to other institutions where the economic and symbolic rewards may be greater.[179]

What is striking about this passage is the emotional and random basis for "esteem," and the fact that the author does not mention any measure of this approval beyond the number of times a work is used or cited or recognized by other readers who bother to give it a footnote. While a supposedly material number may seem like an effective criteria for value, being noticed is purely the effect of whether or not one has conformed to the orthodoxy and can, indeed, be disconnected from the abstract merit or real contribution to the discipline. The fact that an entire intellectual community has allowed itself to be implicated and controlled by what is a belief system (and a belief in footnotes, at that) without any empirical foundation of some vague notion of "quality" is becoming increasing untenable in the 21st century as alternatives to a faith based academic institutions are being developed.

Writing in 2009, scholar Kathleen Fitzpatrick wrote of "Resistance to considering the merits of a mode of publishing freed from the gatekeeping function of peer review…" Noting the "vehemence" of the reluctance to consider democratizing scholarship, she continued,

> …it is only after some initial projection and displacement that the real source of anxiety comes out: the loss of power and prestige…gatekeeping itself is a source of significant privilege.[180]

In the past, any aspirant would have to learn how to navigate the field of his or her chosen discipline and gain what Bourdieu called "habitus" [181] in order to find a foothold within a very narrow space. The terrain is kept artificially small, because Bourdieu's gatekeepers prefer to guard the few rather than corral the many. The gatekeepers are those who read prospective articles or review submitted books, and, consequently, who have the power to make or break an academic career. A mathematician and information systems specialist, Brian Whitworth described this power:

> When a system becomes the mechanism for power,

> profit and control, idealized goals like the search for truth can easily take a back seat. Authors may not personally want their work locked away in expensive journals that only endowed western universities can afford, but business exclusivity requires it. Authors may personally see others as colleagues in a cooperative research journey, but the system frames them as competition for jobs and grants. As academia becomes a business, new ideas become threats to power rather than opportunities for knowledge growth. Journals become the gatekeepers of academic power rather than cultivators of knowledge, and theories battle weapons in promotion arenas, rather than plows in knowledge fields...We have described a feudal knowledge exchange system run by the few for the few, supported ideologically by the church of rigor, financed by university factories of knowledge, whose goal is to dominate and defend the purity of specialized intellectual fiefdoms.[182]

Academic gatekeepers may not have used the power to impact the lives of their colleagues intentionally, but they have certainly deployed this control as the effect of economic factors in the professional structure. The astonishing thing about academia today is how far the humanities are behind twenty-first century thinking, increasing resembling an old-fashioned music industry fighting a futile battle against users and producers of music. In the business of selling music or ideas, it would seem that the last thing desired is the stifling of the production of the very object/product being sold. But rather than expanding the "business" of knowledge and creating new "products" from a widened field of consumers, the feudal non-business model of academic publishing lumbers on to extinction or non-relevance[183] by holding fast to the latches to gates that are increasingly incapable of keeping knowledge corralled.

As Yochai Benkler notes, "we are an information economy," and that this kind of Web exchange is "radically different" from past distribution models. Benkler pointed out that the basic tools for the information economy—computers—are in the hands of a billion people. If, as Benkler asserted in 2005, we are in an information economy, then each of us can contribute our own unique and critical input.[184] As Benkler expressed it, in an important statement,

> What this means is that for the first time since the industrial revolution, the most important means, the most important components of the core economic

> activities—remember, we are in an information economy—of the most advanced economies, and there more than anywhere else, are in the hands of the population at large. This is completely different than what we've seen since the industrial revolution. So we've got communications and computation capacity in the hands of the entire population, and we've got human creativity, human wisdom, human experience—the other major experience, the other major input—which unlike simple labor—stand here turning this lever all day long—is not something that's the same or fungible among people. Any one of you who has taken someone else's job, or tried to give yours to someone else, no matter how detailed the manual, you cannot transmit what you know, what you will intuit under a certain set of circumstances. In that we're unique, and each of us holds this critical input into production as we hold this machine.[185]

Benkler, thinking economically of what he called a "fourth system of social sharing" or "social production," writes of a "decentralized authority," which, as he points out, is threatened by the established "industrial model." The industrial model is the model of monopoly or the system in which one monopolistic entity controls, in this case, knowledge.[186]

Therefore in the midst of an explosion of information and an unprecedented expansion of knowledge, academia remains on the sidelines, a captive of magical thinking enforced by a belief system few dare to question. As a result, journals for academic publishing, supported by institutions funded by taxpayers, tend to be narrow in scope and can publish only on average half-dozen articles a quarter. A fair amount of money is spent to support and promote the careers of a very few people—few relative to the total number of people in the profession[187] while the remainder, those left behind, represent the unrealized investment of those same taxpayers who never see the full return on their investment. From what is a really a very simple economic problem—expensive books printed for a few readers—comes a completely unrelated mystique about "quality" of publication that is an illogical swerve from scarcity of material resources to moral worthiness for publication.[188] This "worthiness" is very specific: one has to publish, not in just any random journal, but in an "approved" publication. One has to be approved, not by just any random reader, but by a very narrow group of reviewers. If, in your heedless rush to publish, you are not selective, then you fall out side of the rules of where and who and when and so on and your efforts towards publication will "not count" for professional advancement.[189]

As anyone who has read academic books can attest, there is no cause and effect relationship between scarcity and "quality,"[190] between being published and being "worthy" of publication, but this untenable belief system about being "accepted" by one's peers endures simply because there is no way of knowing what was not published.[191] There is no way to measure books not written for fear of rejection. There is no accounting for articles that were never resubmitted or rewritten. There is no way to retrieve the intellectual loss to the discipline when perfectly viable scholarship gets caught up in the snare of an un-economic model that is not sustainable and is artificially kept afloat by a non-productive combination of nostalgia and stale habit and fear of the unknown.[192] To argue that the intellectual world daily sustains incalculable loss in stalled careers and silenced voices is to attempt to prove an invisible positive. The restrictive rules of these incredibly complicated games have nothing to do with knowledge *per se* and are founded on the assumption that "quality" resides in only a few locales and that anything produced in the academic territories outside of these selected sites is not "quality." "Quality" is never defined and is separated, like a rogue, conjoined twin from the content or subject matter or topic or text or writing. Such is the hold of magical thinking. Such is the power of faith.

Opening the Gates

Now at the end of the first decade of the twenty-first century, this academic territory that once commanded and controlled publishing can be conceptually expanded into an Internet that does not need to be funded by university endowments and into a Net that is expansive rather than restrictive.[193] The question becomes: can Bourdieu's logic of symbolic capital, obviously based on capitalism, extend to the Internet, which is a gift economy,[194] operating without economic exchange?[195] Fearful of losing prestige or renouncing their vaunted symbolic capital, most academics have been cautious about entering this new territory, perhaps due to its unbounded openness that allows "anyone" to "publish" without peer review or gatekeepers. When the old economic model[196] is replaced by another (non-capitalistic) model, one based in virtual value, then the Old Paradigm changes and a New Paradigm comes to the fore. Unlike print publication, there are no limits on Web publication and approval and esteem can come from anywhere and everywhere.[197]

The Internet has been notoriously resistant to either external control or to monetization. In many ways, as was discussed earlier, the Web is a

Potlatch society: people give gifts—gifts of their time and intellect and talent in what Bill Cope and Mary Kalantzis called "internet socialism." Such is the wealth and such is the promise that here, in cyberspace, that one can begin to measure what was lost in the past—the voices never heard, the words never read—and savor what richness is to come. As Cope and Kalantzis pointed out in 2009, the Internet has caused and is causing disruptions in academic circles, from business practices to the "democratization of knowledge:"

> More knowledge is being produced in the networked interstices of the social Web, where knowing amateurs mix with academic professionals, in many places without distinction of rank. In these places, the logics and logistics of knowledge production are disruptive of the traditional values of the scholarly work—the for–profit, protected knowledge of the corporation; the multimodal knowledge of audiovisual media; and, the 'wisdom of the crowd' which ranks knowledge and makes it discoverable through the Internet according to its popularity. If one wanted to view these developments normatively, one could perhaps describe them as amounting to a democratization of knowledge.[198]

Therefore, today it is possible to escape the siren call of the center, still under the thrall of "publish or perish," and to avoid the lure of publishing in a so-called prestigious journal that claims to be "peer reviewed." The liberated writer moves away from a restricted field that is guarded by gatekeepers to the open field that free and open.[199]

These open areas are called the Commons, a reversion to the feudal era when the "commoners," those who used the "Common" territory, that is land that was shared in "common," were allowed to farm their own acres. The "Commons," as they existed in medieval times were part of a system of responsibility and obligation. The landowner had a responsibility to those who worked the land as free peasants or tenants by protecting them from harm. The tenants, in turn, had an obligation to the owner to work the land for the lord who allowed them to live on the property.[200] Open-field farming on land that was held "in common" by the peasant community who were allowed their own plots. According to Michael Wood in *The Story of England,* these strips were "owned" by families for generations and the individual plots of land were even given names.[201] This system of *noblesse oblige* ended until the eighteenth century when it became more profitable to fence in the land, to close the commons, and to raise sheep. Ownership and property rights pushed peasants off the very lands they had tended for centuries, ending the last bastions of community responsibility and obligation.[202]

In defining the twenty-first century Commons, David Bollier said,

> The commons—a hazy concept to many people—is a new paradigm for creating value and organizing a community of shared interest. It is a vehicle by which new sorts of self-organized publics can gather together and exercise new types of citizenship. The commons can even serve as a viable alternative to markets that have grown stodgy, manipulative, and coercive. A commons arises when- ever a given community decides that it wishes to manage a resource in a collective manner, with special regard for equitable access, use, and sustainability. The commons is a means by which individuals can band together with like-minded souls and express a sovereignty of their own…Commoners realize that this other way of being, outside hierarchical institutions, in the open space where viral spirals of innovation are free to materialize, is an important source of their insurgent power.[203]

The idea of the Creative Commons,[204] occupied by Commoners, is based upon sharing intellectual property by avoiding corporate or institutional control. As Bollier states, these activities, totally outside the established institutions, are called "peer production, "social production," "smart mobs," "crowdsourcing" and are defined as "socially created value," that comes through international interaction.[205] Harvard professor Lawrence Lessing is one of the leading exponents of the "Commons" on the Internet.[206] As Lessing defined the "Commons in his 2001 book, *The Future of Ideas. The Fate of the Commons in a Connected World*,"

> What has determined the commons is the character of the resource and how it relates to a community. In theory, any resource might be held in common (whether it would survive is another question). But in practice, the question a society must ask is which resources *should be*, and for those resources, *how*.[207]

Brian Whitworth referred earlier to the "castles" of the gatekeepers and their "feudal" habits, emphasizing the fortress-like apparatus of academia, which savors the privileges of the ruling class, while shirking the obligations and responsibilities that might be due to the discipline or to colleagues. Along with his writing partner, Rob Friedman, Whitworth recommended that academia act more responsibly and

> ...create a full-access, full-review KES (Knowledge Exchange System) by using proven social computing tools to support open electronic knowledge exchange that accepts everything, rates everything and publishes everything. This is not abandoning the roots of academia but returning to its original goal of seeking truth by publishing knowledge freely for mutual critique and benefit. Such a system could form the basis of an inclusive academic community that invites contributions from other disciplines at the crossroads of technology usage.[208]

The Commons has been revived on the Web and the fields of cultural production are indeed open to the Commoners. The *resources that should be* to which Lessing referred are those of individual creativity and knowledge—that is what should be held in common or accessible to all. The *how* to which Lessing referred is the means of distribution—the Web, free and unfettered and uncontrolled by either government or corporations or by gatekeepers or censors. The Internet has become the new territory for academics interested in distributing their research and scholarship.[209] Here is an abundant field of content production, awash in information and teaming with images—all there for the taking—the blogging, the mashing up, the redistribution, and the dissemination of ideas and research and scholarship. In contrast to closed and restricted and limited fields,[210] the Internet lacks paper and pages. There is only space, empty space waiting to be filled with words and images, a place where an image world can come to life. On the Internet, Culture belongs to the Commons.[211] Internet terminology for academia calls the medieval Commons "Open Access" or OA, which refers to the growing revolt against traditional academic publishing and the attendant scholarly flight from restrictions.[212]

Usually Open Access[213] refers to users or consumers being able to enter into fields of knowledge, such as scientific, or intellectual endeavors, such as academic, or artistic creativity, such as music, without restrictions, such as fees or passwords. Knowledge should be openly distributed; culture should be accessible to everyone. It was the scientists and the early innovators in computer technology who not only expected but who also demanded Open Access: the free exchange of ideas and data and information. Without open access, scientists cannot efficiently function and technology cannot build upon itself.[214] For some reason, the humanities have been slow in coming to the Commons.[215] In contrast to the scientific community, there is no premium put on immediate access to the newest scholarship in, for example, art history. After all, history is in the past, the art isn't going anywhere, and any texts about a distant era can wait, often for years for publication, because the humanities have not traditionally been party to the element of timeliness. In addition, historians or literary theorists are not dependent, as are scientists or technology specialists, on the swift distribution of knowledge. To the contrary, scholars in the humanities tend to hoard their work and jealously guard their chosen territories, often refusing to "allow" interlopers to "publish" in "their" areas.[216]

However, the urge to publish what one has produced has its own professional urgency, especially to younger scholars, who have little patience with an old model of watching and waiting for the gatekeepers' decisions, as scholar Diane J. Bowser wrote,

> …this new younger generation of scholars will be willing to pay their dues for only so long before abandoning traditional organizational structures. Younger scholars are increasingly frustrated and horrified to learn that philosophy alone remains committed to antiquated procedures for journal submission/publication. Discussions amongst younger scholars often focus on ways to change or subvert the current commercial models. This is a generation that grew up on the Internet, regularly abandoning dated domains for new territories. We move on to new social networking sites or adopt cool tools for our iPhones shortly after launch. The choice to abandon commercial for open access models will definitely happen in philosophy as it already has in many other academic disciplines.[217]

The lag time in academia exists because "academia," and all its arcane *habitus*, the rules and regulations that govern its functioning, follows the feudal system of strict and arbitrary hierarchies which are far more important to the institution than innovation. Indeed, following the status quo or respecting the already acquired and already known, and bowing to established knowledge is existential to academia.[218] In contrast to this Knowledge Enclosure is the Open Field of the External Academic Practices, which exist outside the hierarchies of member privilege and are generated on the sole purpose of the practical. Eric von Hippel calls the Internet activity "Information Communities." As von Hippel expressed it:

> It is likely that information communities are getting steadily more pervasive for the same reasons that user innovation communities are: the costs of diffusing information are getting steadily lower as computing and communication technologies. Improve. As a result, information communities may have a rapidly increasing impact on the economy and on the landscape of industry. They are and will be especially empowering to fragmented groups, whose members may for the first time gain low-cost access to a great deal of rich and fresh information of mutual interest. As is the case for user innovation networks, information networks can actually store content that participants freely reveal and make it available for fee downloading...And/or, information networks can function to *link* information seekers and information holders rather than actually storing information.[219]

Scholars began gathering together as "Commoners" in 2006 and attempt to confront the armed resistance of those who still own the means of cultural production. From scientists to Napster, the Commoners come from generations of intellectuals who believe in sharing creative works.[220] The millennium mentality began in the community of software designers who understood what their corporate overlords could not: that if programmers worked together and shared their ideas, then the result should be free and the free exchange of products, which would only result in more innovation. But these new innovators were also part of an old world that understood only ownership and control and profit and property and were protected by a legal system designed to protect corporations. Among those dedicated to Open Source and Open Access was one of the early founders of Creative Commons, Aaron Swartz.[221] Swartz committed suicide after being hounded to death over the issue of distributing academic materials usually reserved for privileged university subscribers.[222]

The two mental landscapes of intellectual productivity and corporate profit continue to clash, and the struggle continues between those who experiment and invent for the sheer satisfaction and those who sell the products based on that work and who, therefore, seek short-term rewards that can be monetized.[223] Although this contest over the proper disposition of intellectual property will take years to settle, the idea and possibility of expanding Open Source and Open Access[224] to intellectual and artistic endeavors has spawned a new generation whose mindset has been formed in this atmosphere of free creativity and sharing and exchange.[225]

Writing in 2012 on the occasion of the Berlin 9 Open Access Conference, Heather Joseph stated that there is now "no debate" about Open Access, only questions of its impact and how to proceed. For the academic areas, "gatekeeping" was no longer a solution but a problem. As Joseph wrote of the conference participants,

> Perhaps the single largest barrier to the adoption of open access publication practices by scholars and researchers is the concern over how publication in an open access journal will be valued by decision makers in the tenure, promotion, and funding processes. Nearly every speaker expressed the need to re-think the current evaluation and merit structure, in light of the new opportunities presented in an open-access environment. Speakers and audience members were deeply engaged in discussing how to construct and deploy new measures of the impact of scholarly research. While journal articles are likely to remain the primary vehicle by which research is evaluated, participants made the case that open access creates new avenues for putting those articles into context against other types of research outputs, and to measure a variety of outcomes in addition to citations. Talk of rethinking the scholarly reward system included a robust discussion of potential changes in not only how the value of results might be measured, but also in how researchers might evaluate one another.[226]

As the century moves into its second decade, the impact of thirty years of personal computers and the Internet has become clear. This Web technology was developed by an odd combination of scientists and geeks, government and garage entrepreneurs, all benefiting from participating in a community that shared ideas and data. Computer technology and the way it has swiftly advanced and expanded itself is an excellent example of how a field can evolve in leaps and bounds when unorthodox outsiders combine forces with university based researchers to bring about change.[227] In contrast, the humanities in university and college communities have stayed firmly planted in the twentieth century and are operating as though nothing has changed: publish or perish, peer review, prestigious publications, tenure, and so on.[228] The system that rules academics is an "enchanted" system which demands that the followers internalize a set of practices that are essentially based upon fear; and this fear—the phrase "publish or perish"[229] is a dire one—reinforces obedient behavior and unquestioning submission to the rules. But it is now possible to not break the rules but to simply walk away from a game that is rigged and to find another way to develop professionally.[230]

For the academic writer, the Web is the logical destination and becomes a new territory for the formation of a more open and accessible academic discourse in the new location where the land, so to speak, is there for the taking, and there is no center, no margin and no borders, just a homesteader's paradise—pick a spot and claim it. Re-locating to the Internet, the writer leaves the twentieth century world of closed scholarship behind[231] and ventures onto or into a new "field" where a new audience is waiting and where there is no one to stop you from writing what you want, when you want, and where you want. Many of us do most of our writing is done on the Web, on our own cyber sites, where we can write what we want, when we want, at our own convenience and, most importantly as much as we desire. The question becomes, once it is placed on the Web, sited in Cyberspace, posted on the Internet, how is scholarly—intellectual—academic writing re-defined?

The Future Art of Writing

I am going to use writing in the arts as an example of the impact of the Internet on traditional academic writing. There are two reasons for this choice of the arts. First, I work in the arts as an art historian and an art critic and these are the areas I know best. And second, unlike other fields in the humanities, art history is about objects: art can be seen in museums and galleries, and art criticism is intellectually accessible to everyone. And unlike traditional academic art history publishing, the images are free and can be obtained by clicking and dragging instead of through royalties. Art writing in Cyberspace has a built-in audience that can extend from career art historians to practicing art critics to university academics to college students to the general art interested public. In fact, there is a huge and varied audience waiting for art topics and issues and the presence of this large and well-educated audience leads to opportunities on the Web and to challenges on the Internet and to new rules about how to write on the Net.

In addition, the result of moving art *reportage* to the Web is a fundamental redefinition of art criticism or art history or art scholarship into "art writing" or writing about art in a hybrid fashion, combining literature, critique, history, and theory with an entirely new audience in mind, an audience that becomes part of what Chris Anderson called "The Long Tail."[232] And be comforted by the thought that, as Anderson put it, "…almost anything is worth offering on the off chance it will find a buyer."[233] Anderson's trailblazing article about the music industry was written for *Wired* magazine in

2004 and the five-page essay subsequently became a best-selling book. The significance of Anderson's thesis is important to academia because he analyzes the difference between what corporations/institutions think/assume the consumer/user wants and the way in which the businesses then decide control the supply of music towards those assumptions.[234]

In practice, corporate assumptions have been proven wrong, and, as Anderson pointed out, that if an open-minded music distributor makes more titles/music available for the buyer, a market exists for items that might never see the light of day otherwise.[235] In other words, if someone is interested in music, chances are this person has wider tastes or more eclectic interests that Wal-Mart could imagine.[236] Equally, if someone is interested in art, chances are that, first, most of those people are not interested in the fares that are offered by the traditional market in academic books and that, second, the majority of readers would welcome less expensive and more accessible materials on art.[237] There is a curious divide in art writing: on one hand, there is a huge amount of art historical material on art hidden in databases that is deliberately withheld from the art public and on the other hand there is a plethora of art criticism, some written for a small and local constituency and some addressing a larger audience.

If we interpret the very large field of art criticism as symptomatic of an equally large interest in the arts, then it is hard to imagine a better example for Chris Anderson's concept of a "niche" market than art writing on the Web. The kind of art writing with which the public is most familiar is the traditional form of art criticism, short reviews, which appear in newspapers and art publications. These texts are usually brief and topical, providing information about current art events and reviewing the art work in question. Competing with "hard" news and sports and local events in a newspaper, there is little space in print publications for art writing on exhibitions, which admittedly have a shelf life. Even in a magazine devoted art reviews, such as *Artforum*, five hundred words is relatively generous in today's world. Even if the publication offers an online version of itself, such as *The New York Times*, the Web review will not necessarily be longer and may even be edited for Internet formatting. Although the traditional publications have not yet allowed their writers the freedom to go over the stipulated word length, the Internet offers a matchless immediacy and the space and place to write as much as one wants. As Anderson himself pointed out,

> I find blogging ruins me for magazine writing. It's difficult to write for magazines right now, which is ironic given

that I'm a magazine editor. It's difficult because magazines are a kind of one-size-fits-all product, and the audience is large, with differing interests. You have to write something that tries to satisfy all of [your readers] or many of them, whereas a blog is very self-selecting. If you're interested in what I have to say, fine. If you're not, that's great—go somewhere else. The book is also self-selecting. If you're not interested in the concepts in the book, don't buy it. If you are, I'm going to go deep, and that's great. But books—and blogs—are focused, whereas magazines are not.[238]

I will come back to Anderson's point about how a writer feels about the ability to write or "go deep," as he said later, but to continue—art writing on the Web could become part of what has already been forming through museum websites: the Long Tail for art. Traditionally, conventional art history and art historians have had little use for the general art audience, from student beginners to museumgoers or art lovers. Prestige is at stake and the professorial writer of survey texts has far less symbolic capital than that of the notoriously difficult author of a notoriously obscure work of scholarship that was bravely read by only a determined few.

If he were alive today, Pierre Bourdieu would be the first to point out that the distribution of symbolic capital in art historical circles is inverse to that of the music industry—the obscure has more prestige than the well-known—meaning that The Long Tail for art writing is the home for an art writing that reaches out to a wide if niche audience. With music, it was impossible to know what would and would not sell until the cost of renting space in a building was eliminated in favor of music in cyberspace.[239] Once artificial constraints are removed then there are no boundaries for music lovers and once the artificial and costly practice of publishing books in paper in advance of sales is unnecessary, an entirely different market is revealed. Just as there is no reason to confine the sales of CDs to racks in a Barnes and Noble bookstore, there is no reason to confine the number of articles offered annually in a print journal.[240] Once these artificial constraints for art critical writing and for art historical scholarship are lifted, two phenomenon will take place: first, more authors, scholars, writers will be revealed, and second, more readers will emerge to receive them. And there is no reason to wait for publishing companies and universities to enter into the twenty-first century. One can simply stop waiting to be published, someday, stop standing in line, and go on line, step into Cyberspace.

The Web forces a separation between writers, those who write to write and authors, those who write to publish. I am using the terms "writer" and "author" to suggest an etymology of the word "writer" in Roland Barthes' term "writerly" from his book *S/Z* and to his 1968 essay, "The Death of the Author." In *S/Z*, Barthes stated that

> The writerly text is a perpetual present, upon which no *consequent* language (which would inevitably make it past) can be superimposed; the writerly text is *ourselves writing* before the infinite play of the world (the world as function) is traversed, intersected, stopped, plasticized by some singular system (Ideology, Genius, Criticism) which reduces the plurality of entrances, the opening of networks, the infinity of languages. The writerly is the novelistic without the novel, poetry without the poem, the essay without the dissertation, writing without style, product, structuration without structure.

In other words, a writer writes and on the Internet writing can be continuous and uncontained and, as Barthes imagined, "writerly." As Chris Anderson said of blogging, this new Cyberwriting is immediate and direct and always alive. In contrast, for an Author to place writing into print and to submit a text to be published is to kill the words. A book becomes a dead thing, dead on arrival, as out of date as the fat yellow-edged telephone book thrown onto your front porch. As Barthes said of the Author, "To give a text an Author is to impose a limit on that text, to furnish it with a final signified, to close the writing."[241] To the Author, the monograph, the book, is the Gold Standard; to the Web writer, the only book can only be an e-book, open to revisions or changes and flexible in a way that no traditional publisher would allow. The writerly book has no Author, only a writer who is constantly rewriting the Cyberbook, a living, breathing object, always subject, not to revision but to constant revitalization.

One can wait for rescue from the invisible gods of the faith-based academic system or one can create a new space for art discourse by writing on the Internet. Why wait? Once art history and art criticism go on the Web, these practices become transformed into a form of cyber "art journalism," but this is not your mother's art journalism. Rather than produce a contribution designated as a "studium," the writer must make a mark, a "punctum."[242] Although in the essay *Camera Lucida,* Barthes was discussing photography, the "studium" of a photograph, its conventional meaning, can be interpreted as parallel to "readerly" or conventional texts, and the "punctum" of an image, become the unexpected and uncontrolled elements is the "writerly" or that which makes a text come to life. Cyberwriting is quite simply the appearance of the unexpected, art writing out of place and replaced on the Net where it floats, free from the rules of an old game. Art writing is, by its very nature, radical, in the sense that Barthes wanted writing to be radical,[243] because it defies convention and distances itself from the previous system of control. The art writer does not ask permission to write; the art writer simply writes. Paralogy has been unleashed.

In contrast to the pleasure of the text and the delight of composing "little narratives," the system of "publish or perish"[244] and peer review is more than a long and time-consuming process and a psychologically draining ordeal, it also discourages scholars from writing. One must write, not because one enjoys research or the life of the mind or even writing itself but to survive and not "perish." One must write, therefore, cautiously and carefully and direct each and every word, not towards to forwarding the discipline or towards advancing knowledge but to pleasing an unknown and unseen reviewer.[245] The predictable result, for the traditional academic or critic, has been an extremely artificial and narrow passage to publication in the "correct" journals[246] and eventual publication of the career-making monograph. But in the twenty-first century world of the Web, the question arises: why accept an old-fashioned model when another and more efficient method of displaying intellectual acumen is available?[247] Why not change the methods? As Pierre Bourdieu said, "To change the world, one has to change the ways of world-making, that is, the vision of the world and the practical operations by which groups are produced and reproduced."[248]

The Web writer, as Chris Anderson put it, can "go deep," or write at will, probing for an audience of "produsers." The idea of art writing as a kind of "journalism" and the *reportage* it implies is indicative of the new power of the audience on the Web. The old model for art publication was what is called "push" publication in which a package of what you should know, i.e. knowledge, is "pushed" upon the reader. It was through this push model that the discipline of art history and the discourse on the arts was formed.[249] Today the model is "pull" journalism, because art writing on the Web is audience driven. In other words it is the readers who select the sites and it is the reader who decides what s/he will read. The goal is no longer to appease the gatekeepers; it is to "pull" in the audience.[250] The Cyber-audience is the new peer review. In contrast to the select readers of traditional art journals, the few, the powerful, the select, the Web readers are self-selected and there are many surfers and browsers available to the writer who has the nerve to move into the wide open range of this new field of content production. The refereeing takes place with your audience on the Web. If you are good, they will come. If you are not good, they will never visit. If you have nothing of value to say, they will leave.[251]

The Cyberwriter needs a place in the spaceless Net: either one's own website or the ability to publish in Open Access publications. The writer on the Internet must be reliable. All content must be consistent in quality because reading on the Web is an activity that is distinct from reading print. The Web writer has less than ten seconds to grab the reader's attention. The reader, in turn, is intent on a specific search and has an immediate need for a certain kind of information or knowledge. Possibly due to the amount of time spent searching for the desired information, the attention span of the viewer is greatly shortened. Reading for contemplation ceases and is replaced by the restless activity of skimming for key words.[252] The Internet reader will quickly scan the article, searching for key words and if the exercise in skimming does not quickly yield results, the reader will move on. A Web reputation is made because the work of the writer is a reliable and responsible source, authoring a website that is readily available and/or publishing content that is constantly new and continually updated. Readers who are pleased in the first few moments and get what they needed will bookmark the site/s will and return.

When the writer is in Cyberspace,[253] Content is King and the name of the new game or the rule of the New Paradigm is simply to generate and supply content. In contrast, the old rules of the old game of the Old Paradigm was to limit content and to control the amount of subject matter, to make material on art scarce through an artificial practice of exclusion to imply that that which was "pushed" was more valuable or prestigious than that which was discarded or rejected.[254] On the Web, no one cares about who is writing in terms of which university s/he attended or under whom s/he studied—one needs to be only respectable and reputable: it is the What that counts—Content.[255] Those who are already on the Web are the forerunners or the advance guard that have acted, for practical reasons, to protect their own careers and to respond to a situation that, in the world of academic publishing, has gone from bad to worse to crisis.[256] In the face of the economic calamity called "the crisis of the monograph,"[257] academia has responded ostrich-like and the result is that, as the second decade of the twenty-first century continues, an entire generation of scholars and scholarship is in danger of being lost. But these people can be found.

Once on the Internet, the new writer meets the new reader,[258] whose reading habits have been reshaped from "book reading" to "screen scanning."[259] Although art history as a discipline was formed within the pages of books and journals, art historians and art critics must take into account the new reading formations on the Internet.[260] There will be unavoidable transformations to the discipline—once art writing goes on line, every aspect of reading and writing must be rethought for Internet publications where none of the old questions apply: Who is an authority? Who is authorized to speak? Who gives permission to write? What is the source or prestige of the publication? Who is allowed to publish in the limited space of the printed page?[261] As Tony Bennett wrote in 1985, thinking not at all of the Internet, "Different reading formations, that is to say, produce their own texts, their own readers, and their own contexts."[262] In fact, the re-location of reading and writing to the Web alters the production of knowledge.

The art writer, who goes on the Web, finds that the audience has changed from one's own peer group to the general art-interested public, students, and fellow scholars—all searching for information, a search, which is fundamentally different from a search for something called "knowledge," which was safely contained safely within the confines of the metanarrative of a discourse: old-fashioned and bounded. While "Information" is ascertainable and is defined by what is on the Web, "Knowledge" is a nostalgic concept and is not a definable word. Rather than creating a discernable discursive formation, these discrete bits of information may or may not coalesce into "knowledge,"[263] if we define knowledge as discourse. But, as was mentioned earlier, Lyotard conflated "knowledge" and "information" as being the same and this sameness, the conflation, is the definition of "The Postmodern Condition," or the Flattening of the World. The Flat World of the Web changes the meaning of knowledge, and knowledge is redefined by that which can be quickly located in Cyberspace. Whether the discipline of art history likes it our not, what matters for any reader of art on the Web is the accessibility and readability of the Websites.[264]

Accessibility to intellectual materials is one of the most currently contentious issues in academia today. While more and more knowledge is being put on line, at the very same time corporations are systematically turning public research into a private good by secreting academic journal articles and books into giant closed databases and, as a result, enraging anyone trying to think critically. In comparison to the corporate management of information, what happens on the Web is that knowledge will be configured in different ways and will be re-defined as an accumulation of units of information which the reader actively pulls from a variety of sources and then puts these discrete "learning objects" into "knowledge." And what is happening is that the researcher becomes the searcher or the seeker, who has criteria that may be different or actually at odds with academia. Rather than gravitating towards a "definitive" book on a topic, the re-searcher on the Internet tends to use what is easily available. In terms of accessibility—any e-journal or Web site that is password protected or that is in any way exclusionary will simply be passed over by the reader. No one wants to take the time and energy to sign up for the privilege of trying to access knowledge that should be accessible to everyone.[265] The Web is inclusive, and exclusion is offensive. One of the rules of the Web is that no one will click more than twice. Moral: if you are published in a prestigious journal and your journal is secreted in JSTOR,[266] you will not be read.[267] If you are published in a book that is offered in print only, you will not be read.

The amount of academic research that has been withdrawn from public access is both still unknown and still growing, leading to a new acronym: AIW or the "Academic Invisible Web." German scholars, Dirk Lewandowski and Philipp Mayr explained,

> ...we define the Academic Invisible Web (AIW) as consisting of all databases and collections relevant to academia but not searchable by the general internet search engines.[268]

The new reader is reluctant to take the time and make the effort to use resources that are not readily available in cyberspace. For the art writer who is willing to make the risky journey out of traditional publishing and onto the Internet, the opportunities are extraordinary. One has the space and the place not only to update the already-written but also to become one of the main sources for information on the arts. Art history is but one of the humanities that traps canonical works on library shelves and secrets authors behind password-protected archives.[269] To be read today, you must be posted in an open site on the Web.[270] A recent article on *Aljezerra* by Sarah Kendizor quoted one of her colleagues who remarked, "Can you imagine if JSTOR was public? That means someone might actually read my article."[271] To those who react in horror at the thought of such intellectual laziness and who insist on preserving the ritual of testing the student's determination to do difficult research as proof of devotion or seriousness need to think about other questions: are you an intellectual? If so, why restrict intellectual development? Are you a teacher who believes in disseminating knowledge? If so, why would be complicit with efforts to block access to scholarly writing?[272]

Readability means not only that the reader has to be able to access art writing but also that the narrow and focused readership, which art historians and art critics have traditionally enjoyed is no longer the target.[273] The readership now is international and diverse and essentially unknown. The result is that art writing as it has traditionally existed—

jargon, code words, insider terminology, unexplained references, name-dropping—cannot thrive on the Web. Readers welcome intelligent writing and look for high quality content and intellectual exchange and have no patience for a style of writing that seems deliberately obtuse and exclusionary.[274] The importance of readability—the ability to read and understand what is written—cannot be overemphasized. On the Internet, readers have a multitude of choices and these Web-readers are exacting and discerning and are as insulted by code words as they are impatient with academic jargon.[275] The new "reading formation" is an ironic inversion of the old "reading formation" that passively accepted information "pushed" upon it, turning the former key to success in academic publishing—the secret language of the discipline—into a sure failure for the writer on the Internet. The issue is not that jargon, aka, disciplinary specific terms, is "bad" or "wrong;" jargon has a purpose to serve. Rather the issue is whether or not inaccessible phraseology serves the needs of the Internet writer.

Just as jargon on the Web will stand in the way of a wide readership, the traditional set up of a "page" in a "book" type format has no reason to exist in cyberspace. Why move a form or a layout lifted from a print medium and accept the material limitation of a "page" in a non-material space where the "page" does not exist? One of the most frequent mistakes academics make when transferring their scholarship to the Web is to replicate the formats and the practices of a print presence in Cyberspace.[276] The possibly instinctive replication of print, often small sized fonts with serifs, which are difficult to read, interferes with readability. First, as has been demonstrated, when databases such as JSTOR lock thousands of scanned journals and their contents behind paywalls, the new generation of Web readers will simply blow past this resource. To cordon off knowledge, making it available to only the few who are affiliated with an educational institution, instead of those who actually paid for it,[277] and, therefore, should own the work, is unethical.[278] Whether the authors whose works are incarcerated in JSTOR want it or not, their research is not being utilized and their scholarship is not part of the conversation.[279] The second problem for those tucked away in databases is that old-fashioned journal pages are scanned in, forcing readers to click from page to page instead of scrolling smoothly down the text. This issue exacerbates the third problem, the scholarly habit of long introductions, with some writers forcing the reader to turn far too many pages before coming to the point of the essay. Once again, if the first page does not yield results, a Web reader will lose patience, and irritated that information is deliberately being withheld, will move on with a click of the touchpad.

The penalty for not being "part of the conversation" is a grave one. Going back to Richard Rorty, to not be a participant in the discursive conversation is to not be part of the discourse. Locked away behind gated databases, many scholars have fallen out of range and are no longer heard: their vaunted articles are now like trees that fall in an increasingly empty forest. In their absence, the louder and more available voices are creating the Rorty-inspired conversation and are peppering the Internet with the paralogy of Little Narratives. Given the sustained and growing chorus of discontent about academic databases and given the natural desire of authors to be read, scholars of the future will undoubtedly be forced to chose between being published in print and hidden away or writing and being read on the Internet.[280] To those accustomed to the Ways of the Web, the sentimental adherence to the idea of publishing an anachronistic "book" and the attachment to the "article" printed in a journal is puzzling and irritating, and the Web writer must understand what it means to work in Cyberspace: no shape, no place, no contours, and most importantly, no time.

Art writers are a group of professionals who, unlike their art historical colleagues, do not have to ask permission to publish: art critics are asked to write by people who want to publish our work. But, this ease of publication has come with a caveat: our writing, most of which has been done on assignment, dates over time. Therefore, the biggest change is the transition to the Web that art criticism must make is from being a temporary account of an art exhibition to a permanent discussion of art.[281] When the review is in print, once the show is over or the museum or gallery event has ended, the value of the information provided diminishes. In contrast, art writing is on the Web forever; it does not fade; it cannot be thrown away; it can be deleted; but it cannot be erased and becomes an "artifact" that is constantly engaged in a continuous "conversation" about art.[282] Once the writer is Web-based, a decision must be made: when an exhibition or event is here today and is gone tomorrow, the question becomes—how can one make this article or post relevant for future readers?[283]

The answer is that performative practice that I would like to call "Long Tail art writing." Long Tail art writing does not "review" an exhibition or critique the art or evaluate the artist but addresses the "event" as an occasion to discuss not just the art being shown but also the issues and concepts surrounding the objects with an eye to adding to the knowledge of the subject.[284] Keeping in mind that corporations (newspapers and magazines) routinely underestimate the intelligence of the consumers, "Long Tail Writing" means that ways must be found to seek out the extended niche audience and to make the texts themselves live beyond their initial posting.[285] As Chris Anderson put it, "Many of our assumptions about popular taste are actually artifacts of poor supply-and-demand matching—a market response to inefficient distribution." In other words, academic publishing, the very living breathing example of "inefficient distribution," might have less to do with distributing knowledge than with celebrating feats of scholarship.[286] In the real world, such as the world of the music business that Anderson studied, an academic article read by a few and purchased by even fewer would become part of "The Long Tail," a suddenly active element in a niche market. Once the work is freely available on line, even the most arcane topic will find its audience, many of which had been denied access by proprietorial databases.

Currently in academia, there is no such thing as a "hit" or a "best seller," or to put it in another way, there is no tail, long or short, because there is no head.[287] Because academic publishing is so deliberately and arbitrarily restrictive, there is no way of knowing whom the audience might be or what the unrestricted audience might want to read. As the system works now, the academic audience/readers get what they are given, or what the referees deemed worthy of being distributed. The academic writers may wait for years to get one article or one book published. However, if opportunities were opened for unrestricted and direct—writer released— academic publication on the Internet, something like a genuine audience would develop, and much of the previously unpublished work would find readers, and writers would be encouraged to produce more knowledge because, suddenly, a Long Tail had been created for even the most obscure and rejected topics.[288]

My proposal that traditional art criticism be replaced by performative art writing is being made in the midst of what has been called—for decades— a "crisis" in art criticism. Art criticism it appears is in trouble; art critics are being fired from newspapers; we are doomed by our theories, strangled by our jargon, done to death by our own cultural irrelevance. Indeed, if the complaints about art criticism are correct—contempt for the popular audience, use of linguistic codes and university language and a general loss of professional purpose—then the field deserves to die and the sooner the better. But, as it has been said, out of crisis comes opportunity. What is striking about the current discussions of the digital age dilemma faced by print art criticism is that among the many writers and many participants in seminars and so on is the adherence to conventional thinking and the unspoken assumption that art criticism should not change—although it is dying.[289]

One of the reasons why art criticism has been in this never-ending "crisis,"[290] is because its role has been artificially limited by the fact that it had to appear in print and by the role that was imposed upon it—that the purpose of art criticism is to evaluate and judge and to pass down an (informed) opinion upon an object offered up for appreciation. But, I contend, this limited ambition, to criticize, probably came about for very simple reasons—newspaper and magazine editors decided that the art audience needed to read a description and a decision five hundred words in length for publication in the weekend edition. The contemporary form of art criticism was contextually created in relation to a social culture that was determined to educate and elevate the masses through a little taste of art. However, the best and the most influential and the most formative art criticism was always Long Tail Art Writing—a potent mixture of art, philosophy, social commentary, critique, all adding up to the kind of writing that was serious and expansive and contextual. There is nothing new in this kind of art writing. Back in the formative years of the discipline, the ranks of art criticism were populated by the likes of the poet Stéphane Mallarmé who edited a fashion magazine and wrote about Impressionism and admired Edgar Allen Poe and revolutionized poetry and was painted by Manet.[291] Mallarmé took advantage of the late nineteenth century system of publishing *petites revues* that allowed the equivalent of Long Tail writing to publish his poems and his critical writing.[292] Often, when it becomes necessary to reform a discipline that has lost its way or has become unsure of its mission, the appropriate solution is a favorite tool of a revolutionary: return to the roots and revisit the precursors.

The current situation of art history and art criticism, frozen in an inert state, is reminiscent of the way in which the Dead-enders of the French Salon System fought futile battles against the insurgency of the outsider artists. The secret irony of the current situation for art writers on the Web is that the very art historians who teach about and celebrate the *avant-garde* of the past century will be the very detractors of this new vanguard practice of publishing in Cyberspace. The art writer on the Internet, the publisher who avoids the gates is the descendant of the Impressionist painter who refused to show in the Salon.[293] While trying to shame writers who try Internet publishing, like the established Salon artist Jean-Léon Gérôme who criticized Édourad Manet's experimental painting, the art history establishment continues to publish many books celebrating *avant-garde* renegades of the past.[294] When the art critic transforms into art writer, s/he is in good historical company as s/he moves to the Web, following in the footsteps of the Impressionists to the gallery space on 25 Boulevard des Capucines in 1874, circumnavigating the game of publish or perish and slipping past the gates of peer review.[295]

Art writing has always been important to the field of art history and performative art writing can be more assertive and significant, allowing critique to take its proper and unrecognized place as a serious player in the art world. For a very long time, the academic field of art criticism was considered a very minor one, with art critics playing the role of the scorned stepsister. Although certain selected famous art critics were studied, mostly in relation to the art they wrote about, few art historians studied criticism seriously as a literary from or as an entity unto itself.[296] Art criticism was and is considered to be a handmaiden to the art, a way to explain the art, and was not analyzed as a very special type of discourse. Rather than being given a proper respect, art writing, whether that of the past or present, is disparaged due to its supposedly "popular" status because the writer must address a general audience.[297] In other words, the profession of art history has internalized the traditional *avant-garde* ideas of "worth." If the public likes the work of an artist or writer, then the writer's texts, like the paintings of Norman Rockwell, are immediately devalued. It is worth noting, however, that those very academics who scorn contemporary art criticism, spend enormous amounts of time and energy studying about and writing about a critic who openly addressed his articles "to the bourgeoisie,"[298] Charles Baudelaire and about a critic who was the first to use radio to broadcast his ideas about art, Walter Benjamin.[299]

Although, on one hand, it was this very writing—art criticism—that was absorbed into the "history" of the art and became the contextual and explicatory foundation for the works of art, it was relegated to a subordinate status.[300] Despite the proven importance of, for example, the writing of Émil Zola for the comprehension of Édouard Manet, contemporary art critics have been given art criticism a second-class status, precisely because of the short-lived relevance of the texts. What Zola did in his writing was not to evaluate Manet or to criticize his paintings[301] but to give the reader a new way of thinking about art. To ask the reader to think is the role and the task of the art writer. It was Charles Baudelaire, who pioneered what could be a once and future manner of writing by discussing art in a developed and substantive manner in *The Painter of Modern Life*.[302] Although Baudelaire wrote his fair share of general art writing addressing the larger public, this 1863 essay was a thoughtful and sustained attempt to define *modernité*, a new urban phenomenon, marked by motley crowds and ephemeral fashions and the fugitive fads that flitted through the consumer culture, creating a new kind of "beauty." What was so extraordinary about this project on modern life was Baudelaire's choice of Constantine Guys, not his friend Édourad Manet, as his "painter of modern life."[303] In selecting Guys, a popular illustrator who made art for the "crowd," the public, Baudelaire pointed the way to the future of art: to be modern, one had to move away from the past, away from the stultifying Salon system, a move that Manet never made.[304] To be modern was to be part of the new urban existence, a world being written into existence through an emerging era of commodities, fashioned to be consumed, regurgitated, and replenished. To paint this life, one had to be, like Guys, outside of the system.

Baudelaire had concerns much larger than that of promoting the career of a particular painter, and, in fact, the very anonymity of "Monsieur C. G." aides his purpose, which to define the fugitive "modern life" and its strange new contingent beauty. However, over time, the larger role for the art writer shrank (or was shrink) and the notion that the role of the critic is to be a talent scout is the opening line of artist Julian Schabel's movie *Basquiat,* when the New York writer for *Artforum,* René Richard, notes that everyone is worried about missing out on the next van Gogh.[305] This concern, about missing the "van Gogh boat," is an art market-driven trope, and this anxiety of omission has driven art criticism for decades. But the best art writing has always been concerned with incoming trends and defining tendencies. However, post-Basquiat, in the wake of Postmodernism, it is no longer possible for a small and devoted coterie of writers either to manufacture a "movement" or defend new artists in a confined space of a local art world. Having written extensively on how "Cubism" was discursively created,[306] I am aware that the literary and intellectual tactics employed by these first critics of Cubism, who wrote exactly one hundred years ago would today simply disappear in the endless cyber space of the Web.

The early twentieth century art critics in Paris were a small group of individuals—writers and poets—who were writing from the perspective of being associates and colleagues of the artists and were well-qualified to write about art that they knew intimately. More often than not they wrote to each other or to an audience of producers: "produsage," as Alex Bruns would have said. As advocates, they were making a case, so to speak, for the legitimation of Cubism as a consecrated art movement. Indeed, the traditional role of the art critic had become, not judgment or evaluation, but discovery, discourse, and canonization of art and artists. These writers on Cubism were "present at the creation," and over time, their accounts, such as André Salmon's[307] account of Picasso's 1907 painting, *Les Demoiselles d'Avignon,* "Anecdotal History of Cubism," become valuable eyewitness testimony for later art historians. Historically, the critical works gained credence when the art of which they wrote became anointed and entered the historical precincts.[308] What the art writers of the early twentieth century achieved was, not a banal description of works of art, but a perceptive articulation of the visionary mind for the future of painting.

Likewise, in New York, the art writers on the scene in the 1940s sensed another such moment of change and tried to assess the passing of time while pondering the next act for art. Once again the best criticism of this time of transition struggled to explain the undercurrents in an art world caught in the paroxysm of formation.[309] Clement Greenberg and Harold Rosenberg "created" an art movement out of rivalrous and disparate artists and called the confrontational situation "Abstract Expressionism." Clement Greenberg borrowed an American style pastiche of strained—as in put through a journalistic strainer—European aesthetics to bring Ab Ex into being through his critical dances with borrowed philosophical language.[310] Although he wrote of individual artists, Greenberg's most elegant and definitive essays were of a time and a place that he himself helped fashion with his own strong and decisive words.[311] In the same way, Harold Rosenberg worked European existentialism into an American tradition of "action,"[312] which re-defined a modern form of expressionism (long outmoded in Europe) into a modern way of existential living as an artist always in a state of becoming. However overblown or overextended these critical expenditures may seem today, the words of the "Twin Mountains" remain those that explain a mood and a moment of art in time.[313]

Looking back, the definitive writings on Cubism and Abstract Expressionism are few in number and short in length, respecting the limitations of their destinations in print. None of the twentieth century writers produced a monograph with the critical weight and intellectual heft of Baudelaire's *The Painter of Modern Life.* Moreover, nineteenth and twentieth century art criticism was grounded in a precise locale, such as Paris or New York. These definitive writings by these well-placed and articulate writers depended upon privileged access to the artists' studios and to the artists themselves. The ability of these writers to become symbiotic with the artists had the result of devaluing second-hand or non-primary sources from other art writers in other cities, not "present at the creation." Indeed the art critical practices of the past were dependent upon a real center, a city, a neighborhood where art was made; a locale that the critic could visit often, cultivate acquaintances, even friendships, and pass on the studio talk, translated for the reader.[314]

Today, the art market is international and so too is the audience. Indeed the artists themselves are nomadic or are scattered across continents. The twenty-first century art market is international and so too is the audience. The print media asks that its critics chase exhibitions at art fairs from continent to continent, and although the eyewitness account is valuable, there is a real question as to whether or not "being there" is a sentimental survival of twentieth century practices. Likewise, museums have not yet realized the capacity and potential of the Internet. The websites resemble the pages of a book: text studded with static images, with the occasional video, often of the old-fashioned talking head of an authority figure, who "explains" art to the masses. Today, there are alternatives to being present. Through a museum or gallery website, art shows can be "visited" from great distances. An art writer does not have to know the artist nor does she have to "visit" a work of art or an artist's studio; he can write about any object as long as it exists in Cyberspace.[315] The obligatory trip to the gallery is no longer obligatory. The art writer can write internationally or locally and is no longer limited to a narrow art scene. Indeed, unlike the importance of New York in the past, no one art site has precedence over any other. Nor will a body of carefully gathered short articles on a group of artists become canonical or foundational for the understanding of a movement. Although it is valued today, Duchamp's two-issue publication, *The Blind Man*, was published only twice and on the Internet, it would not be treasured but scorned as an abandoned site.

By producing a new form of developed and extended writing that addresses itself to a wide range of readers, the Web writer can actually forge a new field that is a hybrid of up-to-date content, sound scholarship, and articulate stylistic and striking language that is attractive to the twenty-first century eye. If, as my famous art critical counterparts insist, art criticism is "in crisis," then producing a new form of content that is a hybrid mash-up of a sampling of criticism and history and theory would invigorate an old and exhausted genre.[316] But, first, it must be pointed out that the "art world" of today is as shapeless and as expansive as the Internet itself and that this New World for the new Web writer does not resemble the Old World and it is my contention that when the art critic tries to proceed as if nothing has changed, the "crisis" will continue.[317] Rather than work with the public who want to participate in the conversation, print publications are more than happy to fire local critics under the guise of saving money and allowing their readers to rely on Rotten Tomatoes.[318] It is time for intellectuals to take their own lives in their own hands, create their own futures and to reclaim the agency to create and to write and to publish. There are no gates in Cyberspace.

For art historians, open access to the Web ends the gatekeeping to publication and ends the traditional territoriality of art history, leading to inevitable changes in the discipline. This openness allows new voices to write of new topics in a new way and the discipline of art history will be enriched.[319] Undoubtedly there are those who cringe at the thought of open access to art writing and who will worry about those ephemeral ideas of "quality" and "standards," but the future of art writing is on the Internet where new definitions of "quality" for writing are being rewritten and new "standards" for presentation are being developed. With unprecedented and unanticipated openness to publication opportunities, art history and art criticism will inevitably change.[320] Colleges and universities will have to accept serious Web publications, whether from an individual's own Web site/s or from an e-journal. In the minds of the older generation, there may be a hierarchy between print and cyber, but for the younger generation, such distinctions are meaningless. New criteria will inevitably evolve—but it is too early to determine what these new considerations may be. Technology is always changing, making any "rules" obsolete and impossible to apply or enforce. Although less than a decade after the publication of his seminal work *The Technological Society*, Jacques Ellul's book was out of date, but his statement, "Technique has become autonomous; it has fashioned and omnivorous world which obeys its own laws and which has renounced all tradition," [321] explains the world we live in today.

At the beginning of the book, I stated that the Web made binaries impossible and yet, it seems as if I have set up a new binary, between an Old Paradigm of publish or perish and peer review and a New Paradigm of open intellectual discourse.[322] However, these two paradigms are quite separate and operate within very distinct conceptual spheres. Open discourse is just that: "open," populated by "little narratives," and is not only resistant to boundaries but also to the limitations of naming and labeling and making neat and tidy divisions. One of the oddities of current culture, especially in America, is the invisibility of personalities from the world of visual arts. While other arts, especially film and music, are prominent in mass media, from Charlie Rose to TED talks,[323] those of the art world are notably absent. It is unclear why this lacuna in the arts exists and why the fine arts have not been able to "cross over" into the mainstream—lack of interest on the part of the mass audience—snobbery on the part of the practitioners? What is clear is that once an artist or an art writer decides to move into the new territory of the Internet, suddenly the potential of such a shift becomes clear: an artist does not have to wait for the occasional gallery exhibition; the art writer does not have to wait to granted access to the publications that "count." One simply moves forward into visibility.

Whatever the uses and abuses of the Old Paradigm in the past, the future could very well be witness to a new generation of scholars, who, in following the footsteps of public intellectuals,[324] such as Malcolm Gladwell and Simon Scharma,[325] will combine multiple roles that were once separated, raising new questions: when one writes in and publishes and performs in an unguarded and unpatrolled sector, how can scholarship, journalism, *reportage*, criticism, history, public service, and social responsibility[326] be separated? This question comes from the performative precincts of paralogy far away from a center that seems to be disintegrating and buckling of its own weight. New languages will be created and new modes of public address will come about as art historians and other scholars in the humanities find themselves speaking, not in the small enclosure of their peers but to an audience seeking a gift. And there is an audience for the visual arts—visit a museum on any given Sunday, go on an "art walk" in a small city, attend the art fairs in Basel, walk through the halls of an art school—and there they are, the people who will read, listen and hear. But the voices must come from the future and be heard on the Web, the texts must be written for a place where they can be found on the Internet, and writing must be re-written for those who compose in Cyberspace.

There is a large and untapped audience for art and art writers if only the arts professionals are wiling to renounce the safety of the protective practices of restricted discourse. For decades, the center of gravity has resided in the Old Paradigm, but although gravity (gravitas) has its own weight, this heaviness can crush intellectual innovation. Nothing new can come from the center, where there is only the fortress of the already-thought and already-written. To humbly borrow a concept from the great bell hooks, who, in 1984, spoke from a feminist perspective of the advantages of being not in the center but in the margins. In 1989, hooks wrote in the article "Choosing the Margin as a Space of Radical Openness,"

> I was not speaking of a marginality one wishes to lose - to give up or surrender as part of moving into the center - but rather of a site one stays in, clings to even, because it nourishes one's capacity to resist. It offers to one the possibility of radical perspective from which to see and create, to imagine alternatives, new worlds.[327]

And so I salute the edge, where we perch. Welcome to the Wild West, bell hook's "Space of Radical Openness."

****

This short book has come, not to an end, but has entered another level of discourse, the footnotes. These footnotes are the foundations of the text and constitute another level of information for the reader. As with all authors who use work available on the Internet, I make no promise that links will still be active, but the references can always be re-located on the Web. Please continue reading.

[1] In fact, on the occasion of an exhibition (*Postmodernism: Style and Subversion 1970-1990*) at the Victoria and Albert Museum on Postmodernity, Hari Kunzru of *The Guardian* made a case that post 9/11, the Internet made Postmodernism commonplace:

> For many, the events of 11 September signaled the death of postmodernism as an intellectual current. That morning it became clear that "hostility to grand narratives", as Jean-François Lyotard defined it, was a minority pursuit, an intellectual Rubik's cube for a tiny western metropolitan elite. It seemed most of the world still had some use for God, truth and the law, terms which they were using without inverted commas. Graydon Carter, the editor of Vanity Fair, was widely ridiculed for declaring that the attacks signaled "the end of the age of irony", but his use of the po-mo buzzword proved prescient. If irony didn't vanish (though during the crushing literalism and faux-sincerity of the Bush-Blair war years it seemed like a rare and valuable commodity), postmodernism itself suddenly seemed tired and shopworn. Use Google's ngram viewer to look at the incidence of the word "postmodernism" in books since 1975 and you find a sharp rise, peaking in around 1997, then an equally sharp decline. Plot this against the use of the word "internet" and the comparison is startling. Almost unused before the mid-80s, "internet" overtakes "postmodernism" in 2000, and carries on rising. All avant-gardes are in the business of futurism. They make an attempt to inhabit the space they predict, and in so doing, they bring it into being. Postmodernism was, crucially, a pre-digital phenomenon. In retrospect, all the things that seemed so exciting to its adherents – the giddy excess of information, the flattening of old hierarchies, the blending of signs with the body – have been made real by the internet. It's as if the culture was dreaming of the net, and when it arrived, we no longer had any need for those dreams, or rather, they became mundane, part of our everyday life. We have lived through the end of postmodernism and the dawning of postmodernity.

Hari Kunzru. "Postmodernism. From the Cutting Edge to the Museum." *The Guardian* (Thursday, 15 September 2011):

http://www.guardian.co.uk/artanddesign/2011/sep/15/postmodernism-cutting-edge-to-museum

[2] One can only imagine the ghost of Walter Benjamin wondering if the author has not at long last become the engaged activist producer he envisioned,

> Namely, instead of asking: what is the relationship of a work of art to the relationships of production of the time? Is it in accord with them, is it reactionary or does it strive to overthrow them, is it revolutionary?---In place of this question, or in any case before asking this question, I would like to propose another. Before I ask: how does a literary work stand in relation *to* the relationships of production of a period, I would like to ask: how does it stand *in* them? This question aims directly at the function that the work has within the literary relationships of production of a period. In other words, it aims directly at a work's literary *technique*. With the concept of technique, I have named the concept, which gives access to a direct social analysis, and thus a materialist analysis of literary products. At the same time the concept of technique gives us the dialectical starting- point from which the sterile opposition between form and content can be overcome. The concept of technique also indicates the way to determine correctly the relationships between tendency and quality about which we asked at the beginning. So if we could make the above formulation, that the correct political tendency of a work includes its literary quality because it includes its literary tendency, now we can state more exactly that this literary tendency can be found in the progress or regression of literary technique.

Walter Benjamin. "The Author as Producer." *New Left Review*. 1/62, July-August, 1970, pg. 2.:
http://roundtable.kein.org/files/roundtable/Walter%20Benjamin_%20The%20Author%20as%20Producer.pdf

[3] Alan Kirby described the end of postmodernity as the beginning of "digimodernity," or a new form of communication:

> The digimodernist text in its pure form is made up to a varying degree by the reader or viewer or textual consumer. This figure becomes authorial in this sense: s/he makes text where non existed before. It isn't that his/her reading is of a kind to suggest meanings; there is no metaphor here. In an act distinct from their act of reading or viewing, such a reader or viewer gives to the world textual content or shapes the development and progress of a text in visible form. This content is *tangible;* the act is physical. Hence, the name "digital modernism" in which the former term conceals a pun: the centrality of digital technology; the centrality of the digits, of fingers and thumbs that key and press and click in the business of material textual elaboration.

Alan Kirby. *Digimodernism: How New Technologies Dismantle the Postmodern and Reconfigure Our Culture* (New York: The Continuum International Publishing Group Inc., 2009) 51.

[4] In 1994, Elizabeth Lane Lawley explained Pierre Bourdieu's concept of symbolic capital and academia:

> While the field and habitus describe, respectively, the environment and rules within which class struggles take place, the concept of symbolic capital defines the tools used by individuals and institutions within a field to gain dominance and thus to reproduce themselves over time. It is in this area that Bourdieu both draws most strongly from Marxist ideas of class and conflict, and also breaks most clearly from the classical Marxist constructions. Rather than defining capital purely in Marx's economic terms, Bourdieu defines two primary types of symbolic capital: economic and cultural. Both describe endowments that individuals bring with them into the field and attempt to augment. Economic capital is equivalent to the capital familiar to students of Marxist theories including both monetary and property assets. Cultural capital, however, is a concept unique to Bourdieu's theoretical model. This is where Bourdieu's use of the narrower definition of culture comes into play. Cultural capital can also be described as cultural competence. Like economic capital, it conveys legitimacy, and a legitimacy regulated by institutions within the

society. In the case of cultural capital, that legitimacy is regulated not by the government but by educational and artistic institutions.

Cultural capital can be converted into economic capital, just as economic capital can be converted into cultural capital. However, these conversions happen at different rates of exchange. Economic capital is more liquid, and more easily transferable from generation to generation, making it particularly useful in continuing the process of reproducing class legitimacy and domination over time. Cultural capital, however, also functions as a major factor in class definition. In order to maintain the legitimacy of cultural capital, and to ensure both its convertibility and its ability to reproduce itself, the educational system creates a market in cultural capital with certificates as the currency.

The real significance of capital in Bourdieu's theoretical model is the role that it plays in the continuing struggle between the dominating and the dominated classes. It is through the acquisition of capital, and the use of symbolic capital to perpetrate symbolic violence, that classes ensure their own legitimacy and reproduction. Like Marx, Bourdieu believes that the more this process of symbolic violence is hidden from sight and left unchallenged, the more powerful it is in reproducing class dominance. Thus, when we take as an absolute given that individuals with advanced degrees are best qualified to teach in universities, and do not challenge the assumptions behind that assertion, we leave power structures unchanged and allow the continuation of the symbolic violence that Bourdieu calls "pedagogic action."

Elizabeth Lane Lawley. "The Sociology of Culture in Computer-Mediated Communication: An Initial Exploration:"
http://www.itcs.com/elawley/bourdieu.html

[5] Intellectual capital has different meanings, depending upon whether or not one is referring to the ideas of Pierre Bourdieu or to the cloistered world of the university to the pragmatic world of business. The latter actually values the "knowledge workers" or those who possess knowledge

that in business parlance must be "managed." An article on Intellectual Capital traces the early beginnings of the concept:

> ...intellectual capital is also irrevocably bound up with the notion of the knowledge worker, and here, as with so many other ideas, we can turn to the thinking of Peter Drucker. In his 1969 book, *The Age of Discontinuity*, Drucker introduced the term knowledge worker to describe the highly trained, intelligent managerial professional who realises his or her own worth and contribution to the organisation. "The knowledge worker sees himself just as another professional, no different from the lawyer, the teacher, the preacher, the doctor or the government servant of yesterday," wrote Drucker. "He has the same education. He has more income, he has probably greater opportunities as well. He may well realise that he depends on the organisation for access to income and opportunity, and that without the investment the organisation has made – and a high investment at that – there would be no job for him, but he also realises, and rightly so, that the organisation equally depends on him." Drucker recognised the new breed, but key to his contribution was the realisation that knowledge is both power and ownership. If knowledge, rather than labour, is the new measure of economic society, then the fabric of capitalist society must change. In his 1992 book, *Managing for the Future*, he developed this idea: "From now on the key is knowledge. The world is becoming not labour intensive, not materials intensive, not energy intensive, but knowledge intensive."

----"Intellectual Capital." *The Management Lab:*
http://www.managementlab.org/files/u2/pdf/classic%20innovations/Intellectual_Capital.pdf

[6] There are articles, too numerous to mention, or cite, much less to read, addressing the current crisis in academic publishing. This crisis, which has existed for twenty years, has resisted publishing on the Internet as a solution. As Colin Steele reported in 2008:

> When it comes to the relationship between publishing and promotion and tenure, academic perceptions remain

rooted in historical models. As Richard Fisher has noted, "putting the finished copy of [your book] in the hands of your Dean or Head of Department remains a tangible moment that no click can yet replicate, and one to which tenure and promotional committees in our worlds remain highly susceptible". A recent survey notes the printed journal, compared to e-versions, faces a steep decline in the coming five to ten years in the institutional marketplace. The limited distribution of print monographs may also be contributing to destroying the intellectual vitality that monographs were originally meant to foster. One of the major issues for getting E-press monographs accepted is faculty conservatism, for example, in terms of the use of print books for review purposes and the belief that electronic content is somehow less prestigious than its print equivalent. The restructuring by Columbia University Press of its Gutenberg-e monographs to open access has highlighted some of the structural issues in regard to faculty perceptions.

Colin Steele. "Scholarly Monograph Publishing in the 21st century: The Future More Than Ever Should be an Open Book." *The Journal of Electronic Publishing* (Volume 11, Issue 2, Spring, 2008): http://quod.lib.umich.edu/cgi/t/text/text-idx?c=jep;cc=jep;rgn=main;view=text;idno=3336451.0011.201

[7] In writing about "Intended or Unintended Consequences of a Publish-or-Perish Culture: A Worldwide Survey," authors Hendrik P. van Dalen and Kène Henkers wrote,

> To attain promotion within academia and in the end full professorship, one must have a solid publication record. Even after attaining full professorship, the ambition shifts to securing a position at a more prestigious university. The higher productivity of full professors combined with the observation that they do not feel less pressure than lower-ranked professors suggests that self-selection mechanisms are at work. Low- productivity scholars move to institutes or universities that do not put too much pressure on them, whereas highly productive scholars move to higher-ranked universities where productivity standards are also higher. Due to this

> treadmill effect, scholars can arrive at the conclusion that in order to stay in the same place one must continuously run harder.

Hendrik P. van Dalen and Kène Henkers. "Intended or Unintended Consequences of a Publish-or-Perish Culture: A Worldwide Survey," *CentER Discussion Paper Series No. 2012-003* (January 11, 2012): http://papers.ssrn.com/sol3/papers.cfm?abstract_id=1983205

[8] Mario Biagioli presented what Raymond Siemens called "the argument *ad fontes*," or back to the origins, of peer review in "From Book Censorship to Academic Peer Review." Biagioli noted that peer review was rooted in the need of the seventeenth century state to control publication and distribution of ideas and developed, over time, into what the author, a follower of Michel Foucault, called "disciplinary practices." As he stated,

> Along with the institutionalization of scientific disciplines, peer review also moved from a filtering function (to stop 'unsuitable' books from being printed) to an editorial function (to intervene on texts to make them conform to disciplinary standards). The development of such parameters of quality or publishability did not represent a simple freeing of science from the legalities of censorship but the articulation of a new, more specialized and internalized kind of disciplining. When, from the end of the 18th century on, state censorship systems faded out with the absolutist regimes on which they hinged, peer review did not follow their demise. It lost its legal role within the licensing system of scientific publications, but it persisted unchallenged as a selection practice that eventually came to characterize the whole of academic and university science.

Biagilio's title is interesting, pointing to a direct conceptual link of state control of thought to academic control of the disciplines and of the thinking of those who operate within the discipline---all in the name of controlling the production of content.

Mario Biagiloi. "From Book Censorship to Academic Peer Review." *Emergences* (Volume 12, Number 1, 2002): http://innovation.ucdavis.edu/people/publications/Biagioli%202008%20Censorship_review.pdf

And as Raymond Siemens stated in "The Credibility of Electronic Publishing,"

> In general circulation for some time, the argument *ad fontes* suggests that we consider the source of our formalized academic publication process; it operates, in essence, as follows. In earlier times, when formal methods of inquiry and dissemination as we now know them were being shaped, the exchange of ideas and knowledge and the advancement of scholarship was facilitated as much by private exchanges and the circulation of private manuscripts and correspondence as by other means. The establishment of the first scientific journals, in Britain and France during the seventeenth century, saw the beginnings of academic publication's formalized dissemination, concurrent with the development of the role of scholarly editor -- the scholarly editor, in this case, being someone who took on the task of re-circulating materials of interest to a community of scholarly readers. In addition to being responsible for disseminating those materials, the editor also helped determine which materials were of value enough to warrant dissemination to that community. While editorial boards and methods of review (methods that act, to this day, as additional assurances of value) would soon rise out of this, much of value still happened outside the more formalized processes of exchange that were emerging, and much of value would continue to be exchanged in forums outside of those vetted by editor and editorial board; and so it does to this day.

Raymond Siemens. "The Credibility of Electronic Publishing. Introduction and Overview:" http://web.viu.ca/hssfc/final/Overview.htm

[9] Cathy Davidson, co-founder of Humanities, Arts, Science, and Technology Advanced Technology or HASTAC, wrote an interesting article on peer review in 2011, where she recounted her experiences:

> I have given a number of talks about how shocking it was to inherit the files of *American Literature*, to read decades' worth of reader's reports on articles, and see

> how often, before around 1970, articles were accepted or rejected on quite personal terms, based on who the author was, who the author studied with, who the author knew, and, even more shockingly, overtly what race, gender, or sexuality the author was said to possess. "XX, isn't that a Hebraic-sounding name?" one rejection report began. "He's a fairy," another said. *Really.* There was no sense of accountability to some anonymous, institutionally-approved standard. Those sound like the kind of anonymous, hateful comments people leave on blogs or YouTube, but these were delivered by the top people, the arbiters of tenure and promotion, in the whole profession. They wrote with a tacit idea that "we" knew who was or wasn't worth publishing. The "we" was the in-group then running AL; there were some horrible people calling the shots but, at the same time, there were also wonderful people, some of the finest and most generous and I read their comments too. But no one else did. Because it was a closed system. Abuses occur in open systems; abuses happen in closed systems. That's the point. The contemporary system of anonymous double-blind or single-blind and multiply-read peer review can stink...but even worse was the old-fashioned prejudice or the too-chummy Old Boy idea of "it's who you know/are/studied under that counts."

Cathy Davidson. "Does Digital Publishing Need Peer Review?" HASTAC (July 20, 2011): http://hastac.org/blogs/cathy-davidson/does-digital-publishing-need-peer-review

[10] In 2004 David Shatz published *Peer Review: A Critical Inquiry*, which began with a brief overview demonstrating how unreliable the system of peer review had become. Shatz noted that while the scholars in the sciences had published many reports of the corruption within the practice, the humanities have continued to shy away from dealing with what is clearly a problem for the field.

> Surprisingly, this is the first book-length study of peer review that utilizes methods and resources of contemporary philosophy. In fact, this is the first wide-ranging treatment of the subject by a scholar in the

humanities. I say "surprisingly" because given the ubiquity and importance of evaluation in academia, and the frustrations aroused by the difficulty of publishing in the humanities due to high rejection rates in peer reviewed journals and publishing houses, one would expect that peer review would be existentially crucial and therefore be extensively discussed in print (peer reviewed or otherwise). Furthermore, peer evaluation raises issues about the import and basis of evaluative judgments and the value of free expression, issues of interest to scholars in the humanities. Because of its ethical aspect, the topic also has dimensions of epistemological significance, since it implicates such concepts as truth, bias, relativism, conservatism, consensus, and standards of good argument. Philosophers and other humanities scholars have produced a voluminous literature on these subjects. Yet they have not applied their approaches to these topics to peer review itself, that is, to the very procedures and practices that produced much of the voluminous literature in ethics, epistemology, and so many other fields. Specialists in fields of the humanities have not organized and sparked a systematic and ongoing debate. Why is this?

David Shatz. *Peer Review: A Critical Inquiry* (Lanham, Maryland: The Rowman Littlefield Publishing Group, Inc., 2004) 4.

[11] In February of 2013, Daniel Leszczynski wrote of yet another problem with peer review. Interestingly, the sciences are where examples of incompetence of peer review can come to light. In the sciences, it is possible to discover actual errors or dubious methodologies. However, in the humanities, which are inherently more subjective, the objective standards are less rigorous. In "Opinion: Scientific Peer Review in Crisis," Leszczynski recounted a problem with "the Danish Cohort study,"

> Peer-review failed, and a study that should never have got published due to its unfounded conclusions remains as a valid peer-reviewed article in the *British Medical Journal*. As long as the flawed study is not withdrawn it will be used by scientists and by decision makers to justify their actions—e.g. a reference to the Danish Cohort study was recently used as supporting evidence in

failing to indicate a causal link between cell phone radiation and brain cancer by the US Government Accountability Office. How is it possible that the *British Medical Journal* allowed such a poor quality peer review? Were the peer reviewers incompetent or did they have conflicts of interest? What was the involvement of the *BMJ*'s editors? Why, once alerted to serious design flaws by readers, have *BMJ* editors not taken any action? In my opinion the Danish Cohort study should be retracted because no revision or rewriting can rescue it. The study is missing crucial data on exposure to cell phone radiation. Furthermore, an investigation should be launched to determine why such a flawed study was published. Was it peer reviewer and *BMJ* editor incompetence alone or was a conflict of interest among reviewers involved? (The authors of the study declared no conflicts of interest, but the original cohort was reportedly established with funding from a Danish phone company.) Answering these questions is important because it might help to avoid similar mistakes in the future.

Daniel Leszczynski. "Opinion: Scientific Peer Review in Crisis." *The Scientist Magazine* (February 25, 2013): http://www.the-scientist.com/?articles.view/articleNo/34518/title/Opinion--Scientific-Peer-Review-in-Crisis/

Another problem in studying the peer review process is the fact that the Internet is progressing and growing faster than the research, which now has to assess the role of the web in allowing publication to take place without peer review. A case in point is an excellent article on peer review written in the early 2000s and, not unexpectedly, the author and the works he cites are from the scientific community. The Joint Information Systems Committee is United Kingdom based organization that researches the intersection between technology and university education.

Fytton Rowland. "The Peer Review Process. A Report to the JISC Scholarly Communications Group"
http://www.jisc.ac.uk/uploaded_documents/rowland.pdf

[12] One of the more interesting "war stories" came from Katherine Fitzpatrick whose first book, *The Anxiety of Obsolescence,* had a long and

hard road to publication, as recounted in her second book, *Planned Obsolescence: Publishing, Technology, and the Future of the Academy*. As the new title implies, the earlier event apparently changed the career trajectory of Fitzpatrick, who, and I would agree with her, feels that it is unwise to simply move the system of peer review to Cyberspace. Fitzpatrick's book explored what it now means to be an "author" now that one's text can be repeatedly overwritten as readers/peers comment. Her book provides an excellent overview (up to date of publication) of the new situation in university scholarship and she stated,

> ...the real call for open-access publishing models has its roots not in the subversion of market forces in the distribution of scholarship, but in the ethical desire to break down the barrier between the information "haves" and "have-nots" of the twenty-first-century university structure. Proponents of open access hope to enable institutions without substantive endowments, and those in less-wealthy states and developing nations, to have access to the most important new developments in scholarly research. Such access is arguably most crucial in medical and other scientific fields, but we must resist the suggestion that the humanities, and particularly fields such as literary and media studies, are relative luxuries that do not demand similar openness of distribution; fields such as these continue to represent the central interpretive and analytical skills of our, and our students', being in the world, and it is therefore no less important for the products of research in these fields to be made as widely available as possible. If part of the core mission of the university—particularly state-funded institutions, but including those private institutions that, as New York University's motto would have it, consider themselves to serve the public interest—is the production and dissemination of new forms of knowledge, then open-access modes of distribution would seem to be far more in keeping with that mission than would the closed, cost-recovery model.

Kathleen Fitzpatrick. "Chapter 5. The University." *Planned Obsolescence: Publishing, Technology, and the Future of the Academy* (NYU Press: 2011)

[13] As Cathy Davidson pointed out there are thriving communities of alternative academic publishing that utilize some form of "peer review:"

> If we want digital scholarship to "count" for tenure within currently existing institutions of tenure, then the fact that it is peer reviewed--that it has to pass through a certain process of feedback, evaluation, and revision (even if it holds to the internet dictum of "publish first, revise later") is important; specifying the means of evaluation and assessment should be part of the portfolio that leads to tenure. It may not be traditional peer review (whatever "traditional" means there--each press and journal has its own forms of "traditional") but that makes it even more urgent to spell out its process, the means by which a given community ensures the quality and calibre of contribution, decides on its norms of openness and expertise.

Cathy Davidson. Op cit.

[14] The importance of exposing intellectual studies to the largest and most public audience possible is illustrated by the recent scandal of an now-infamous "austerity" study, "Growth in a Time of Debt," by Harvard economists Carmen Reinhart and Ken Rogoff which was revealed to be the result of a misuse of methodology, i.e. e., eliminating data that contradicted a conclusion that seemed to be foregone. The interesting aspect of the paper is that it was initially presented at the American Economic Association in 2010, and presentations do not require peer review. Once presented, the paper was released into the wild, without rigorous vetting. Once the work product---materials used in the study--- was given over to other economists the basic errors in data entry were discovered.
Mark Gongloff. "Influential Reinhart-Rogoff Pro-Austerity Research Riddled with Errors: Study." *Huffington Post Business* (04/16/2013):
http://www.huffingtonpost.com/2013/04/16/reinhart-rogoff-austerity-research-errors_n_3094015.html
The authors of the report defended themselves against the onslaught of criticism, following what economist Paul Krugman noted was a long-standing and on-going concern as to the validity of the study. The errors that undermined the study came to light only when the authors allowed another university access to their original spread sheet. The fact that, as Krugman pointed out, the authors already had "status" when their paper was circulated and eventually published may have led to the lack of substantive peer review. However, no one could replicate the results, giving rise to concerns that something internal to the study had gone very

wrong. This high-profile case illustrates the flaws of the traditional peer review system, which rests upon intellectual nepotism, but also shows the value of public exposure of not just the study but also of the revelation of its underlying data that resulted in a corrected version of the study laid out for all to evaluate and debate.
Paul Krugman. "The Excel Depression." *The New York Times* (April 18, 2013): http://www.nytimes.com/2013/04/19/opinion/krugman-the-excel-depression.html
The fact that the reasons for erroneous conclusions of the "study" were finally uncovered by a graduate student added to the public embarrassment and international exposure of what seemed to be either frighteningly bad methodology or deliberate manipulation of numbers in order to get to the desired result. Needless to say the authors vigorously defended their reputations, but as investigative reporter Matt Taibbi pointed out in the June 6 2013 (print edition) issue of *Rolling Stone*, "...the two Harvard windheads reversed course arguing that they had been in favor of using debt to stimulate growth all along."
Matt Taibbi. "The Mad Science of the National Debt." *Rolling Stone* (May 22, 2013): http://www.rollingstone.com/politics/news/the-mad-science-of-the-national-debt-20130522

Carmen Reinhart and Kenneth Rogoff. "Debt, Growth, and the Austerity Debate." *The New York Times* (April 25, 2013):
http://www.nytimes.com/2013/04/26/opinion/debt-growth-and-the-austerity-debate.html?pagewanted=all

Then on May 25, 2013, in a "Dear Paul" letter, the duo got quite personal: "So it has been with deep disappointment that we have experienced your spectacularly uncivil behavior the past few weeks."
http://www.carmenreinhart.com/letter-to-pk/

To which Dr. Krugman replied on Farred Zakaria's June 2, 2013 *Global Public Square* television program that, although Rogoff was a "magnificent economist, the paper was "thrown out hastily." And so the spat continued because the peer review system broke down and was not fixed until the work was released to the public, where, at last it was properly and humiliatingly vetted:
http://globalpublicsquare.blogs.cnn.com/2013/06/01/krugman-on-the-rogoff-reinhart-spat/

[15] There has been a trend away from full time work towards part time work in universities and colleges since the end of the 20th century. For most institutions, the majority of the faculty is part time, nameless,

unrepresented individuals, who nevertheless carry the burden college education. An interesting report issued in 2012 highlighted a few aspects of contingent last-minute hires.
Steve Street, Maria Maisto, Esther Merves, and Gary Rhoades. "Who is Professor 'Staff' and How can this Person Teach so Many Classes?" *Center for Higher Education Policy Report #2* (August 23, 2012): http://www.insidehighered.com/sites/default/server_files/files/profstaff(2).pdf

[16] Kathleen Fitzpatrick argued for Open Access in the face of the rising costs of publication, which are stifling opportunities to create and publish and to distribute ideas.

> Publishing is never free, of course; it either costs us in dollars or in labor (and often both), and sustainability in scholarly publishing has often been equated with the need to produce revenue based on the sale of publishing's products. As I've argued at length, however, the current system of scholarly publishing is already not sustainable for most not-for-profit organizations, and some of the ostensible solutions – such as handing journals over to the commercial publishers who seem to have found a viable profit model – are only making things worse. One might see here the cautionary tale of a fellow humanities scholarly organization that, facing a budgetary crisis, contracted with a commercial publisher to distribute its journals. That organization received a nice bit of income in the short term – but the commercial publisher involved immediately more than doubled the institutional subscription fees for the journals involved, ensuring that more libraries would be forced not to carry those journals, and thus reducing the potential impact of the work published in them. And needless to say, however much the organization involved earned in this exchange, the corporate publisher earned more.

Kathleen Fitzpatrick. "Giving it Away: Sharing and the Future of Scholarly Education." *Planned Obsolescence* (January 2012): http://www.plannedobsolescence.net/blog/giving-it-away/

[17] Another upstart writer, criticizing the Old Paradigm, but for very different reasons was *Enemies of Promise: Publishing, Perishing and the Eclipse of Scholarship*, a short 2004 book by Lindsay Waters, published by

Prickly Paradigm Press. This book is concerned with the linkage of publishing and tenure, which is an argument against how tenure is determined.

[18] As early as 2001, Jean-Claude Guédon and Raymond Siemens did a study on peer review and electronic publishing. Guédon described the connection between print and prestige:

> Visibility is a function of prestige and technology. A very prestigious journal will always be very visible, but an average-prestige journal can see its visibility enhanced by technology as well as a change in language. In the bilingual journal on geology and physical geography published in the Université de Montréal, the same author sees his articles cited twice as much if he or she publishes in English rather than French. A journal that is better distributed, promoted, located within good baskets of similar periodicals, well referenced by many bibliographies, etc., will obviously be more visible and there is no question that a powerful publisher capable of printing lavish catalogs, offering easy subscription services to dozens of journals through one procedure, etc., will make a journal more visible than would a small university press or a small learned society. Big publishers have often played on this capability to convince interesting journals supported by weak infrastructures to move into their private collection. Small, weak journals will probably see their visibility increase quite a bit through electronic publishing, and this is probably true for a fair proportion of HSS journals in Canada. And this increased visibility will also probably result in enhanced prestige and authority. However, one must keep in mind that such elusive variables as prestige or authority are built only gradually and that it takes time. As a result, a paper journal going toward a digitized version can expect temporary set backs in visibility, particularly if its reader community is known to be somewhat more resisting to technological innovations than is the norm. This also means that particular attention must be paid to the transition period through which we are presently going.
>
> Prestige is very much tied to tradition and/or the prestige of the evaluators themselves. It is clear that if an

electronic journal in literature were supervised by several Nobel prizes that would allow themselves to be actively engaged in its day to day activities, there is no question that such a journal would not suffer from any lack of prestige, on the contrary. The problem that new electronic journals face is that they have not had real time yet to establish a reputation and, as the technology, until recently, filtered the reading public in way that had nothing to do with their excellence, but rather with their proficiency in the new technologies, such journals were suffering -- and may still be -- suffering from an artificially truncated audience. This situation is evolving positively and ever more rapidly now, but the question nevertheless remains to some extent. Authority is different from prestige and, on that score, digital material do not have to envy their paper counterparts. In effect, any electronic journal that would have authoritative editorial boards, that would develop particularly rigorous (and also innovative) peer review processes and that would manage to throw effective light on their best published pieces would certainly gain unquestionable authority without many problems. And if a journal enjoys visibility plus authority, prestige is not far behind.

Imprint, in a sense, is short hand for prestige. I have an article published in the American Historical Review and that means a lot more than the Canadian Historical Review for some mysterious reason, one of which being the relative size of the communities and the degree of competition to be accepted (measured in rejection rates). Presently, the Canadian and USA efforts work in parallel and with communities that overlap only slightly. However, in a distributed, digitized environment, being present at the same time as the other journal is not a threat, but an advantage on the contrary, as the strategy of web-rings amply demonstrates. In other words, articles from these two journals (and many other similar journals) could be joined in the same, large, archive. But what of Canadian individuality, identity, etc., questions that loom large in the HSS field (and factually repeated, so to speak, in the French-language journals of Québec and the rest of French Canada)? The answer, actually, is simple: nothing prevents one or several Canadian editorial board to select specific articles that they find particularly interesting and do or invent all they want to bring attention to these publications. In other words, electronic publishing distinguishes between the phase where documents are placed at the disposal of the public (publishing proper) and the phase where « distinctions » are being attributed. It used to be that being printed was « the » distinction; electronic publishing changes this and leads us to think of the distinction phase completely separately from the publishing phase.

However, doing so changes the means by which distinction is imparted and imparting distinction is a sure sign of power. In other words, those who now hold that privilege are afraid of losing it ("gate keepers") and they will every possible argument to protect it without, if possible, ever mentioning it.

Jean-Claude Guédon. "The Credibility of Electronic Publishing: A Report to the Humanities and Social Sciences Federation of Canada." (2001) http://web.viu.ca/hssfc/final/credibility.htm

[19] There are a number of books, all of which become unavoidably out of date as soon as they are published, about researching on the Internet. Some of the newer ones include
Annette N. Markham and Nancy K. Baym, Editors. *Internet Inquiry: Conversations about Method* (Sage Publications, 2009)
Roger D. Wimmer and Joseph R. Dominick. *Mass Media Research: An Introduction* (Boston: Wadsworth, 2011)
Daniel Araya, Yana Breindl, Tessa J. Houghton. *Nexus: New Intersections in Internet Research* (New York, Peter Lang Publishing, Inc., 2011)

[20] One of the new generation of scholars who are dubious about the value of traditional journals, is Kevin Bonham who wrote,

> We don't need any academic journal's services anymore. If you publish in any journal, you are making it easier for them to take action that harms academic institutions, so you shouldn't... the truth is, journals add very little value to science, and impose huge monetary costs, as well as costs in terms of delayed publication and limited distribution.

Kevin Bonham. "Peerj—the Science Journal we Need and Deserve." *ScienceBlogs* (February 12, 2013):
http://scienceblogs.com/webeasties/2013/02/12/peerj-the-science-journal-we-need-and-deserve/

[21] It is likely that a new kind of Public Intellectual will emerge: people who create and distribute knowledge, not only in the sciences where the dissemination of research is often government mandated but also in the humanities. These more academic types could emerge and are emerging on the Internet. In 2001 Richard Posner wrote *Public Intellectuals: A Study in Decline* and then updated it in 2003. However, it is now, predictably out of date, as he was thinking mostly of print media and of intellectuals who write outside of their academic fields. But today, it is possible to foresee academia continually moving to a new domain: the Web and the profile of "public intellectuals" will undoubtedly become more strongly etched on line.
Richard Posner. *Public Intellectuals: A Study in Decline* (Harvard University Press, 2001/2003)

[22] Mark Poster, one of the scholars who has been among the most perceptive of those who analyze media, commented that

> The question of the culture in relation to the Internet involves a risk, a step into the unfamiliar precisely with respect to the figure of the self. If this question is foreclosed, one cannot examine critically the political culture of the new media. One can merely put forward existing cultural figures of the self---race, class, and gender, or citizen, manager, and worker---to test the role of new media in furthering their positions as they see themselves and as they are. Such a framework is instrumental and overlooks systematically the constitutive character of media not in some form of technological determinism but as a space that encourages practices that, in turn, serve to construct new types of subjects. There is perhaps a more subtle way in which critical studies refuses the cultural question of the Internet. In this case scholars do not so much presuppose existing forms of race, class, and gender. The Internet is here fully recognized. Bit it is configured as a threat, not to specific groups but to general types of practice that are characterized as "human."

Mark Poster. *What's the Matter with the Internet?* (University of Minnesota, 2001) 4.

Poster's point can be illustrated by a section from a chapter by Johanna Drucker in which she states,

> Positivistic, strictly quantitative, mechanistic, reductive and literal, these visualizations and processing techniques preclude humanistic methods from their operations because of the very assumptions on which they are designed: that objects of knowledge can be understood as self-identical, self-evident, a historical, and autonomous. Within a humanistic theoretical frame, all of these precepts that have been subject to serious critical rethinking. So can we engage in the design of digital environments that embody specific theoretical principles drawn from the humanities, not merely work within platforms and protocols created by disciplines whose methodological premises are often at odds with---even hostile to---humanistic thought?

Johanna Drucker. "Humanistic Theory and Digital Scholarship." *Debates in the Digital Humanities.* Edited by Matthew K. Gold (University of Minnesota Press, 2012) 86.

[23] An excellent example of applying critical theory to the Internet can be found on YouTube by the theorist, Christian Fuchs, "Critical Theory in the Age of the Internet, Part One:"
http://www.youtube.com/watch?v=qPr8qof8YtQ
and "Part Two:" http://www.youtube.com/watch?v=LQ6xyJYdFKY
where he discusses the gift economy of the Internet. Fuchs is also the author of *Foundations of Critical Media and Information Studies* (New York: Routledge, 2011) and *Internet and Society: Social Theory in the Information Age* (New York: Routledge, 2008)

[24] As early as 1995, Mark Poster attempted to analyze the new highways and byways of information that he correctly understood would change the world of the future. His words and language choices---all that was available at the time seem both quaint and insightful:

> The effortless reproduction and distribution of information is greeted by modern economic organizations, the corporation, with the same anxiety

that plagues nation states. Audio taping was resisted by the moguls of the music industry; video taping by Hollywood; modems by the telephone industry giants. Property rights are put in doubt when information is set free of its material integument to move and to multiply in cyberspace with few constraints. The response of our captains of industry is the absurd one of attempting vastly to extend the principle of property by promulgating new "intellectual property laws," flying in the face of the advance in the technologies of transmission and dissemination. The problem for capitalism is how to contain the word and the image, to bind them to proper names and logos when they flit about at the speed of light and procreate with indecent rapidity, not arborially, to use the terms of Deleuze and Guattari, as in a centralized factory, but rhyzomically, at any decentered location. If that were not enough to daunt defenders of modern notions of property, First Amendment issues are equally at risk. Who, for example, "owns" the rights to and is thereby responsible for the text on Internet bulletin boards: the author, the system operator, the community of participants? Does freedom of speech extend to cyberspace, as it does to print? How easy will it be to assess damages and mete out blame in a communicative world whose contours are quite different from those of face-to-face speech and print? These and numerous other fundamental questions are raised by Internet communications for institutions, laws and habits that developed in the very different context of modernity.

Mark Poster. "Postmodern Virtualities." *The Second Media Age* (Blackwell, 1995): http://www.hnet.uci.edu/mposter/writings/internet.html

[25] For many writers, post 911, it is a given that Postmodernism, like Modernism, is a historical artifact and should be treated as such. As Alan Kirby wrote in *Philosophy Now*,

> Along with this new view of reality, it is clear that the dominant intellectual framework has changed. While postmodernism's cultural products have been consigned to the same historicized status as modernism and romanticism, its intellectual tendencies (feminism, postcolonialism etc.) find themselves isolated in the new

philosophical environment. The academy, perhaps especially in Britain, is today so swamped by the assumptions and practices of market economics that it is deeply implausible for academics to tell their students they inhabit a postmodern world where a multiplicity of ideologies, world-views and voices can be heard. Their every step hounded by market economics, academics cannot preach multiplicity when their lives are dominated by what amounts in practice to consumer fanaticism. The world has narrowed intellectually, not broadened, in the last ten years. Where Lyotard saw the eclipse of Grand Narratives, pseudo-modernism sees the ideology of globalised market economics raised to the level of the sole and over-powering regulator of all social activity – monopolistic, all-engulfing, all-explaining, all-structuring, as every academic must disagreeably recognise. Pseudo-modernism is of course consumerist and conformist, a matter of moving around the world as it is given or sold.

Secondly, whereas postmodernism favoured the ironic, the knowing and the playful, with their allusions to knowledge, history and ambivalence, pseudo-modernism's typical intellectual states are ignorance, fanaticism and anxiety: Bush, Blair, Bin Laden, Le Pen and their like on one side, and the more numerous but less powerful masses on the other. Pseudo-modernism belongs to a world pervaded by the encounter between a religiously fanatical segment of the United States, a largely secular but definitionally hyper-religious Israel, and a fanatical sub-section of Muslims scattered across the planet: pseudo-modernism was not born on 11 September 2001, but postmodernism was interred in its rubble.

Alan Kirby. "The Death of Postmodernism and Beyond." *Philosophy Now. A Magazine of Ideas* (January/February 2013): http://philosophynow.org/issues/58/The_Death_of_Postmodernism_And_Beyond

[26] In writing of scholarship in the field of media, John Hartley began his article by addressing a historical split in the intellectual world between

knowing and doing or to put it another way, between art and craft, and all the hierarchical implications heretofore entailed:

> There are two aspects to the problem of digital scholarship and pedagogy. One has to do with scholarship, the other with pedagogy. In scholarship, the association of knowledge with its printed form remains dominant. In pedagogy, the desire to abandon print for "new" media is urgent, at least in some parts of the academy. Film and media studies are thus at the intersection of opposing forces pulling the field "back" to print and "forward" to digital media. These tensions may be especially painful in a field whose own object of study is an analogue form of communication, neither print nor digital. Although print has been overtaken in the popular marketplace by audiovisual forms, this was never achieved in the domain of scholarship. Even when it is digitally distributed, the output of research is still a "paper." Meanwhile, in the realm of teaching, production- and practice-based pedagogy has become firmly established. Nevertheless, a disjunction remains between high-end scholarship in research universities and vocational training in teaching institutions. Neither is well equipped to deal with the digital challenge.

John Hartley. "Digital Scholarship and Pedagogy, the Next Step: Cultural Science." *Cinema Journal* (Volume 48, Number 2, Winter 2009): http://muse.jhu.edu/login?auth=0&type=summary&url=/journals/cinema_journal/v048/48.2.hartley.pdf

[27] In an otherwise stunningly outmoded approach to publication (written in 2010!), Sarah Jones provided a ray of common sense:

> As metrics of scholarly authority, university-press books are supposed to reflect prestige, rigor, and accomplishment. What makes the scholarly book a hotbed of discussion about authority in academe is the recent increase in the digital publication of books. As the costs of print publication continue to rise and the numbers of books acquired by libraries and individual users have decreased, the expectation of having your own book when the tenure and promotion committee is waiting, persists. This tension has made the digital

publication of a scholarly book tempting to many researchers. In addressing the Sixth Scholarly Communication Symposium at Georgetown University Library, Professor Stephen Nichols of Johns Hopkins University, explains that many in the academic community believe that peer-review processes are only possible for print publications, so digital scholarship is belittled and younger scholars are discouraged from pursuing such avenues. This perception of digitally published scholarship—including books—reduces the legitimacy of an online book as a metric of scholarly authority according to members of the academic community. This point is important to remember as we consider books as metrics of authority. The digitization of information is happening; it is now a question of the extent to which academic information will go digital and the correlation of that shift to academic perceptions of print and digital books as scholarly metrics. While many scholarly authority metrics such as the h-index, the journal impact factor, and Web of Science citation patterns seek to quantify objectively the research output of academics, it is my contention that scholarly books as metrics of authority may tell us more about the individuals applying that metric than the scholar being considered.

Sarah Jones. "Scholarly Books." *Measuring Scholarly Metrics.* Edited by Gordon R. Mitchell (Lincoln, Nebraska: Oldfather Press, 2011) 33.

[28] This loss of a fixed location brings to mind, of course, Frederic Jameson who in an interview in 1989 interview answering a question about the loss of a "whole," Jameson stated,

> One of the ways to describe this is as a modification in the very nature of the cultural sphere: a loss of the autonomy of culture or a case of culture falling into the world. As you say, this makes it much more difficult to speak of cultural systems and to elevate them in isolation. A whole new theoretical problem is posed. Thinking at once negatively and positively about it is a beginning, but what we need is a new vocabulary. The languages that have been useful in talking about culture and politics in

the past don't really seem adequate to this historical moment.

Anders Stephanson and Frederic Jameson. "Regarding Postmodernism---A Conversation with Frederic Jameson." *Social Text. Universal Abandon? The Politics of Postmodernism* (No. 21, Duke University Press: 1989):
http://postcolonial.net/@Backfile/_entries/3/file-pdf.pdf

[29] Doris Teske took up this issue of the relevance of Postmodernism in his 2003 anthology,

> Cyberspace can be read as turning these theories into reality, as the created and virtual space has come to materialise the hypothetical constructs of many theories of postmodernity. In the space of its virtual communities, location and distance have become irrelevant so that questions of margin and center seem obsolete in initial idealistic views of the Internet, the public space of the virtual world seemed to be accessible to all, as traditional channels of distribution were circumvented.

Doris Teske. "Beyond Postmodernist Thirdspace?---The Internet in a Post-Modern World." *Beyond Postmodernism: Reassessments in Literature, Theory, and Culture* edited by Kalus Stierstorfer (Berlin: Walter de Gruyter gmbH & Co., 2003) 102.

[30] George Ritzer. *Contemporary Sociological Theory and its Classical Roots: The Basics* (McGraw-Hill, Incorporated, 2009)
 Postmodern Social Theory (McGraw-Hill, 1997)

[31] George Ritzer. "The Internet Through a Postmodern Lens." *The Society Pages*. November 19, 2012:
http://thesocietypages.org/cyborgology/2012/11/19/the-internet-through-a-postmodern-lens/
or
http://www.youtube.com/watch?v=BqZ5w2dw4AU&feature=player_embedded

[32] Jean Baudrillard. *Simulacra and Simulations*. Translated by Shelia Faria (University of Michigan Press, 1995):
http://www9.georgetown.edu/faculty/irvinem/theory/baudrillard-simulacra_and_simulation.pdf

[33] ibid. n. p.

[34] McLuhan wrote in 1964,

> In a culture like ours, long accustomed to splitting and dividing all things as a means of control, it is sometimes a bit of a shock to be reminded that, in operational and practical fact, the medium is the message. This is merely to say that the personal and social consequences of any medium—that is, of any extension of our- selves—result from the new scale that is introduced into our affairs by each extension of ourselves, or by any new technology.

Marshall McLuhan. "Chapter One." *Understanding Media: The Extensions of Man* (New York: McGraw Hill, 1964)

[35] Baudrillard continued,

> But it would be useful to posit the opposite hypothesis: INFORMATION = ENTROPY. For example: the information or knowledge that can be obtained about a system or an event is already a form of the neutralization and entropy of this system (to be extended to science in general, and to the social sciences and humanities in particular). Information in which an event is reflected or broadcast is already a degraded form of this event.

Baudrillard. Op.cit., n. p.

[36] To those who might wonder what negentropy might mean, it is a term that comes from a 1944 book by Erwin Schrödinger, *What is Life? The Physical Aspect of the Living Cell.* Mae-Wan Ho wrote of negentropy as "mobilizable energy" and "free energy," and Schrödinger himself defined the term as "positive entropy," which is how the living organism sustains itself, or the production of life itself in contrast to entropy, which implies death.
Linus Pauling. "Schrödinger's Contribution to Chemistry and Biology." in *Schrödinger: Centenary Celebration of a Polymath.* C. W. Kilmister, editor (Cambridge University Press, 1989) 229.
Mae-Wan Ho. "What is Schrödinger's Negentropy?" Institute of Science in Society. *Modern Trends in BioThermoKinetics* (Number 3, 1994) 50-61: http://www.i-sis.org.uk/negentr.php

[37] Mark Nunes. "Jean Baudrillard in Cyberspace: Internet, Virtuality and Postmodernity." *Style.* Summer 1995 (Volume 29, Number 2): 314-327. See also a six-page book by Frank Andres. *Jean Baudrillard on the Internet.* July 9, 2012.

[38] "Jean Baudrillard---Baudrillard on the New Technologies. An Interview with Claude Thibault," March 6, 1996. Translated by Suzanne Falcone. The European Graduate School. Graduate and Postgraduate Studies.
http://www.egs.edu/faculty/jean-baudrillard/articles/baudrillard-on-the-new-technologies-an-interview-with-claude-thibaut/

[39] Despite the sad fact that Baudrillard was somewhat out of sync with the computer, there is an internet journal, open to all, dedicated to studies of his work: *The International Journal of Baudrillard Studies.* The development and launching of this journal is described by its founder, Gerry Coulter in "Launching (and Sustaining) a Scholarly Journal on the Internet: the International Journal of Baudrillard Studies" (Volume 13, Issue 1, Winter 2010):
http://quod.lib.umich.edu/j/jep/3336451.0013.104?rgn=main;view=fulltext

[40] Most postmodern theorists (Baudrillard denied being a "postmodernist.") assumed something called "power," however disseminated, and they also assumed a waning of the individual subject who disappears into a system of some sort. However, the most important insight of both Baudrillard and other postmodern philosophers, such as Jacques Derrida, is that all information or all text became equalized in "value" in cyberspace.

Few of the late twentieth century philosophers foresaw the possibility that the Internet might become a democracy, assessable to anyone and everyone. The Web is now a place where "experts" write in a flattened universe and we all live in a system of representation in which the representations are based (not based) and/or are baseless in simulacra. The famous assertion of a "post truth" society came from the Bush Administration and was articulated in a 2004 article by Ron Suskind:

> In the summer of 2002, after I had written an article in *Esquire* that the White House didn't like about Bush's former communications director, Karen Hughes, I had a meeting with a senior adviser to Bush. He expressed the White House's displeasure, and then he told me something that at the time I didn't fully comprehend --

> but which I now believe gets to the very heart of the Bush presidency. The aide said that guys like me were "in what we call the reality-based community," which he defined as people who "believe that solutions emerge from your judicious study of discernible reality." I nodded and murmured something about enlightenment principles and empiricism. He cut me off. "That's not the way the world really works anymore," he continued. "We're an empire now, and when we act, we create our own reality. And while you're studying that reality -- judiciously, as you will -- we'll act again, creating other new realities, which you can study too, and that's how things will sort out. We're history's actors . . . and you, all of you, will be left to just study what we do.

Suskind was writing about a president, George Bush, in clearly over his head, who fell back on (Christian) faith, which was substituted for knowledge or information. The unnamed aide who made the statement is now thought to be Karl Rove, but the idea of the facts being immaterial was not symptomatic just of one administration but of an entire political party and ultimately of a divided and polarized nation, in which one "side" strove to retain a foothold in reality and the other lived in an almost completely fabricated universe, often called "parallel." Indeed in the past Presidential contest an aid to Mitt Romney said that the campaign would not be hampered by "fact-checkers."

Ron Suskind. "Faith, Certainty, and the Presidency of George W. Bush." *The New York Times Magazine.* October 17, 2004.
http://www.nytimes.com/2004/10/17/magazine/17BUSH.html?ex=1255665600&en=890a96189e162076&ei=5090&partner=rssuserland

[41] In an interesting short article written in the aftermath of September 11th, Stanley Fish discussed the end of sympathy for relativism among the neo-conservatives:

> In general two arguments are being run (often at the same time) in these pieces: first, the events of September 11 prove postmodernism to be wrong; second, postmodernism is somehow responsible for September 11—if not responsible for the fact, responsible for a diminished American resolve. Thus in the *Chicago Tribune,* Julia Keller proclaimed "the end of

postmodernism" on the reasoning that no postmodernist could possibly retain his or her views *and* acknowledge the reality of a plane hitting a tower. But no postmodernist would deny this or any other reality. What would be denied is the possibility of describing, and thereby evaluating, the event in a language that all reasonable observers would accept. That language, if it were available, would be hostage to no point of view and just report things as they are, and many postmodernists do hold that no such language will ever be found.

Stanley Fish. "Can Postmodernists Condemn Terrorism? Don't Blame Relativism.:" http://www.gwu.edu/~ccps/rcq/Fish.pdf

[42] The most obvious instances of lying and the consequent fact-checking is today's partisan politics. Ironically, the rise of outright lying in politics has been paralleled by the technological ability to hear all and record and to reveal all. When Jim Tharpe of the *Atlanta Journal-Constitution's PolitiFact* Georgia said, "It's a complete reversal of traditional journalism," he may have meant that, in the past traditional newspapers monopolized the "news." Now independent organizations have created niche operations, somewhat related to *reportage* without being strictly reportorial.

Cary Spivak."The Fact-Checking Explosion." *American Journalism Review*. (December/January 2011): http://www.ajr.org/article.asp?id=4980

[43] In *Twilight Memories,* postmodern theorist, Andreas Huyssen wrote of Baudrillard in a dramatic but startlingly prophetic fashion. Not only did Huyssen foresee the disconnection from the real world, he also predicted one of the more salient aspects of the Internet---the propensity for gift giving:

> ...Baudrillard's discourse leaves the realm of history and contemporary culture and somersaults into a kind of catastrophic theology that will leave us forever, I presume, with simulation, the hyperreal, and capital as a system of floating signifiers unchained from any referent whatsoever. Simulation, indeed. A melancholy fixation on the loss of the real flips over into the desire to get beyond the real, beyond the body, beyond history. It is a religious desire, a desire for ultimate transcendence, achieved in Baudrillard, as in McLuhan, through the media. So what are we to find at the end of implosion,

inside the black hold about which Baudrillard keeps phantasizing? Perhaps a postmodern potlatch in a global village. But we will never know, since the black hold will have absorbed all light, all images, all simulations. Iconoclasm writ large will have won the day, or rather: the night when television has finally gone off the air.

Andreas Huyssen. *Twilight Memories: Marking Time in a Culture of Amnesia* (New York: Routledge, 1995) 190.

[44] Baudrillard stated,

> To a system whose argument is oppression and repression, the strategic resistance is the liberating claim of subjecthood. But this strategy is more reflective of the earlier phase of the system, and even if we are still confronted with it, it is no longer the strategic terrain: the current argument of the system is to maximize speech, the maximum production of meaning. Thus the strategic resistance is that of the refusal of meaning and of the spoken word - or of the hyperconformist simulation of the very mechanisms of the system, which is a form of refusal and of non-reception. It is the strategy of the masses: it is equivalent to returning to the system its own logic by doubling it, to reflecting meaning, like a mirror, without absorbing it. This strategy (if one can still speak of strategy) prevails today, because it was ushered in by that phase of the system, which prevails. To choose the wrong strategy is a serious matter. All the movements that only play on liberation, emancipation, on the resurrection of a subject of history, of the group, of the word based on "consciousness raising," indeed a "raising of the unconscious" of subjects and of the masses, do not see that they are going in the direction of the system, whose imperative today is precisely the overproduction and regeneration of meaning and of speech.

Baudrillard. Op.cit., n. p.

[45] As Baudrillard commented,

> ...power itself, after knowledge, has taken off, has

> become ungraspable - has dispossessed itself. In a now uncertain institution, without knowledge content, without a power structure (except for an archaic feudalism that turns a simulacrum of a machine whose destiny escapes it and whose survival is as artificial as that of barracks and theaters), offensive irruption is impossible. Only what precipitates rotting, by accentuating the parodic, simulacral side of dying games of knowledge and power, has meaning.

Baudrillard. Ibid. n. p.

[46] Writing of Ferdinand Saussure, Jonathan Culler explained,

> Saussure asserted unequivocally that language is a system of differences in which all elements are defined solely by their relations with one another...the prominence Saussure gives to binary oppositions has born fruit. Most work in phonology has been based on a reduction of the sound continuum to discrete element, which can be defined as the point of intersection of several distinctive features...

Culler continued, by noting that linguist Roland "....Jakobson and others argue that the use of binary oppositions to describe structure is not simply a methodological device but a reflection of the nature of language itself." Jonathan Culler. *Ferdinand De Saussure* (Ithaca: Cornell University, 1976, 1986) 102.

[47] In fact, the very translation of Foucault's famous triad: *voir, savoir, pouvoir* or to see is to know is to have power over has been under close scrutiny by several scholars. The English language does not distinguish, as does the French, between *"pouvoir"* which is power over (someone) and *"puissance"* which means power to do something. In other words, there is a fine but important distinction between "over" and "to." Without getting too deep into the weeds of theory, it should be noted here that, to be very precise indeed, that the Web is without *pouvoir* or power "over" but is a place when one has the power "to" act. For more on this matter read:
Judith Revel. *Michel Foucault. Expériences de la pensée* (Paris: Bordas, 2005)
Gayatri Chakravorty Spivak. *Outside the Teaching Machine* (New York: Routledge, 1993)

[48] The original title of Jeremy Bentham's proposals for prisons, work houses, mad houses, hospitals and schools---all gathered together under the Panopticon conception is long and all inclusive:
PANOPTICON; OR THE INSPECTION-HOUSE: CONTAINING THE IDEA OF A NEW PRINCIPLE OF CONSTRUCTION APPLICABLE TO ANY SORT OF ESTABLISHMENT, IN WHICH PERSONS OF ANY DESCRIPTION ARE TO BE KEPT UNDER INSPECTION; AND IN PARTICULAR TO PENITENTIARY-HOUSES, PRISONS, HOUSES OF INDUSTRY, WORK-HOUSES, POOR-HOUSES, LAZARETTOS, MANUFACTORIES, HOSPITALS, MAD-HOUSES, AND SCHOOLS: WITH A PLAN OF MANAGEMENT ADAPTED TO THE PRINCIPLE: IN A SERIES OF LETTERS, WRITTEN IN THE YEAR 1787, FROM CRECHEFF IN WHITE RUSSIA. TO A FRIEND IN ENGLAND BY JEREMY BENTHAM, OF LINCOLN'S INN, ESQUIRE.
http://luci.ics.uci.edu/websiteContent/weAreLuci/biographies/faculty/djp3/LocalCopy/PANOPTICON.pdf

In *Discipline and Punish*, Michel Foucault clearly considered Bentham's architecture of control as the modernist move towards greater consolidation of central power over an increasingly mass and urban society. As Foucault wrote in 1975, long before the Internet:

> Bentham's Panopticon is the architectural figure of this composition. We know the principle on which it was based: at the periphery, an annular building; at the centre, a tower; this tower is pierced with wide windows that open onto the inner side of the ring; the peripheric building is divided into cells, each of which extends the whole width of the building; they have two windows, one on the inside, corresponding to the windows of the tower; the other, on the outside, allows the light to cross the cell from one end to the other. All that is needed, then, is to place a supervisor in a central tower and to shut up in each cell a madman, a patient, a condemned man, a worker or a schoolboy. By the effect of backlighting, one can observe from the tower, standing out precisely against the light, the small captive shadows in the cells of the periphery. They are like so many cages, so many small theatres, in which each actor is alone, perfectly individualized and constantly visible. The panoptic mechanism arranges spatial unities that make it possible to see constantly and to recognize immediately. In short, it reverses the principle of the dungeon; or rather of its three functions - to enclose, to deprive of

light and to hide - it preserves only the first and eliminates the other two. Full lighting and the eye of a supervisor capture better than darkness, which ultimately protected. Visibility is a trap.

Until the extent of NSA "spying" on Americans was revealed in the summer of 2013, it was doubtful that, in an age of the Patriot Act, CCTV, Facebook and "sexting" that the idea of surveillance was alarming today to most people. Indeed, the opposite effect seemed to have taken effect: as people become used to being watched, many increasingly "show themselves" and make themselves more visible. However, the idea that the government routinely accessed the deepest secrets of the public for years has rufled the complacency of naïve Internet users.

Michel Foucault. *Discipline and Punish.* Translated by Alan Sheridan (New York: Random House, 1977) http://foucault.info/documents/disciplineAndPunish/foucault.disciplineAndPunish.panOpticism.html.

[49] At the end of 2012, China set about closing more loopholes. No doubt more openings will be found by ever resourceful and desperate users continue to poke halls in the Great Wall.

Keith Bradsher. "China Toughens its Restrictions on the Use of the Internet." *The New York Times* (December 29, 2012): http://topics.nytimes.com/topics/news/international/countriesandterritories/china/internet_censorship/index.html

[50] In March 2012, China, which has more than twice the Internet users than America, continues to tighten its grip of censorship, fighting the constant attempts to break through the Firewalls. As Robert Olsen in *Forbes* reported,

> "People now go online to find solidarity with other citizens who see problems in Chinese society—such as corruption, abuse of power, and environmental degradation—in their day-to-day lives," writes Sophie Beach, the executive editor of China Digital Times, a website that maintains a list of the government's 2,000 banned or temporarily banned search terms.

Robert Olsen. "China's Shifting Censorship Regime Puts Squeeze on Internet Giants." *Forbes* (March 12, 2013):

http://www.forbes.com/sites/robertolsen/2013/03/12/chinas-shifting-censorship-regime-puts-squeeze-on-internet-giants/

[51] As Bentham wrote,

> To prevent thorough light, whereby, notwithstanding the blinds, the prisoners would see from the cells whether or no any person was in the lodge, that apartment is divided into quarters, by partitions formed by two diameters to the circle, crossing each other at right angles. For these partitions the thinnest materials might serve; and they might be made removeable at pleasure; their height, sufficient to prevent the prisoners seeing over them from the cells. Doors to these partitions, if left open at any time, might produce the thorough light. To prevent this, divide each partition into two, at any part required, setting down the one-half at such distance from the other as shall be equal to the aperture of a door.

Bentham. Ibid. *Letter II., n. p.*

[52] One of the early theorists of the Internet, Andrew L. Schapiro, laid out how the Web slips the controls of capitalism. In his second chapter, "The Politics of Code," Schapiro links the increase of control by the individual made possible by technology with a free-market capitalism. As he stated in 1999,

> In the case of the control revolution, the significance of the surrounding environment is abundantly apparent. This shift in control is reinforced by---and it reinforces---current trends in political and social thought that emphasize the power of the individual. One of the most prominent of these trends is the exaltation of the free market that has occurred in the recent decades. Public, collective control of resources has given way to private, individualized control. *Laisez-faire* economic polities have become dominant in the major nations of the world because of the belief that the economy works best when actors in the private sector control the production and distribution of goods and services. Public policy is driven less by abstract principles of social justice and the common good than by a desire to achieve efficiency and to satisfy the "revealed preferences" of consumers. Autonomy is favored; restraints on choice are frowned

upon. Indeed, notions of market freedom and personal freedom have become intertwined in public discourse (and sometimes confused as well).

The author was writing in 1999 and could not have foreseen how the corporations and private businesses would soon seek and acquire monopolistic control over individuals, all while charging far more money than a government entity would dare. The current state of cable companies is a case in point and ironically the younger generation has fled the corporate world and has found entertainment their own way---on the Internet. But, that said, Shapiro's larger point still holds true: technological changes have allowed for individual autonomy and on the Internet, the "free market" is indeed a truly "free" marketplace of ideas.

Andrew L. Shapiro. *The Control Revolution* (The Century Foundation, 1999) 13 -24.

[53] Barbara Warnick wrote an early article that puzzled over the possible impact of the Internet on discourse.
Barbara Warnick. "Rhetorical Criticism of Public Discourse on the Internet: Theoretical Implications." *RSQ: Rhetoric Society Quarterly* (Volume 28, Number 4, Fall 1998)

[54] In her --- book on Foucault, Sara Miles elegantly and succinctly summarized the philosopher's idea on discourse,

> A discourse is a regulated set of statements, which combine with others in predictable ways. Discourse is regulated by a set of rules which lead to the distribution and circulation of certain utterances and statements...Rather than seeing discourse as simply a set of statements which have some coherence, we should, rather thank of a discourse as existing because of a complex set of practices which try to keep them in circulation and other practices which try to fence them in circulation and other practices which try to fence them off from others and keep those other statements out of circulation.

Sara Miles. *Michel Foucault* (New York: Routledge, 2003) 91.

[55] Michel Foucault. *The Archaeology of Knowledge.* (Vintage Books Edition, January 2010) 76.

[56] In examining the role of scholarship and publication in higher education, Morton Winston remarked,

> Demographic pressures on higher education following the Second World War, that is, the shift from the elite to mass access to higher education, and more recent demands that the academy serve the interests of more culturally, racially, and ethnically diverse students, did little to change the dominance of the professionalized disciplinary elites and of the research-publishing ethos in American higher education.

Discussing the "disciplinary elites," Winston continued,

> These elites consist mainly of senior, tenured professors holding chairs that the more prestigious research and doctoral-granting universities who, by and large, have advanced to their current position of power paradigms. The way one this, of course, is by delivering invited lectures and talks on the circuit of speakers hosted by the major research universities, by giving lectures and symposia at major professional meetings, and, most importantly, by the writing and publishing of learned articles and scholarly books in which authors attempt to shape the opinions of other professional practitioners of their disciplines. The journal article is the unit of capital in the academic marketplace; it is the record of one's "research" at the frontiers of knowledge of one's discipline, and it is thus the basis of any credible claim one might have to be one of the keepers and shapers of the disciplinary paradigm. However, individuals rarely become members of their respective disciplinary elites only through publishing in specialty journals. The single-authored scholarly book is the real marker of academic prestige and respectability, but only, of course, if it is published in the "right" university press, and only then if it is favorably reviewed by acknowledge masters of the field in the leading scholarly journals devoted to that subject. Thus, research and publication have come to be regarded as the necessary activities of those who aspire to power within the academy, for only through them

does a professor have the chance of becoming a member of a disciplinary elite.

Morton Wilson. "Prospects for a Reevaluation of Academic Values." Edited by Joseph M. Moxley and Lagretta T. Lenker. *The Politics and Processes of Scholarship* (Westport, CT: Greenwood Press, 1995) 54-55.

[57] Douglas Kellner, the recognized authority and explicator of Jean Baudrillard, compared Baudrillard to McLuhan but what is interesting about his chapter is that he does not update his concepts to present day. Both writers, McLuhan and Baudrillard live in and assumed that "media" was a one-way street, in which the views/listeners passively consumed the "dominate" ideology of the ruling class. But in an age of Internet, the audience is transformed into the user, a personage totally different from the consumer, and these active participants not only talk back but also take back media.

Douglas Kellner. "Reflections on Modernity and Postmodernity in McLuhan and Baudrillard." *Transforming McLuhan: Cultural, Critical, and Postmodern Perspectives.* Edited by Paul Grosswiler (New York: Peter Lang Publishing, Inc., 2010) 179-202.
See also: *Baudrillard Now: Current Perspective in Baudrillard Studies.* Edited by Ryan Bishop (New York: Polity Press, 2009)

[58] The Internet seems to be but is not entirely democratic. For our purposes, the search engine itself, for example Google, becomes, as A. Diaz argues, a kind of gatekeeper that might well be fueled by monetary goals rather than by a simple need to distribute information on a level playing field.

> As the primary gatekeepers of the Web, search engines not only direct users to particular pages but can also direct consumers towards particular services and products...But by selling advertising, Google and its competitors have an enormous financial incentive to direct users away from the "free," "organic" results and towards the sites of its sponsors.

A. Diaz. "Through the Google Goggles: Sociopolitical Bias in Search Engine Design" in *Web Search: Multidisciplinary Perspectives.* Edited by Amanda Spink and Michael T. Zimmer. (Berlin: Springer-Verlag Berlin Hedelberg, 2007) 20.

[59] Charles Lemert wrote about discursive violence in *Durkheim's Ghosts: Cultural Logics and Social Things.* Lemert stated,

> True discourse only surfaces in a form twisted by violence. The face it turns toward men...is the calm exterior visage of power. The domineering free gaze of the clinic is matched by the cold, calculating gaze inhabiting Bentham's Panopticon. The reverse side of the liberation of truth is the subjection of all to its gaze. Subjection and freedom intermingle. Power-knowledge is originally a violence done to the truth in which truth appears as idea, original, and innocent. Transgression takes the form of knowledge and power...Archaeology, or what, after *The Archaeology of Knowledge,* Foucault calls genealogy, is the transgressive knowledge in which the taboos thrown up around the will to truth are violated.

Charles Lemert. *Durkheim's Ghosts: Cultural Logics and Social Things.* (Cambridge University Press, 2006) 243.

[60] A very early article on Foucault and the Internet was written in 1997 and is now out of date but in some respects—the continual threat of censorship and control on the Web---are still relevant.

James Boyle. "Foucault in Cyberspace. Surveillance, Sovereignty, and Hard-Wired Censors. *Duke University School of Law:* http://law.duke.edu/boylesite/foucault.htm

[61] One of the most interesting acts of "transgression" in relation to knowledge is the current uprising against database subscriptions, especially the Dutch firm, Elsevier, which manages or controls the distribution of scientific knowledge through the control of over 2000 journals, which give the firm a 36% profit margin. The journals and who can read them and when and where are totally controlled by the corporation, hurting the distribution of knowledge. These journals are made by the scientists who write the articles, gifts that are taxpayer funded, and should be freely accessed by the public that paid for them. What is a public good has become a privately owned and regulated corporation. The boycott of this behemoth that controls the distribution of knowledge flared up despite the corporation's claims that its business model is based upon the necessary of peer review. As leader of the boycott math superstar, Fields medal Timothy Gowers, suggested building a website for a petition. Tyler Nayland put up this site and thousands joined

the boycott and Nayland explained that the content of scientific journals is "given" by experts in the fields to a business that then proceeds to make a profit from the uncompensated contributions. The result is an "academic spring," a phrase modeled after the "Arab spring." Nayland explains that today there is no need to follow this system which was useful historically…but not now.

Rick Karr. "Trouble for Elsevier, the Leading Academic Publisher." *NPR* broadcast posted on [BLOG] Alex Goldman. "Harvard Library: Subscribing to Academic Periodicals is Too Expensive" (April 24, 2012): http://www.onthemedia.org/blogs/on-the-media/2012/apr/24/harvard-library-subscribing-academic-periodicals-too-expensive/?utm_source=/2012/feb/17/trouble-elsevier-leading-academic-publisher/&utm_medium=treatment&utm_campaign=morelikethis

In starting the "Cost of Knowledge Boycott" of Elsevier, a group of mathematicians wrote of the incoherence of corporate control of knowledge that now costs little to disseminate,

> …the world has changed in significant ways. Authors typeset their own papers, using electronic typesetting. Publishing and distribution costs are not as great as they once were. And most importantly, dissemination of scientific ideas no longer takes place via the physical distribution of journal volumes. Rather, it takes place mainly electronically. While this means of dissemination is not free, it is much less expensive, and much of it happens quite independently of mathematical journals. In conclusion, the cost of journal publishing has gone down because the cost of typesetting has been shifted from publishers to authors and the cost of publishing and distribution is significantly lower than it used to be. By contrast, the amount of money being spent by university libraries on journals seems to be growing with no end in sight. Why do mathematicians contribute all this volunteer labor, and their employers pay all this money, for a service whose value no longer justifies its cost?

The petition contains the beginning of what would become almost 2000 names of academics protesting the current situation on the *Cost of Knowledge.com* website.

Timothy Gowers. "Cost of Knowledge Petition":

http://gowers.files.wordpress.com/2012/02/elsevierstatementfinal.pdf

[62] The best-known essay on gift giving is Marcel Mauss's 1925 work *The Gift*. Written in the shadow of the destructive reparations imposed upon Germany, *The Gift* implied, in the conclusion, that the modern notion of exchange was narrow and calculating and based upon purely economic or capitalist considerations, i.e. profit-making or obligation-creating. Mauss contrasts "interest" in gift giving with disinterested gift giving, a more moral form of donating that still exists in more "primitive" cultures. As Mauss wrote,

> It is only our Western societies that quite recently turned man into an economic animal. But we are not yet all animals of the same species. In both lower and upper classes pure irrational expenditure is in current practice: it is still characteristic of some French noble houses. *Homo oeconomicas* is not behind us, but before, like the moral man, the man of duty, the scientific man and the reasonable man. For a long time man was something quite different; and it is not so long now since he became a machine—a calculating machine.

The larger mission of Mauss---to convince the French to treat the Germans with generosity----failed but his account of the moral content of the "Gift" suggests that one hundred years later, the Internet has created a new form of a potlatch culture.

Marcel Mauss. "Conclusions." *The Gift. Forms and Functions of Exchange in Archaic Societies* Translated by Ian Gunnison (W. Norton Library, 1967) 9.

[63] Writing of the Internet as a site of innovation within its own free market economy, Lawrence Lessig stated,

> Innovators nevertheless innovate. And they innovate because the return to them from deploying their ideas is high, even if others get the benefit of the new idea as well. Innovators don't simply sit on their hands until a guaranteed return is offered; real capitalists invest and innovate with the understanding that competitors will be free to take their ideas and use them against the innovators.

Lawrence Lessig. *The Future of Ideas: The Fate of the Commons in a Connected World* (Random House, 2001) 71.

[64] Marcel Mauss. Op. cit., 11.

[65] For a succinct overview of Mass and the other scholars, from Hyde to Derrida, who have discussed his ideas, see religious scholar Erik Davis. "The Gift—Mauss, Bataille, Hyde and Derrida." *Imagining the Real World*. October 26, 2006: http://erikwdavis.wordpress.com/2006/10/26/the-gift-mauss-bataille-hyde-and-derrida/

[66] Marcel Mauss also stated,

> The gift received is in fact owned, but the ownership is of a particular kind. One might say that it includes many legal principles which we moderns have isolated from one another. It is at the same time property and a possession, a pledge and a loan, an object sold and an object bought, a deposit, a mandate, a trust; for it is given only on condition that it will be used on behalf of, or transmitted to, a third person, the remote partner (murimuri}.

Mauss. Op.cit., 22.

[67] Jacques Derrida. *Given Time. I: Counterfeit Money*. Translated by Peggy Kamuf (University of Chicago Press, 1994)
See also a brief discussion of how Derrida discussed Mauss by Tim Jenkins. "Derrida's Reading of Mauss." *Marcel Mauss: A Centenary Tribute*. Edited by Wendy James and N. J. Allen (Berghahn Books, 1998) 83-94.

[68] In a very brief abstract, Mike Greer wrote,

> The exponential growth of the Internet is discussed focusing on whether the decentralisation of p2p servers has created smaller, less apparent social groupings, or whether the internet (or the p2p software) itself has taken on the mantle of the giver, with the user's/receiver's expectations shifting to view these files as permanently available. Finally, moving away somewhat from the 'impossible gift', the extreme ease with which electronic files can now be transferred will be considered, examining whether they might now be of

such insignificance as to fall below the status of gift – effortless to give away, often without knowledge of how many copies might have been distributed – resulting in the 'pure gift' falling out with the realms of both economic transactions and gifts.

Mike Greer. "Has the Internet allowed Derrida's 'impossible gift' to Become an Everyday Occurrence?" *Media and Culture*
David Zeitlyn wrote another interesting and brief "note" on the gift culture vis-à-vis software sharing. "Research Note. Gift Economics in the Development of Open Source Software: Anthropological Reflections." *Research Policy* 32 (2003) 1287-1291.

[69] As Derrida said,
> The symbolic opens and constitutes the order of exchange and of debt, the law or the order of circulation in which the gift gets annulled. It suffices therefore for the other to *perceive the* gift---not only to perceive it in the sense in which, as one says in French, "on perçoit," one receives, for example, merchandise, payment or compensation---but to perceive its nature of gift, the meaning or intention, the *intentional* meaning of the gift, in order for this simple *recognition* becomes *gratitude.* The simple identification of the gift seems to destroy it. The simple identification of the passage of a gift as such, that is, of an identifiable thing among some identifiable "ones," would be nothing other than the process of the destruction of the gift. It is as if, between the event or the institution of the gift as such and its destruction, the difference were destined to be constantly annulled. *At the limit, the gift as gift ought not appear as gift: either to the done or to the donor.* It cannot be gift as gift except by not being present as gift.

Jacques Derrida. Op. cit., 14.

[70] Richard A. Posner wrote of the possible future of public intellectuals, including academics,

> The pool of academic public-intellectual eligibles--- academics for whom there is sufficient potential demand in the public-intellectual market to induce the media to give them a platform if they want it---is larger than the

actual number of "performing" public intellectuals. This implies that there are costs involved in being a public intellectual. The principle costs are two. The first is the opportunity cost: the time that is expended on writing for or engaging in other expressive activities oriented toward the general public is unavailable for teaching, scholarly research, consulting, and leisure. All these activities---the last obviously, the third rarely---yield non-pecuniary benefits, and it primarily these that are sacrificed to don't public-intellectual work, since the celebrity yielded by that work may generate an increase in one's academic salary and one's hourly consulting fee, though it can also reduce the former by lessening the academic repute in which the professor is held.

Indeed, as the recent film, *Inside Job* made clear, academics who are paid consultants (in this economists) put their reputations and that of their fields in jeopardy for their roles in the financial collapse of 2008. However, their fellow professionals closed ranks and no one, beyond the general public, was harmed.
Richard A. Posner. Op. cit., 62

[71] It is interesting to note that the "gift economy" of the Internet emerged from two distinct communities dedicated to sharing: the scientific community and the tech community. The sharing ethos went mainstream due to the subversive activities of Napster, who/which is now shut down but symptomatic of the expansive ethos of free exchange. Some writers have attempted to politicize activities, which are anarchistic enough to escape politics. Jeff Shantz referred to the "anarchy" of the Internet as DIY:

> Contemporary usage of the term DIY in underground movement comes from punk rock and its visceral attack on the professionalization of rock ad the related distance between fans and rock starts. This anti-hierarchical perspective and the practices hat flow from it are inspired by a deep longing for self-determined activity that eschews reliance on the products of corporate culture. As an alternative to market valorization and production for profit embodied in the corporate enterprises, anarchist DIYers turn to self-valorization production rooted in the needs, experiences, and desires of specific communities. In place of a consumerist ethos that encourages consumption of ready-made items,

anarchists adopt a productivist ethos that attempts a re-integration of production and consumption. It is perhaps highly telling that in an age of multinational media conglomerates and gargantuan publishing monopolies a number of younger people have turned towards artisanal forms of craft production in order to produce and distribute what are often very personal works. Even more than this, however, are the means of production, involving decision-making as well as collective labor in which participants are involved, to the degree they wish to be, in all aspects of the process from conception through distribution.

Jeff Shantz. *Constructive Anarchy: Building Infrastructures of Resistance* (Surrey: Ashgate Publishing Limited, 2010) 167. This essay, "Punk as...Book Making: DIY Theory and Post-Political Politics" can also be found in Editors G. F. Mitrano and Eric Jarosinski. *The Hand of the Interpreter: Essays on Meaning After Theory* (Bern: Peter Lang AG, 2009)

[72] Justyna Hofmoki wrote of the gift-giving practices on the Internet,

> The rapid expansion of a networked information economy paves the way for broadening the spectrum of gift giving behaviours, eventually challenging the currently predominant 'exchange economy'. The Internet spectrum offers particularly favourable conditions, enabling and, in fact, encouraging the proliferation of gift-sharing attitudes. First, the cost of sharing information is practically negligible. Second, there is great flexibility in the gift giving process, in terms of the size and timing of the donation. Third, the effects of gift giving, in terms of added social value, can be recognized easily without additional effort. Even if the sharing of information, as such, is not driven by the expectation of reciprocal rewards, the visible effects can serve as a strong incentive for continuing said behaviours in the future. At the same time, Internet commons represent a totally different framework for gift sharing than that of small communities with established direct relationships and shared values between members. Information shared via the Internet typically is offered to a much larger and unknown set of recipients. Kollock points out that such a 'general exchange system' is more generous;

but, at the same time, it is riskier than a traditional gift exchange.

Justyna Hofmokl. "The Internet Commons" Towards an Electric Theoretical Framework." *International Journal of the Commons* (Volume 4, Number 1, 2010)
http://www.thecommonsjournal.org/index.php/ijc/article/view/111/106

[73] Rudi Laermans and Pascal Gielan who stated,

> Foucault formulated his views before the advent of 'the digital age' or the breakthrough of 'the information society'. Hence it is all the more interesting to confront his insights with the reality of the digital archive. More particularly, we will argue that Foucault's epistemological re-interpretation of the archive-notion in terms of 'the system of "utterability"', or 'the law of what can be said', offers the possibility to conceptualise the deep structure of every database or computer system in terms of 'the archive of a digital archive'. In the last section, we return to the notion of 'the digital an-archive' and briefly highlight its specific performative nature...At first sight, Foucault's first re-articulation of the notion of archive seems of little or no use for the understanding of the contemporary digital archive. Yet, one may detect a very direct link. Seen from the point of view of new media, the archive as 'the system of "utterability"' is very close to, if not identical with, the technological notion of program. No digital database, and no access to and use of such an information bank, without all sorts of algorithms or instructions that frame the abstract data and make commands possible, which specify in the form of particular filters and applications the informational nature of the uncountable bits and bytes (for instance in terms of pixels, voxels or letters), and which ensure an always specific interface between the digital data, their specification and the user (on these three levels, see Simons, 2002). The structural or temporal couplings between different programs in public or private data-networks function as an *invisible system* which makes possible a vast array of operations, resulting in an always specific patchwork of 'utterances' - of texts, sounds, images. In general, and this notwithstanding the many

> existing forms of so-called open sources and open netware, one therefore operates in the final instance within *the digital realm of the non-operative,* which consists of excluded operations and therefore of utterances impossible to produce.

Rudi Laermans and Pascal Gielen. "The Archive of the Digital Non-Archive." *Image [&] Narrative*, Issue 17, "The Digital Archive." April 2007
http://www.imageandnarrative.be/inarchive/digital_archive/laermans_gielen.htm

[74] Of course Foucault, like the other postmodern thinkers, was not thinking of the Internet as a new kind of Archive. For him, the archive is neither a library nor an institution where documents are kept but a system which orders the discourse which is, in turn, analyzed in terms of archaeology or the study of discursive formations. In other words, it is not necessarily the history of ideas but how certain discourses are formed or come into being as knowledge "ordered" or shaped or constructed in a certain way. Each era fabricates what passes for knowledge in a particular manner or episteme and it was impossible for Foucault to have followed the trail of changes from classical to modern to our postmodern era that Lyotard began to discern. Foucault and Lyotard were dead before the Internet entered actively into the business of actively creating knowledge and while Foucault was never concerned with the subject and more with how serious speech utterances come together and coalesce into a "discourse," the Web is very much generated by active subjects, marked by strong agent subjectivity.

For Foucault, the concern is always with the link between power and knowledge. For him knowledge is always a reflection of power and the fusion of *pouvoir* and *savoir* is always an abstract one and should not be thought of in a literal fashion. It does not matter, for example, that a state, such as Texas or Tennessee, denies science. The concern of archaeology how an anti-science standpoint comes into being: how does such a discourse form? What social and political forces occur that make such statements possible---possible to be uttered or to be heard or to enter into the mainstream and to gain weight or credibility?

Michel Foucault. *The Archaeology of Knowledge and the Discourse on Language.* Translated by Rupert Swyer (Tavistock Publications, Ltd. 1969/1972) 11 and 12.

⁷⁵ Lyotard began by saying,

> We may thus expect a thorough exteriorization of knowledge with respect to the "knower," at whatever point he or she may occupy in the knowledge process. The old principle that the acquisition of knowledge is indissociable from the training (*Bildung*) of minds, or even of individuals, is becoming obsolete and will become ever more so. The relationships of the suppliers and users of knowledge to the knowledge they supply and use is now tending, and will increasingly tend, to assume the form already taken by the relationship of commodity producers and consumers to the commodities they produce and consume – that is, the form of value.

Jean-François Lyotard. *The Postmodern Condition.* Translated by Geoff Bennington and Brian Massumi (University Of Minnesota Press; 1st edition, June 21, 1984) 4.

⁷⁶ One must point out in passing that Derrida dismissed the center from its governing role in the structure as early as 1966. In his seminal essay, "Structure, Sign, and Play in the Discourse of the Human Sciences," he stated,

> The function of this center was not only to orient, balance, and organize the structure-one cannot in fact conceive of an unorganized structure-but above all to make sure that the organizing principle of the structure would limit what we might call the *freeplay* of the structure.

Derrida continued,

> It would be easy enough to show that the concept of structure and even the word "structure" itself are as old as the *episteme* -that is to say, as old as western science and western philosophy-and that their roots thrust deep into the soil of ordinary language, into whose deepest recesses the *episteme* plunges to gather them together once more, making them part of itself in a metaphorical displacement. Nevertheless, up until the event which I wish to mark out and define, structure-or rather the structurality of structure-although it has always been

> involved, has always been neutralized or reduced, and this by a process of giving it a center or referring it to a point of presence, a fixed origin. No doubt that by orienting and organizing the coherence of the system, the center of a structure permits the freeplay of its elements inside the total form. And even today the notion of a structure lacking any center represents the unthinkable itself. Nevertheless, the center also closes off the freeplay it opens up and makes possible. *Qua* center, it is the point at which the substitution of contents, elements, or terms is no longer possible. At the center, the permutation or the transformation of elements (which may of course be structures enclosed within a structure) is forbidden. At least this permutation has always remained *interdicted* (*I* use this word deliberately). Thus it has always been thought that the center, which is by definition unique, constituted that very thing within a structure, which governs the structure, while escaping structurality.

Jacques Derrida. "Structure Sign, and Play in the Discourse of the Human Sciences." Reprinted in *Writing and Difference*, trans. Alan Bass (London: Routledge,1978) 278-294.

[77] R. J. Bernstein discusses the famous essay in "Serious Play. The Ethical-Political Horizon of Derrida."
http://www.google.com/#hl=en&tbo=d&sclient=psy-ab&q=r.j.+bernstein%2Bserious+play&oq=r.j.+bernstein%2Bserious+play&gs_l=hp.3...807.8557.0.8941.27.27.0.0.0.1.346.3582.6j20j0j1.27.0.les%3Bcpsugrpq1..0.0...1.1.gWGWgrS25pY&pbx=1&bav=on.2,or.r_gc.r_pw.r_qf.&fp=488ae73babd585f2&bpcl=38897761&biw=1196&bih=702

He continued his discussion of Derrida in *The New Constellation: The Ethical-Political Horizons of Modernity/Postmodernity* (MIT Press. 1992)

[78] The personal computer, which could be used by scholars, intellectuals and ordinary people, was not launched for public use until 1977. The pioneer in making computers for home users was Apple and the visionary Steve Jobs. That said, it was not until 1981 that IBM, a much more powerful company was convinced that the computer would be useful for homes and businesses. In these early years, some universities used a primitive version of a computer, a word processor. Over the eighties,

beginning with the young generation, the academic community began to adopt computers for daily use.

[79] Now that the Web has changed the nature of "knowledge," academics are beginning to reconsider Lyotard. For example, Peter Roberts remarked, writing on "the collapse of grand narratives," that

> Lyotard happens to have advanced a position on these matters, as have other professors. But messages about the postmodern condition might be conveyed by any number of different individuals and groups -- and indeed by institutional structures, practices and processes, or by machines. The manner through which the message is conveyed in such cases may differ from that employed by a philosopher, but these alternative modes of transmitting ideas may -- if Lyotard is correct -- be more in keeping with our (postmodern) times. If at this moment in our history relentless consumption provides the dominant motive behind human activity, ideas generated in an 'easy to consume' form are likely to be more palatable. Regrettably, perhaps, the utterances of 20th century philosophers and others in academic positions have only infrequently been given serious consideration by many beyond the confines of the university. There are, of course, some important exceptions here -- ranging from Jean Paul Sartre to Allan Bloom -- but by comparison with television personalities, popular music heroes and newspaper commentators, academics have exerted relatively little influence in shaping (and challenging) public opinion. There are few readily discernible signs that the professoriate will be granted greater respect, or listened to more attentively, as we move into the new millennium. The need for professors as people who will explain the postmodern condition is thus, in the eyes of many, highly questionable.

Peter Roberts. "Rereading Lyotard: Knowledge, Commodification and Higher Education." *Electronic Journal of Sociology* (1998) http://www.sociology.org/content/vol003.003/roberts.html

[80] Martin also stated that

If we turn to the social problem that Lyotard confronts in *The Postmodern Condition,* then it can be seen that the issue of legitimacy is centred around the structural separation of science and culture, for Lyotard foregrounds the question of whether the scientific method possesses an internal mechanism for legitimating the knowledge that it produces. At the beginning of the book, Lyotard identifies the field of inquiry as "knowledge in computerized societies", and from an empirical point of view, observes that the knowledge produced by science can no longer be separated from the infrastructure that is used to produce it. Indeed, it is no coincidence that Lyotard focuses upon the invention of the computer to designate this social field of this new era, for this tool involves the integration of software and hardware components that makes the mental activity of programming dependent upon physical activity of performing calculations (and vice-versa). When the production of scientific research becomes bound to the operation of computers, quantification and calculability become the minimum conditions for the production of knowledge as information. Although Lyotard never makes the distinction explicit, it can be inferred that knowledge becomes information when the means of producing it becomes bound to the possession of fixed capital (the computer), and the means of distributing it dependent upon the market (the commodification of knowledge as information). Traditionally, the knowledge of science has been communicated to the citizens of a democracy through the education system or the public sphere, but with the computerization of scientific research access to information becomes restricted, either because the general public lacks the infrastructure to process it, or the competence to understand it. When Lyotard was writing *The Postmodern Condition* in the 1970s, access to computers was still limited to state institutions and large corporations, for the "personal computer" (PC) had not yet been invented, and the Internet was still in its infancy. For this reason, he interpreted the structural differentiation between science and culture as the source of a "legitimation crisis", because he believed that the knowledge of science could no longer be unified by the university system or disseminated via the public sphere.

William Martin. "Re-Programming Lyotard: From the Postmodern to the Posthuman Condition." *Parrhesia* (Number 8, 2009) 60-75

[81] For Lyotard, performativity is linked to a technological determinism. We see the same thinking in the work of Jacques Ellul: that which is efficient will simply continue to move "forward" on its own terms. "Technique" or *techne* emphasizes means; ends are irrelevant. Whether one reads Ellul or Lyotard, industrialization/technology is a force in culture that has a life of its own. Lyotard realized that this new "force" or drive or engine, as Marx would put it, ran counter to not just belief systems but also to the ability to believe. Lyotard called the resulting "condition" "incredulity" and he directed it towards "metanarratives," but what is lost is faith. The process is complete, he asserted, by the 1950s, and we can assume that what we have been witnessing in this curious "post" time is a nostalgic re-creation of new and doomed belief systems.

See: William Schultz. "J. F. Lyotard. The Ambivalence of our Postmodern Condition. Lyotrad's Diagnosis and Prognosis."
http://www.costis.org/x/lyotard/schultz.htm

[82] Lyotard. "The Postmodern Condition: A Report on Knowledge." Reprinted as an excerpt in *A Postmodern Reader*. Edited by Joseph Natoli and Linda Hutcheon (Albany: State University of New York, 1993) 73.

[83] Simon Malpas stated that,

> ...paralogy...can literally be defined as bad or false logic, Lyotard is describing the way in which a language move has the potential to break the rules of an existing game (which is why it seems bad or false) in such a way that a new game needs to be developed.

Simon Malpas. *Jean-François Lyotard* (New York: Routledge, 2003, 2005) 31.

[84] In fact, in the closing chapter of his book on the Postmodern, Alan Kirby noted the bad translation of metanarrative and the resulting misreading of not just the term but also the thesis of Lyotard's "Report." Widely understood in the 1980s as a renunciation of Marxism or Capitalism of any overarching theory of history or science and so on, Lyotard's "incredulity"

is better comprehended today as an inability to "believe" as an article of faith in a centered body of knowledge, if only because of the proliferation of alternative accounts.

Alan Kirby. "The Return of the Poisonous Grand Narrative." *Digimodernism: How New Technologies Dismantle the Postmodern and Reconfigure our Culture* (New York: The Continuum International Publishing Group Inc., 2009) 225-245.

[85] Lyotard. Ibid. 61, 64, 67.

[86] As Martin Halbert of Emory University wrote in 1998,

> Lyotard believes that current trends in society are moving toward paralogy as a legitimizing principle. He allies the trend toward temporary contracts rather than permanent institutions with paralogy, although he acknowledges that this evidence is equivocal. He does not specifically say whether paralogy will completely overthrow performativity, or simply act in concert with it. This is one of the most problematic areas of his project. The component of the paralogy concept which may initially appears most utopian to our current way of thinking is the idea that data banks can be made freely available to everyone in society. If anything, corporations are inclined to zealously guard access to their databases and provide access to them only through expensive fees. Lyotard describes in great detail the importance of information in world competition for power and economic dominance. He makes an intellectual case for open access to information by a loose appeal to perfect information competitions in game theory, but offers no clear mechanism for moving toward free access to data in society.

Halbert continued,

> When considered in this light, something like paralogy looks increasingly likely. The Internet is a vast ocean of shared information. What becomes significant is the clear identification of what in this ocean is worthy of attention. This is where paralogy comes in. Lyotard's paralogy can be taken to mean exactly this notion of

identifying the worthy new concepts that emerge from the sea of research. This inversion of the rules of the economic game has definite ramifications for higher education's research activities. Quite apart from the ramifications of this point, Lyotard's work makes many specific recommendations that have bearing on the question of the Internet as a medium for scholarly communication. These points must be explored to gain a full sense of how Lyotard's Report addresses the central concerns of my project.

Martin Halbert. *Performitivity, Cultural Capital, & The Internet.* "Lyotard: Postmodern Condition." See also "Performitivity & Paralogy." *First Year ILA Research Paper* (15 April 1998): http://userwww.service.emory.edu/~mhalber/Research/Paper/pci-internet.html

[87] In his great poem of 1919, *The Second Coming,* William Butler Yeats wrote,

> *Turning and turning in the widening gyre /The falcon cannot hear the falconer; /Things fall apart; the centre cannot hold; /Mere anarchy is loosed upon the world, /The blood-dimmed tide is*
> *loosed, and everywhere /The ceremony of innocence is drowned; /The best lack all conviction, while the worst /Are full of passionate intensity.*

William Butler Yeats. "The Second Coming." Published in *Michael Robartes and the Dancer* (Churchtown, Dundrum, Ireland: The Chuala Press, 1920)

[88] In his article outlining the current absurdity of academic publishing, Mike Taylor discussed the possibilities of what publishing could be---possibilities that were held back by tradition.

> Well, so much for the dream. What about the reality? The sad truth is that we are hobbled by the tyranny of tradition. Researchers are used to publishing papers in traditional journals: this is what we are rewarded for and measured by. Publishers are used to being paid every time they deliver an article to a reader. The rational response to the internet would be for the whole community to transition to a service model: instead of

charging for access, publishers would provide services like co-ordinating peer-review, formatting, Web-hosting and archiving, and charge for those services.

Mike Taylor. "The Future of Academic Publishing." *The Independent.* 9 February 2012. http://blogs.independent.co.uk/2012/02/09/the-future-of-academic-publishing/

[89] Jay Rosen wrote on his blog *PressThink.Ghost of Democracy in the Media Machine.* "The People Formerly Known as the Audience."

> The people formerly known as the audience are those who *were* on the receiving end of a media system that ran one way, in a broadcasting pattern, with high entry fees and a few firms competing to speak very loudly while the rest of the population listened in isolation from one another— and who *today* are not in a situation like that *at all*.

- Once they were your printing presses; now that humble device, the blog, has given the press to us. That's why blogs have been called little First Amendment machines. They extend freedom of the press to more actors.
- Once it was *your* radio station, broadcasting on *your* frequency. Now that brilliant invention, podcasting, gives radio to us. And we have found more uses for it than you did.
- Shooting, editing and distributing video once belonged to you, Big Media. Only you could afford to reach a TV audience built in your own image. Now video is coming into the user's hands, and audience-building by former members of the audience is alive and well on the Web.
- You were once (exclusively) the editors of the news, choosing what ran on the front page. Now we can edit the news, and our choices send items to our own front pages. A highly centralized media system had connected people "up" to big social agencies and centers of power but not "across" to each other. Now the horizontal flow, citizen-to-citizen, is as real and consequential as the vertical one.

Jay Rosen. "The People Formerly Known as the Audience." *PressThink.Ghost of Democracy in the Media Machine:* http://archive.pressthink.org/2006/06/27/ppl_frmr.html

[90] As Lyotard remarked,
> These technological transformations can be expected to have a considerable impact on knowledge. Its two principle functions---research and the transmission of acquired learning---are already feeling the effect, or will in the future.

Jean-François Lyotard. Op.cit., 4.

[91] Lyotard. Ibid. XXIV-XXV.

[92] Ian H. Angus. "Learning to Stop: A Critique of General Rhetoric." Ian H. Angus and Lenore Langsdorf, Editors. *The Critical Turn: Rhetoric and Philosophy in Postmodern Discourse* (Southern Illinois Press, 1993) 192.

[93] An exception would be Mark Poster who wrote, rather quaintly, of "computer science" and Lyotard in 1990. Declaring Lyotard as "ambivalent" about the role of computers in changing the mode of knowledge, Poster preferred to discuss the philosopher in relation to philosophers and philosophers. In the 1990s, it was still not possible to fully comprehend the impact of computers and the Internet on the production of knowledge.

Mark Poster. "Lyotard and Computer Science." *The Mode of Information: Poststructuralism and the Social Context* (Chicago: The University of Chicago Press, 1990) 145.

[94] Lyotard. Op.cit. 67.

[95] Lyotard. Op.cit. 53.

[96] At this transitional moment in time MOOCs depend upon a "star" professor who is out of reach of the thousands of students. This star is an artifact of a dying system and, being a single human being, cannot possibly be the repository of all knowledge in his or her field. In addition by relying on the old-fashioned lecture format which is limited in time, MOOCs are restricting knowledge for sentimental reasons. But, as I said, this is a liminal passage. In spring 2013, reporter A. J. Jacobs described the experience of being enrolled in a MOOC:

> As these online universities gain traction, and start counting for actual college course credit, they'll most likely have enormous real-world impact. They'll help in getting jobs and creating business ideas. They might just

live up to their hype. For millions of people around the globe with few resources, MOOCs may even be life-changing. As for whether MOOCs will ever totally replace colleges made of brick, mortar and ivy, however, count me as a skeptic. A campus still has advantages for those lucky enough to afford the tuition — networking being one.

A. J. Jacob. "Two Courses for Web U!" *The New York Times* (April 20, 2013): http://www.nytimes.com/2013/04/21/opinion/sunday/grading-the-mooc-university.html?pagewanted=all&_r=0

[97] As WIRED magazine put it,

> In MOOCs today there is almost zero student choice, no curriculum integration, no sense of brain-learning interjected into the curricula, a lack of modeling or showcasing creativity and/or critical thinking, and the top-down model promotes a sterile, impersonal experience. Finally (at least for this list), is the data captivity by MOOC platforms. While most believe the data will soon be available for a price, most have made it clear that the data is THEIRS and not a school's.

Dr. Jeff Borden. "The MOOC Heard Around the World." *WIRED* (May 13, 2013): http://www.wired.com/insights/2013/05/the-mooc-heard-around-the-world/

[98] There is Facebook today, maybe not tomorrow, were private communications take place and all attempts to substantially monetize it have proved to be a sputtering capitalist dream. Facebook is the great meeting room for friends and family and its users are barely tolerant of overt advertising and resent any attempts to make money off of their exchanges. The fact that people reveal themselves so freely in this site implies a level of privacy that resembles a home. Forbes reported on how Facebook has finally succeeded in linking the sense of community and connectedness to commerce in ways that suit its users.
As the Trefis Team wrote,

> Facebook has been placing higher priority on e-commerce with some recent initiatives. The company launched its Gifts feature in late September, leveraging

its acquisition of mobile commerce start-up Karma. This feature allows users to easily buy and send gifts to each other based on suggestions, and Facebook keeps a share of the purchases made. In addition, the company has also been testing a feature called collections, aimed at promoting e-commerce on Facebook. With this feature, Facebook users can add items they like from certain retailers to their wishlist for purchase. Social commerce, which contributes less than 10% to Facebook's value, could see some boost from these new features.

Trefis Team. "Facebook Earnings: Revenue Growth and Mobile Monetization in Focus." *Forbes* (January 29, 2013): http://www.forbes.com/sites/greatspeculations/2013/01/29/facebook-earnings-revenue-growth-and-mobile-monetization-in-focus/

[99] One of the early and often referred to articles on the gift economy on the Internet was written by Richard Barbrook for the e-journal *First Monday* in the ancient era of 1998.

Richard Barbrook. "The Hi-Tech Gift Economy." *First Monday* (Volume 3, Number 12) December 7, 1998: http://firstmonday.org/htbin/cgiwrap/bin/ojs/index.php/fm/article/view/631/552

[100] For a history of the Internet, see Johnny Ryan who remarked that "on the Web, the user was now king" and that corporations and investors had "fundamentally misunderstood the Internet." Certainly the misunderstanding of the potlatch nature of the Internet led to the strange belief that Wall Street had that *Facebook* could be somehow monetized in the usual fashion. True, anything can be given over to business needs but, given that *Facebook* functions as a kind of scrapbook, advertising needs to be discrete and non-invasive.

Johnny Ryan. *A History of the Internet and the Digital Future* (Wilshire: Anthony Rowe, 2010)

[101] Although highly technical, one of the most recent books on the current state of the Internet was written by Christopher Yoo. *The Dynamic Internet. How Technology, Users and Businesses are Transforming the Network* (Washington, D. C.: American Enterprise Institute, 2012)

[102] Tiziana Terranova has written an interesting article on how people participate collectively and tirelessly on the Web to build the Internet.

> The pervasiveness of the collective intelligence within both the managerial literature and Marxist theory could be seen as the result of a common intuition about the quality of labor in informated societies. Knowledge labor is inherently collective; it is always the result of a collective and social production of knowledge. Capital's problem is how to extract as much value as possible (in the autonomists' jargon, to "valorize") out of the abundant, and yet slightly intractable, terrain. Collective knowledge work, then, is not about those who work in the knowledge industry. But it is also not about employment...Labor is not the equivalent to waged labor...To emphasize how labor is not equivalent to employment also means to acknowledge how important free, affective and cultural labor is to the media industry, old and new.

Tiziana Terranova. "Free Labor." in Trebor Scholz, Editor. *Digital Labor. The Internet as Playground and Factory.* (New York: Routledge, 2013) 33-57. Also see her book, *Network Culture: Politics for the Information Age* (The University of Michigan: Pluto Press, 2004)

[103] The Internet has opened spaces allowing an entirely new class of political intellectuals to emerge. Ronald N. Jacobs and Eleanor Townsley discuss this phenomenon:

> Among the different online developments, the user-authored content proved to the most consequential for increasing the influence and circulation of media commentary. Importantly, it was not just the mainstream newspapers and television stations that were creating forums and Weblogs for individuals to participate in discussions about new of the day. Even more significant, perhaps, were the blogs that developed outside the established news organizations. Web sites like *Daily Kos, Huffington Post, Instapundit* and *Talking Points Memo* created intensely interactive spaces of media commentary, which were updated almost continuously. Importantly, the initial point of departure of a new discussion was more often than not a comment on something that was said or written in the mainstream

> spaces of media commentary, with a hyperlink to the original provided.

Of particular interest is the chapter "Who Speaks in the Space of Opinion?" in which the authors employ the ideas of Pierre Bourdieu to discuss the question of access in different fields.

> This involves considerations about what constitutes good art, literature, journalism, or science, as well as a consideration of the history of debates about these matters within the field. For Bourdieu, internalist principles of distinction define the "privileged social universes" constructed by specific cultural groups who have established both the right to control the "means of cultural production and diffusion" and also "the power of evaluating themselves according to their own criteria." It is these internalist principles of distinction that are related to the demand for autonomy. In other words, within a cultural field, the quest for autonomy will be driven by at least as much by a concern for professional and intellectual control with the filed as it is by, say, an interest in critical rationality or commitment to demographic representation (although these principles are not necessarily mutually exclusive).

Ronald N. Jacobs and Eleanor Townsley. *The Space of Opinion: Media Intellectuals and the Public Sphere* (New York: Oxford University Press, 2011) 49, 79.

[104] The debate in the Western world veered back and forth between the "idealist" and the "materialist" arguments: reality is understood only through the realm of ideas or *a priori* functions of cognition and the exterior reality which is received, perceived and acknowledged by the brain. For a brief discussion of the history and development of the two traditions in philosophy see Wendy Griswold. *Cultures and Societies in a Changing World* (Pine Forge Press, 2008)

[105] John Willinsky noted that in the year 2000, there was already a "crisis" in academic publishing, a crisis that is not yet resolved. The Association of American Universities and the Association of Research Librarians had no solution, in the year 2000, other than proposing that "the evaluation of faculty should place a greater emphasis on quality of publications and a

reduced emphasis on quantity." Willinksy was impatient with such reiteration of the old in the face of the new:

> Focusing on quality over quantity as a means for containing subscription costs is a bit like having fewer, better children to reduce the risk of child-napping – to continue the ransom metaphor. The problem is rather the assumption that publishers alone can guarantee the quality and distribution of this public good, which has allowed them to drive scholarly publishing to the brink of unsustainability. Yet these commercial publishing interests are, in many cases, latecomers to an enterprise that has otherwise run as a sponsored exchange economy. That is, the university (with public and private money for salaries and grants) sponsors its faculty's participation in a knowledge economy that is organized around the exchange of research. Faculty are paid by their own university to do research, to publish research, to review research, and to edit research, in addition to the teaching and service they provide. These research activities, once paid for or sponsored, then lead to the exchange through correspondence, conferences, and journals. In offering this research for exchange, the faculty member is not required to recover salary and grant costs.
>
> This exchange is as vital to research as motion is to sharks, and it is undoubtedly facilitated by those who publish it. The cost of an academic journal subscription only covers the publication costs (principally editorial, printing, and distribution) rather than the actual cost of producing the content. The information is not free (whether it wants to be or not), although the journal publisher gets it for that price; it has been sponsored for the purposes of exchange, most often I would hazard, at public expense. Given this way of thinking, the crisis in scholarly publishing could be cast as an imbalance between the exchange and service economies of scholarly communication, with the (publishing) services currently driving the process to the brink.

John Willinsky. "Proposing a Knowledge Exchange Model for Scholarly Publishing." *Current Issues in Education* (Volume 3, Number 6, 2000): http://cie.asu.edu/volume3/number6/

[106] David Shatz explored the notion that there is a "marketplace of ideas" for academic thought and has found the concept to be countered by gatekeepers who control their disciplines.

> There is also a problem of authority. If one or two of the peer referees do not like an author's ideas, arguments, orientation, methodology, organization, or even writing style, that will often ensure (pending whether revisions are invited) that the ideas will not appear in print where the author wants them and will not reach the hoped-for audience.

David Shatz. Op cit., 17.

[107] In writing to the interconnections between the Internet and knowledge, Julianne Cortese, explained,

> Pathfinder networks are similar to concept mapping but allow for easier comparison between human knowledge structures and information structures presented on a website. Pathfinder networks provide a technique to analyze connections between nodes by examining the link structure between these nodes…Pathfinder networks can be applied to both human knowledge and web-based information structures, allowing the two to be compared for similarities.

Julianne Cortese. *Internet Learning and the Building of Knowledge* (Youngstown, New York: Cambria Press, 2007) 16.

[108] See Brian Whitworth's two part article "Reinventing Academic Publishing Online Part I: Rigor, Relevance and Practice" and "Part II: A Socio-Technical Vision." *First Monday* (Volume 14, Number 8, 3 August 2009) and (Volume 14, Number 9, September 2009).

[109] Brian Whitworth and Rob Friedman. "The Challenge of Modern Academic Knowledge Exchange." SIGITE Newsletter (Volume 5, Number 2, 2008): http://brianwhitworth.com/Rigor-SIGITEJune2008.pdf

[110] Apparently the production and control of knowledge was so important to God that to "eat" from the Tree was to bring about a death sentence:

> But of the tree of the knowledge of good and evil, thou shalt not eat of it: for in the day that thou eatest thereof thou shalt surely die.

"Genesis 2: 17." *King James Version*

[111] Whitworth and Friedman write that

> Naturally change will be opposed by those vested in academic power structures and feared by those dependent upon them. Yet fear of change is not, and has never been, a good reason to avoid progress. The study of hard drive technology evolution illustrates how initially *disruptive innovations* morph into constructive successes (Christensen, 1997). The lesson is that so–called disruptive change is an opportunity if one does not try to deny it. So let us not try to impose on the age of electronic knowledge exchange the rules of the previous printed age (Pinter, 2008). Universities currently outsource the marketing and distribution of their knowledge to publishers with little interest in their communities. If knowledge distributors who create no knowledge dominate its exchange, then the publishing tail is wagging the academic dog. This is not good for anyone, publishers included, since as we have argued here, it is a recipe for academic decay. If universities let publishers kidnap their knowledge and hold them to copyright ransom (Willinsky, 2000), they fail their public duty of knowledge guardianship.

Frankly, I, personally, am dubious of the elaborate charts and diagrams the authors produce to create a new way of moving peer review to an online site. Until proven otherwise, the act of elaborating an already questionable practice to a new location may not solve the problem, which is restricting knowledge through gatekeeping.

Brian Whitworth and Rob Friedman. "Reinventing Academic Publishing Online, Part II: A Socio-Technical Vision." *First Monday. Peer Reviewed Journal on the Internet* (Volume 14, Number 9, September 2009): http://firstmonday.org/ojs/index.php/fm/article/view/2642/2287

[112] Poster stated,

> The hyperreal, though, remains tied to the real, and simulacra sustain their character by their difference from copies with originals. When the question turns to the new media, and, in particular, to the Internet, it is no longer clear if this is the case. The simulacral culture of broadcast media, then, in part strengthens the modern subject, in part constructs new objects without originals, and in part constructs new subjects as multiple and diffuse. With the Internet, by contrast, we find objects before us whose determination is to a very considerable extent underdetermined. The Internet carries forward the modern subject/object relation by vastly increasing the efficiency of producing mass cultural objects and distributing them around the globe. The Internet carries forward the late modern broadcast subject/object by incorporating radio, film, and television and distributing them through "push" technology. But the Internet transgresses the limits of the print and broadcast models by (1) enabling many-to-many communications; (2) enabling the simultaneous reception, alteration, and redistribution of cultural objects; (3) dislocating communicative action from the posts of the nation, from the territorialized spatial (5) inserting the modern/late modern subject into an information machine apparatus that is networked. The result is a more completely postmodern subject or, better, a self that is no longer a subject since it no longer subtends the world as if from the outside but operates within a machine apparatus as a point in a circuit.

Mark Poster. Op.cit., 16.

[113] Mark Poster. *Information Please: Culture and Politics in the Age of Digital Machines* (Duke University Press, 2006) and with David Savant *Deleuze and New Technology* (Edinburgh University Press, 2009)

[114] Richard Rorty. *Philosophy and the Mirror of Nature* (Princeton, N. J.: Princeton University Press, 1979/2009) 378-379.

[115] Ibid. 389.

[116] Media philosopher, Mike Sandbothe, linked Richard and Rorty and Jacques Derrida,

> The project of media philosophy is liked with a new orientation of philosophical self-understanding that Rorty has called the "pragmatic turn." By this is meant the transition to a form of philosophy activity whose focus is no longer the theoreticist question of the representational or constructivist reference of our linguistic cognitive achievements to reality, but instead of the pragmatic question of the utility of our thinking in contexts of action, contexts to be determined morally, politically and socially…a medially deepening of the linguistic turn can be paradigmatically illustrated using the example of Jacques Derrida's *Of Grammatology*…I call the problem area taken up and further developed in a deconstructionist manner by Derrida "theoreticist" because it targets set by human communities. The theoreticist demarcation of understanding of both self and the world, and hence a domain beyond all practical horizons of utility, a domain that is supposed to produce, found or legitimize those horizons. In contrast to this theoreticist version, the pragmatist definition of the tasks of media contexts emerges from culturally and historically given practical contexts of interest and socio-political targets. This can be illustrated by taking as examples selected considerations set out by Richard Rorty, the American figurehead of neopragmatism. Unlike Derrida, Rorty is no concerned with the deconstructionist deepening of the linguistic turn…Rorty takes the linguistic turn more as an occasion for a change of subject and a side stepping of the issues of the epistemological tradition in their linguistic reformulation.

Mike Sandbothe. "Media Philosophy and Media Education in the Age of the Internet." Geoffrey H. Satchell. *Physiology and Form of Fish Circulation* (Blackwell Publishers, Inc. 2000) 64 and 66.

[117] Rorty, Op.cit.

[118] In *Rorty and the Mirror of Nature*, James Tartaglia noted that Richard Rorty took a metaphilosophical approach to write about philosophy as a genre of texts. This stance, taken in 1979, was an early iteration of

Postmodernism in America, an echo of what had been going on for a decade in Europe.

> 1979 was also the year that PMN was published. Apart from its impact in philosophy, it became hugely influential in the humanities generally. This seems to have been a genuine surprise to Rorty, since the book was aimed squarely at professional philosophers. Nevertheless, its conclusions were plain enough for all to see, and appeared to legitimise new directions being taken in critical theory and literary, sociological and cultural studies, directions already taken by continental thinkers like Derrida and Foucault. By breaking down the hegemony of knowledge which natural science and philosophy had enjoyed over social science and literature, and by seeking to undermine any notion of a universal, atemporal truth, Rorty's book seemed to provide a theoretical sanction for the exploration of traditionally philosophical themes such as freedom, truth and power within the context of literature, contemporary culture, history and economics. Thus Rorty came to be seen as the principal English- speaking representative of postmodernism.

James Tartaglia. *Rorty and the Mirror of Nature* (London: Routledge, 2007) 14.

[119] According to Rorty,

> To see keeping a conversation going as a sufficient aim of philosophy, to see wisdom as consisting in the ability to sustain a conversation, is to see human beings as generators of new descriptions rather than beings one hopes to be able to describe accurately. To see the aim of philosophy as truth---namely, the truth about the terms which provide ultimate commensuration for all human inquiries and activities---is to see human beings as objects rather than subjects, as existing *en-soi* rather than as both *pour-soi* and *en-soi*, as both described objects and describing subjects. To think that philosophy will permit us to see the describing subject as itself one sort of described object is to think that all possible descriptions can be rendered commensurable with the

aid of a single descriptive vocabulary---that of philosophy itself.

Rorty. Ibid. p. 378.

[120] Wolfgang Welsch. "Richard Rorty: Philosophy beyond Argument and Truth?" from the home page of the Institut für Philosophie. Friedrich-Schiller-Universität Jena (22 January 1999): http://www.ifp.uni-jena.de

[121] Alex Bruns in "Produsage, Generation C, and Their Effects on the Democratic Process" explained "produsage:"
The four core characteristics of produsage, then, are these:

- Community-Based – produsage proceeds from the assumption that the community as a whole, if sufficiently large and varied, can contribute more than a closed team of producers, however qualified they may be.

- Fluid Roles – producers participate as is appropriate to their personal skills, interests, and knowledges, and may form loose sub-groups to focus on specific issues, topics, or problems; this changes as the produsage project proceeds.

- Unfinished Artefacts – content artefacts in produsage projects are continually under development, and therefore always unfinished; their development follows evolutionary, iterative, palimpsestic paths.

- Common Property, Individual Merit – contributors permit (non-commercial) community use, adaptation, and further development of their intellectual property, and are rewarded by the status capital they gain through this process.

Alex Bruns. "Produsage, Generation C, and Their Effects on the Democratic Process:" http://web.mit.edu/comm-forum/mit5/papers/Bruns.pdf

[122] A rather awkwardly translated article by three digital scientists discusses Lyotard and "Information and Communication Technologies." Areif Ramadhan, Dana Indra Asesuse, Aniati Murni Arymurthy. "Postmodernism in e-Government." *International Journal of Computer Science Issues* (Volume 8, Issue 4, Number 1, July 2011): http://ijcsi.org/papers/IJCSI-8-4-1-623-629.pdf

[123] Bruns defined "produsage" in 2006 as

> ...that within the communities which engage in the collaborative creation and extension of information and knowledge...the role of "consumer" and even that of "end user" have long disappeared, and the distinctions between producers and users of content have faced into comparative insignificance...Produsage exists within a wider context of new and emerging concepts for describing the social, technological, and economic environment of user-led content creation.

Alex Bruns. *Blogs, Wikipedia, Second Life, and Beyond. From Production to Produsage* (New York: Peter Lang Publishing, Include, 2008) 2 – 3.

[124] Alex Bruns. "Unfinished Artefacts, Continuing Process." *Blogs, Wikipedia, Second Life, and Beyond: From Production to Produsage* (Peter Lang Publishing 2008) 27-28

[125] "Trenddriver/Collapse of Conventions." *Trendwatching.com.* September 2010.
http://www.trendwatching.com/trends/maturialism/

[126] Bruns discussed "causal collapse" in a mode more substantive than in *trendwatching* by stating,

> A casual collapse of established hierarchies and institutions is the typical outcome of a paradigm shift---and produsage-driven collapses can already be observed in *Encyclopaedia Brittanica*'s rear-guard battle with *Wikipedia*, the news industry's struggle with citizen journalism, and the software industry's gradual transition towards open source-based business models.
> Bruns discussed the casual collapse of conventional education or the twenty-first century mode of delivering culture in his 2008 book.

Axel Bruns. Op.cit., 344.

[127] Bruns compared corporate or mainstream journalism with "citizen journalism:"

> ...whatever the terms we use to describe it, such probabilistic, debate-driven story development does offer significant advantages over closed-shop, commercial models. Its open processes avoid the impact of personal or institutional bias on behalf of individual journalists and editors; misrepresentations in the initial gatewatcher story, for example, are usually corrected almost immediately as other community members exercise their evaluative role and comment on the story. As such comments are added, stories necessarily begin to involve a wider range of perspectives on the implications of the news story than is possible (even with the best intentions) under the limitations of conventional industrial journalism.

Alex Bruns. Op. cit. 76.

[128] Todd May wondered if Foucault was relevant to today's society:

> We cannot avoid a conversation with the question of Foucault's relation to the present. There is no philosophical fiat by which we can spare him scrutiny, any more than there is a philosophical manoeuvre that would allow him to be dismissed without being read (although there are some who would wish the latter). Even if we cannot, and we will not, close the debate on this question, we must surely open it. After all, the stakes concern who we are now. Are we now still who Foucault says we are?

Todd May. *The Philosophy of Foucault* (McGill-Queen's University Press, 2006) 133.

[129] As the authors said,

> Let us summarize the principle characteristics of a rhizome: unlike trees or their roots, the rhizome

> connects any point to any other point, and its traits are not necessarily linked to traits of the same nature; it brings into play very different regimes of signs, and even nonsign states. The rhizome is reducible neither to the One nor the multiple...It is composed not of units but of dimensions, or rather directions in motion. It has neither beginning nor end, but always a middle (*milieu*) from which it grows and which it overspills.

Gilles Deleuze and Félix Guattari. *A Thousand Plateaus: Capitalism and Schizophrenia* (New York: Continuum Publishing Company, 1987, 1988, 2004) 23.

[130] In their introduction to *A Thousand Plateaus*, Deleuze and Guattari define "rhizome" as

> Let us summarize the principal characteristics of a rhizome: unlike trees or their roots, the rhizome connects any point to any other point, and its traits are not necessarily linked to traits of the same nature; it brings into play very different regimes of signs, and even nonsign states. The rhizome is reducible neither to the One nor the multiple. It is not the One that becomes Two or even directly three, four, five, etc. It is not a multiple derived from the One, or to which One is added (n + 1). It is composed not of units but of dimensions, or rather directions in motion. It has neither beginning nor end, but always a middle (milieu) from which it grows and which it overspills. It constitutes linear multiplicities with n dimensions having neither subject nor object, which can be laid out on a plane of consistency, and from which the One is always subtracted (n - 1). When a mul- tiplicity of this kind changes dimension, it necessarily changes in nature as well, undergoes a metamorphosis. Unlike a structure, which is defined by a set of points and positions, with binary relations between the points and blunivocal relationships between the positions, the rhizome is made only of lines: lines of segmentarity and stratification as its dimensions, and the line of flight or deterritorialization as the maximum dimension after which the multiplicity undergoes metamorphosis, changes in nature. These lines, or lineaments, should not be confused with lineages of the arborescent type, which

are merely localizable linkages between points and positions. Unlike the tree, the rhizome is not the object of reproduction: neither external reproduction as image-tree nor internal reproduction as tree-structure. The rhizome is an antigenealogy. It is a short-term memory, or antimemory. The rhizome operates by variation, expansion, conquest, capture, offshoots. Unlike the graphic arts, drawing, or photography, unlike tracings, the rhizome pertains to a map that must be produced, constructed, a map that is always detachable, connectable, reversible, modifiable, and has multiple entryways and exits and its own lines of flight. It is tracings that must be put on the map, not the opposite. In contrast to centered (even polycentric) systems with hierarchical modes of communication and preestablished paths, the rhizome is an acentered, nonhierarchical, nonsignifying system without a General and without an organizing memory or central automaton, defined solely by a circulation of states. What is at question in the rhizome is a relation to sexuality-but also to the animal, the vegetal, the world, politics, the book, things natural and artificial-that is totally different from the arborescent relation: all manner of "becomings."

A plateau is always in the middle, not at the beginning or the end. A rhizome is made of plateaus.

And they conclude by saying, "A rhizome has no beginning or end; it is always in the middle, between things, interbeing, intermezzo."

Gilles Deleuze and Felix Guattari. Op. cit., 21.

However, Robin B. Hamman of the University of Essex expressed doubts as to whether one could appropriately compare the rhizome to the Internet:

...using the Internet as a model of the rhizome arises when discussing the principle of the rhizome which requires that rhizomes have multiple entryways. Typically, an Internet user will only have one Internet access account, and thus one entryway on to the Internet. To resolve this problem, I move to a theoretical level. In theory, anyone can set up a computer or server on the Internet which would allow them to create their own access point or node as it called by computer networking professionals. Similarly, anyone can sign up for Internet access with any of the companies that provide such a service. In theory, this resolves the problem of multiple access points, however things do not always work out in the same way that things on a theoretical level would make us believe. What is happening in today's world is that class, race, and gender divisions determine who has access to computer equipment and to the knowledge to use this technology. This means that, although those without financial restraints can have access to the Internet from multiple entryways, most people will not have such access at anytime in the foreseeable future. So the Internet is not truly a rhizome for all it's (sic) users, but for a select few it remains a rhizome with multiple entryways.

Robin B. Hamman. "Rhizome @Internet. Using the Internet as an Example of Deleuze and Guattari's 'Rhizome.'" *Cybersociology Magazine*. (1996): http://www.socio.demon.co.uk/rhizome.html

[131] Christian Fuchs. "Towards Marxist Internet Studies." *Triple C* (10(2): 392-412, 2012 ISSN 1726-670X): http://www.triple-c.at)

This article provides an extensive presentation of the works of various scholars who are using Marxism to analyze the Internet.

[132] Timo Beck described "user-generated content:"

People benefit from the contributions of others in online communities, from the information and support that is provided, and the conversations they participate in. To survive and thrive, online communities have to promote the benefits the members seek---social exchange and the possibility to present oneself are the basic mechanisms by which participants derive benefit. Therefore people or members, who develop new ideas and continually changing content, build the heart of any online community---they make it unique and valuable…

Timo Beck. *Web 2.0: User-Generated Content in Online Communities. A Theoretical and Empirical Investigation of its Determinants.* (Hamburg: Diplomica Verlag GmbH, 2007) 20.

[133] Eric von Hippel discussed his concept of "democratizing innovation," which is the relationship between innovators who welcome users as co-inventors. His book *Democratizing Innovation* published in 2005 is available to all under a Creative Commons license. That said, for the past thirty years, von Hippel has studied the shift from the traditional passive model, or the advertiser "giving" the product to the public to the collaborative model between maker and user. However, his research showed that many innovative devices were actually created by users who desired or needed the product and, once these objects captured the attention of the manufacturer, the origins of the process were lost. Von Hippel speaks of the users as active *bricoleurs*, who "take what is around." Following von Hippel's concept, the Web is now the idea site for users who want to customize knowledge toward their owns ends and, according to the logic of the Long Tail, consumers of this specialized information will come.

Eric von Hippel. "Democratizing Innovation and Norms-based Intellectual Property Rights:" http://www.youtube.com/watch?v=m6RttLCiKxI
Von Hippel makes the important point that communities who share innovation thrive and grow:

> The collective or community effort to provide a public good---which is what freely revealed innovations are---has traditionally been explored in the literature on "collective action." However, behaviors seen in extant innovation communities appear to be more robust with respect to recruiting and rewarding members than the literature would predict.

Eric von Hippel. *Democratizing Innovation* (Creative Commons, 2005) 11.

[134] As Barthes wrote in *S/Z*,

> ...literature itself is never anything but a single text: the one text is not an (inductive) access to a Model, but entrance into a network with a thousand entrances; to take this entrance is to aim, ultimately, not at a legal structure of norms and departures, a narrative or poetic Law, but at a perspective (of fragments, of voices from other texts, other codes), whose vanishing point is nonetheless ceaselessly pushed back, mysteriously opened: each (single) text is the very theory (and not the

> mere example) of this vanishing, of this difference which indefinitely returns, insubmissive.

Roland Barthes. *S/Z*. Translated by Richard Miller (Farrar, Straus, and Giroux, Inc. 1974) 12.

[135] For example the founder of *The Victorian Web* an excellent site, George P. Landow, wrote that in *S/Z*,

> "Roland Barthes describes an ideal textuality that precisely matches that which has come to be called computer hypertext -- text composed of blocks of words (or images) linked electronically by multiple paths, chains, or trails in an open-ended, perpetually unfinished textuality described by the terms link, node, network, web, and path..."

However, Professor Landow also credited Theodor H. Nelson, who coined the term. In his 1992 book *Hypertext. The Convergence of Contemporary Critical Theory and Technology,* he noted that readers of Barthes and Foucault found these authors easier to read because they were familiar with the Internet. He also quotes J. David Bolter as saying, "...what is unnatural in print becomes natural in the electronic medium and will soon no longer need saying at all, because it can be shown."

George P. Landow. "The Definition of Hypertext and its History as a Concept."
http://www.cyberartsweb.org/cpace/ht/jhup/history.html
George Landow. *Hyptertext. Contemporary Critical Theory and Technology* (Baltimore: The Johns Hopkins University Press, 1992)

[136] As Bush wrote:

> The human mind does not work that way. It operates by association. With one item in its grasp, it snaps instantly to the next that is suggested by the association of thoughts, in accordance with some intricate web of trails carried by the cells of the brain. It has other characteristics, of course; trails that are not frequently followed are prone to fade, items are not fully permanent, memory is transitory. Yet the speed of action, the intricacy of trails, the detail of mental pictures, is awe-inspiring beyond all else in nature.

> Man cannot hope fully to duplicate this mental process artificially, but he certainly ought to be able to learn from it. In minor ways he may even improve, for his records have relative permanency. The first idea, however, to be drawn from the analogy concerns selection. Selection by association, rather than indexing, may yet be mechanized. One cannot hope thus to equal the speed and flexibility with which the mind follows an associative trail, but it should be possible to beat the mind decisively in regard to the permanence and clarity of the items resurrected from storage.
>
> Consider a future device for individual use, which is a sort of mechanized private file and library. It needs a name, and, to coin one at random, "memex" will do. A memex is a device in which an individual stores all his books, records, and communications, and which is mechanized so that it may be consulted with exceeding speed and flexibility. It is an enlarged intimate supplement to his memory.

Vannebar Bush. "As We May Think." *The Atlantic Magazine.* July 1945. http://www.theatlantic.com/magazine/archive/1945/07/as-we-may-think/303881/?single_page=true

[137] As Thierry Bardini wrote,

> What actually differentiates hypertext systems from information –retrieval systems is not the process of "association," the term Bush proposed as analogous to the way the individual mind works. Instead, what constitutes a hypertext system is clear in the definition of hypertext already cited: "a style of building systems for information representation and management around a *network of nodes connected together by typed links.*" A hypertext system is constituted by the presence of "links." And a process of association analogous to the way the individual mind works is not the only way of establishing links. The most important ones are established in natural language.

Thierry Bardini. *Bootstrapping: Douglas Engelbart, Coevolution, and the Origins of Personal Computing* (Stanford: Stanford University Press, 2000) 40.

[138] Bush. Op. cit.

[139] Michael Worton. *Intertextuality: Theories and Practice* (New York: Manchester University Press, 1990). This book, written in 1990, predictably does not mention the Internet but Graham Allen, writing in 2000, reprinted in 2011 mentioned the Internet three times. Allen asked,

> Is intertexual as hypertextual reading ultimately not a kind of surfing rather than reading/ The serious answer to that rather rhetorical question would be that the nature of reading is obviously being affected, in ways we are hardly aware of as yet, by the radical change from print to digital technology...The answer to the question just posed clearly involves the future of the concept of intertextuality. Whatever that future is to be it is bound to involve a process of naming and renaming...In a process which is in itself intertextual, we have seen the concept renamed and renamed again during the course of this book. In the context of new media studies and digital culture the pressure to generate terms which reflect the significant change in the object of study will inevitably mean that the focus alters from text to media, from textuality to mediality and mediation.

Graham Allen. *Intertextuality* (New York: Routledge, 2000, 2011) 213-214.

[140] As Kristeva explained,

> The three dimensions or coordinates of dialogue are writing subject, addressee and exterior texts. The word's status is thus defined *horizontally* (the word in the text belongs to both writing subject and addressee) as well as *vertically* (the word in the text is oriented towards an anterior or synchronic literary corpus)...Dialogue appears most clearly in the structure of carnivalesque language, where symbolic relationships and analogy take precedence over substance-causality connections. The notion of *ambivalence* pertains to the permutation of the two spaces observed in novelistic structure: dialogical

space and monological space. From a conception of
poetic language as dialogue and ambivalence, Bakhtin
moves to a re-evaluation of the novel's structure. This
investigation takes the form of a classification of words
within the narrative---the classification being then linked
to a typology of discourse.

This seminal 1966 article has been reprinted in "Word, Dialogue and Novel." *The Kristeva Reader*. Edited by Toril Moi (New York: Columbia University Press, 1986). 36 and 43

[141] Arkady Plotnitsky. "Un-Scriptible."*Writing the Image After Roland Barthes*. Edited by Jean-Michel Rabate (Philadelphia: University of Pennsylvania Press, 1997) 243-257.

[142] Jacques Derrida. *Of Grammatology.* (Baltimore: The Johns Hopkins University Press, 1967, 1976) 163.

[143] The original book, *Dream Machines: New Freedoms Through Computer Screens---A Minority Report* was self-published by Nelson in 1974 and is now available through Hugo's Book Service, 1974
Nelson imagined a place where hypertext could explode or as *The New Media Reader* put it:

> ...he was called a crackpot (and worse) for his strong
> conviction that Xanadu's fundamentals represented the
> future of media and culture. The general belief was that
> there simply was not demand for a public, hypertext-
> enabled publishing network. This belief was resisted,
> however, by small groups around the world who created
> and worked with various types of hypertext-enabled
> networks. Although we have not yet reached Xanadu,
> when one of these systems, the World Wide Web, began
> to explode in popularity during the 1990s, the voices of
> Nelson naysayers were drowned forever in a flood of
> international hypertext publishing.

Theodor P. Nelson. *Computer Lib/Dream Machines:*
http://www.newmediareader.com/book_samples/nmr-21-nelson.pdf

[144] The premier writer on the relationships between intertextuality and hypertext is the important scholar and web designer, George P. Landow. What is interesting about Landow and many other writers on the Internet

is that he assumes "empowerment" as something possessed by the reader who is now free to link and relink and to move here and there at will. That said Landow, like many other writers on the Web, has not yet come to terms with the power that Internet writers may have gained. That said, he has conscientiously updated his seminal books on hypertext over the years.

George P. Landow. *Hypertext 3.0: Critical Theory and New Media in an Age of Globalization* (Baltimore: The Johns Hopkins University Press, 1992,1997, 2006)

[145] Nelson, Op. cit.

[146] The term originated with Bela Julesz in 1981 in "Textons, the Elements of Texture Perception, and their Interactions," published in *Nature,* and referred to a distinction between pre-attentive vision and attentive vision. Researchers use "textures" to test human vision at different stages of attention.

Bela Julesz. "Texton Gradients: The Texton Theory Revisited." *Biological Cybernetics* (Volume 54, 1986)

[147] Bernard Reber and Claire Brossard, editors. *Digital Cognitive Technologies: Epistemology and Knowledge Society.* "Chapter 10: Hypertext, an Intellectual Technology in the Era of Complexity." (Hoboken, N. J. John Wiley & Sons, 2010) n. p.

[148] Although Deleuze and Guattari professed to be tired of trees, the roots of their concept of the rhizome have spread to the Internet. Connections to the Web is explored by Ian Buchanan, editor of *Deleuze Studies,* who makes the point that the searches on the Web are "interested" as opposed to disinterested, as with the rhizome's activity:

> Yet, if we were to grant that the Internet is acentred, nonsignifying, and acephalous in appearance and indeed in its very construction, the reality of its day-to-day use still does not live up to this much-vaunted Deleuzian ideal. Here we have to remind ourselves that Deleuze and Guattari regard the rhizome as a tendency rather than a state of being. It must constantly compete with an equally strong tendency in the opposite direction, namely towards what they term the 'arboreal'. The Internet exhibits arboreal tendencies as well rhizomatic tendencies and any balanced assessment of it would

have to take these into account too and weigh up their relative strength.

Ian Buchanan. "Deleuze and the Internet." *Australian Humanities Review* (Issue 43, December 2007): http://www.australianhumanitiesreview.org/archive/Issue-December-2007/Buchanan.html

[149] Christian Vandendorpe wrote,

> Whereas a book intrinsically has a totalizing function and aims to cover a whole area of knowledge, hypertext encourages the use of a large number of links in order to explore associations between ideas, to "spread out" rather than to "dig" in the hope of engaging readers whose interests are constantly changing, moving from association to association. Every concept referred to in a hypertext is thus potentially a distinct entry that can in turn generate new branchings, or more precisely, new rhizomes. It should be added that hypertext is by nature opaque, unlike a book, which has multiple, constantly accessible reference points. While reading a book is marked by duration and a certain continuity, reading hypertext is marked by a sense of urgency, discontinuity and constant choices. In fact, every hypertext link challenges the ephemeral contract with the reader: will the reader click on the hyperlink and continue his or her quest or abandon the quest?

Christian Vandendorpe. Translated by Phyllis Aronoff. *From Papyrus to Hypertext: Toward the Universal Library* (University of Illinois Press, 1999, 2009) 2.

[150] Martin Weller discusses the strange and exploitative nature of academic publishing by comparing a scholarly writer to an inventor of a product. An inventor would never sign over control of the product to the manufacturer but an author must sign away all rights to an article over to the publisher who then goes on to reap royalties, especially through library subscriptions or purchases. But in addition to the loss of rights and ownership, the unhappy author also may have lost months of years in waiting to be exploited. As Weller described the situation:

> The process can take up to two or even three years from submission to final publication. Much of this is taken up by the peer-review process, but many journals will still be restricted by the length of each issue and frequency of publication, with many journals only releasing one or two issues per year. The delay in publication reveals a print mentality still in operation in many cases, and for a fast-moving field it renders journals almost redundant as the main source of scholarly exchange…The main reason that academics are beginning to question the publishing model is that they are finding alternative methods for communication, publishing and debate which are more rewarding and have none of these restrictions in place. For most authors academic writing is a creative process, and that personal satisfaction gained from engaging in a creative pursuit is something that can be found elsewhere now.

Martin Weller. *The Digital Scholar: How Technology is Transforming Scholarly Practice* (New York: Bloomsbury Academic, 2011) 13.

[151] Given the importance of "publish or perish" for getting hired in academia and for getting promoted in academia, little has been written on the topic. Like peer review, publish or perish operates according to unwritten rules and unspoken customs and unstated practices. The fact that there is a veil of silence and privilege that drops down and blocks inquiry only enhances this unchecked power that is fueled largely by non-empirical emotions. Lives, careers and the quality of life of university professionals depend upon a system that is inherently unfair, has no defendable criteria, and yet remains powerful because so many intelligent people genuflect to the fearsome words, "publish or perish." The entire edifice, like a religion, rests upon a belief system that cannot be challenged, except at one's peril. One of the few books that even mentions "publish or perish," *Assessing What Professors Do: An Introduction to Academic Performance,* treats this important topic with deadpan dismissiveness:

> Publish or perish may be the easiest of all performances based appraisal systems to administer. Each year an administrator or committee adds up the number of publications for each faculty member and awards salary increases on the basis of who published the most. After some specified period of time, generally seven years, if a

faculty member published an adequate number of
quality studies, tenure and promotion are awarded.

Not only do the writers not define "quality," they spend only two pages on the topic.

David A. Dilts, Lawrence J. Haber and Donna Bailik. *Assessing What Professors Do: An Introduction to Academic Performance. An Introduction to Academic Performance Appraisal in Higher Education* (Westport, CT: Greenwood Press, 1994) 42.

I also came across a very early article by an assistant professor, who did not get promoted at Tufts due to lack of publications. Woodrow Wilson Sayre protested that the emphasis on research was harmful to teaching. This short essay, written in 1965 and published in *Life* magazine, undoubtedly reflects the post-war shift from teaching to research that caught an entire generation of teachers off guard. The essay was preceded by a photo essay, "A Teacher Sweats It Out," an article on UCLA professor, Bill Gerberding. One of the headlines in this story reads, "Though students rate him one of the best at UCLA TEACHING WON'T GET HIM TENURE."

Woodrow Wilson Sayre. "It's Publish or Perish." *Life* (January 29, 1965) 66.

[152] In 2005, Kathleen Fitzpatrick wrote of her case---a situation I had actually heard of---in which her book was rejected, not due to the quality but due to the cost of publication, on the eve of the awarding of her tenure. In an attempt to see into the future she wrote of the perils that await those who venture onto the Internet and into Cyberspace:

> ...creating something new also creates a series of dangers: those pioneers who first make the leap to a new system of open-source electronic publishing risk having traditionalists distrust their vitae. It is perhaps no accident that the first experiments in online journal publication in the humanities were by and large conducted by those whose research took as its object new media and contemporary technologies: scholars who could convincingly argue to promotion committees that the new form of publication itself was part of the research...scholars in non-contemporary nonmedia-related fields will not accept electronically delivered monographs until the mode of delivery has first been

proven viable, or more to the point, until other scholars take material published in such a mode seriously...

Kathleen Fitzpatrick. "From Crisis to Commons." *Cinema Journal* (Volume 44, Number 3, Spring, 2005) 94.

[153] It is well known, for example, that women and minorities publish less than their male counterparts, a condition that is defined as "less prolific," a term that places the blame on the individual. Rather than inquire as to why certain groups publish less and some publish more by examining a system, the responsibility is shifted in such a fashion that the real question---why is there a two tiered academic system of the privileged and unprivileged is not answered. Elizabeth G. Creamer stresses "productivity," rather than publishing in her study:

> Prolific writers are disproportionately likely to be white males because the primary criteria used to define productivity, quantity of journal articles and citations to them, reflect career paths, work assignments, interests, and access to resources that are much more characteristic of white men than most women and minorities. This suggests that, in addition to examining the question of whether traditional productivity criteria are equitably applied, it is essential to examine the question of whether productivity criteria are equitable.

Elizabeth G. Creamer. "Addressing Faculty Publication Productivity: Issues of Equity. ERIC Digest:" http://www.ericdigests.org/1999-1/equity.html

[154] A 2007 study of graduate programs determined that the attrition rate in the humanities at the ten-year mark was 45%, nearly half of those who started dropped out ABD and probably went on to other fields.

Scott Jaschik. "Hope on Ph.D. Attrition Rates---Except in the Humanities." *Inside Higher Ed* (December 7, 2007):
http://www.insidehighered.com/news/2007/12/07/doctoral

[155] A study done at the beginning of the 21st century (now outdated) expressed concern about the attrition rate among graduate students, those who would educate the next generation in the classrooms of the colleges and universities. But even fifteen years ago, the old fashioned method of preparing graduate students was ill-suited for the future. As the study's authors noted,

It may be argued that, given the changing expectations for faculty work and the range of types of faculty positions, it is no longer adequate or appropriate for current faculty members to prepare graduate students as "clones" of themselves. Gaff, Pruitt-Logan, and Weibl (2000) suggested that, although the nineteenth-century model of graduate education grounded in German models of research and scientific discovery is widespread, "it is inadequate for the challenges confronting the professoriate of the twenty-first century." They argued that "a mismatch exists between doctoral education and the needs of colleges and universities that employ new Ph.D.'s."

Ann E. Austin and Donald H. Wulff. "The Challenge to Prepare the Next Generation of Faculty." *Paths to the Professoriate: Strategies for Enriching the Preparation of Future Faculty* (Jossey-Bass, 2004): http://media.johnwiley.com.au/product_data/excerpt/47/07879663/0787966347.pdf

[156] Joseph C. Hermanowicz has long been interested a psychological condition experienced by academics, anomie, a term he borrowed from Emile Durkheim. He interviewed faculty in the late nineties and the early 2000s, a time of degenerating conditions for college professors. As Hermanowicz explained, universities are in a time of change and thus of stress for the faculty. "Anomie refers to a collective breakdown of order instigated by a divide between the realities of everyday situations and the needs and wants of a future," Hermanowicz explained. He continued,

> If anomie arises from a disjuncture between expectations for the present and future, then an absence of opportunity to achieve recognition originates from a discrepancy between individuals' desired recognition and present conditions.

The point the author makes in an important one, for as was noted by another writer, *esteem* is the reward sought by academics, not money, but recognition. Hermanowicz ended his article by describing a variety of reactions to anomie: first, *retreatism* or giving up, second, *ritualism* or carrying on, third, *innovation* or cheating, and fourth, *rebellion*, of which he wrote,

> Rebels may reject the standards by which their work is judged in their professional community and insist on their own criteria to assess the importance of their work.

Joseph C. Hermanowicz. "Chapter Eight. Anomie in the American Academic Profession." *The American Academic Profession: Transformation in Contemporary Higher Education* (Baltimore: The Johns Hopkins Press, 2011) 216-240.

[157] Anna Neumann wrote rather movingly of the dedication of faculty to "scholarly learning" or the simple joy of intellectual stimulation:
> As a personal activity, scholarly learning reflects who and why many individuals choose to enter scholarly careers within the American research university; it also may peak to why a fair number of these individuals persist in those careers. Asked to describe their professional paths, the majority of university professors In interviewed spoke at length and often emotionally about how they found or selected their professorial careers. The academic career that they pursued, along with the academic profession they joined in so doing, was, for many, a vehicle for pursuing their more personal scholarly learning.

Anna Neumann. "Scholarly Learning and the Academic Profession in a Time of Change." Edited by Joseph C. Hermanowicz. *The American Academic Profession: Transformation in Contemporary Higher Education* (Baltimore: The Johns Hopkins Press, 2011) 210.

[158] Whitworth's two part article on Information Systems continued,

> Academics are now gate-keepers of feudal knowledge castles not humble knowledge gardeners. They have for over a century successfully organized, specialized and built walls against error. However the problem with castles, whether physical or intellectual, is that they dominate the landscape, they make the majority subservient and apathetic, and battles for their power reduce productivity. As research grows, knowledge feudalism, like its physical counterpart, is a social advance that has had its day.

Brian Whitworth. "Reinventing Academic Publishing Online Part I: Rigor, Relevance and Practice." *First Monday* (Volume 14, Number 8, 3 August 2009) 2.

[159] Read Bourdieu's rather scathing description of academia in France: *Home Academicus* (Stanford: Stanford University Press, 1984)

[160] The increasing and unconsciousable rise of library databases has created a boycott and has led to new questions, such as that asked by author Matthew Ingram, "…in an era of democratized distribution of information, why do we need expensive distribution paywalled journals in the first place?" The sad answer is, according to Ingram,

> …the biggest obstacle to this happening — and to the spread of open access or open science as a whole — isn't the control that publishers like Elsevier have over the professional publishing process. The biggest obstacle is the role that these journals play in academia itself, and how important publishing in a specific journal can be when it comes to promotions, granting of tenure, research grants and other aspects of academic life. Even some researchers who support the Elsevier boycott have said they will continue to publish in its journals because they feel that they have to.

Matthew Ingram. "Why do we need Academic Journals in the First Place?" *Gigaom* (February 22, 2012): http://gigaom.com/2012/02/22/why-do-we-need-academic-journals-in-the-first-place/

[161] For example a 2011 book on Pierre Bourdieu mentioned the Internet only in passing, and Simon Susen's "Bourdieu and Adorno on the Transformation of Culture in Modern Society: Towards a Critical Theory of Cultural Production" does not take the production of culture on the Web at all.
Simon Susen and Bryan S. Turner, Editors. *The Legacy of Pierre Bourdieu. Critical Essays* (London: Anthem Press, 2011)

[162] Pierre Bourdieu. *Homo Academicus* (Stanford: Stanford University Press, 1984) 100.

[163] In a very strange book of an intellectual life mis-spent in the service of an uncaring institution, V. A. Howard wrote, "from a laborer's point of view," of the class system at Harvard and admitted to his "mistake."

> My mistake...was a naïve trust in universities as places of nurture and reward for intellectual excellence, or what amounts to the same thing, attachment to obsolete institutional values that led us down the garden path to exploitation.

As he was writing of his thirty-five year career in 1999, Howard laid out two class systems, first the divide between the

> ...well funded fields such as biotechnology, business strategies, medical research, computer-software development, and government policy studies...Relieved of faculty responsibilities for teaching and governance...they are free to pursue their research full time...The system of university, government and industrial research collaboration serves their interests well. Not so for those of us in the low-end, poorly funded arts and humanities struggling to get back into a normal academic environment virtually the only setting where we are employable...

V. A. Howard. *Gambling Up to Nowhere: Publishing and Perishing at Harvard* (Bloomington, Indiana: iUniverse, 2008) 2 and 4.

[164] Pierre Bourdieu wrote long and hard of the university system in France. As a new book on Bourdieu as a revolutionary, by Gad Ya'ir, who wrote,

> The persistence of class society bothered Bourdieu. Like many of his French colleagues---predecessors, contemporaries, or followers---he was pledging allegiance to the republican ideals of the French Revolution. Like many other French scholars, he advocated justice, universality, and egalitarianism, and he sought solidarity and fraternity. But perhaps more than other scholars, Bourdieu explicitly referred to the connections between the counter-revolutionary events of 1789 and contemporary ones; he saw a clear line connecting the hierarchical structure of the three estates before the Revolution and the unequal and unjust order of social classes in the Fifth Republic.

Gad Ya'ir. *The Last Musketeer of the French Revolution* (Lanham, Maryland: The Rowman & Littlefield Publishing Group, Inc., 2009) 83.

[165] Martin Halbert."Bourdieu. *Home Academicus." Performity, Cultural Capital, and the Internet.* Emory University: http://userwww.service.emory.edu/~mhalber/Research/Paper/pci-internet.html

[166] Edward Jay Epstein. "The Diamond 'Overhang.'" *The New York Times* (December 3, 2009): http://www.nytimes.com/2009/02/23/opinion/23iht-edepstein.1.20368819.html?_r=0

[167] As Nick Bontis pointed out,

> ...knowledge as a resource does not comply with the scarcity assumption. The more knowledge is supplied (or shared) the more highly it is valued. Furthermore, when was the last time the demand for knowledge went down?

Nick Bontis. "Managing Organizational Knowledge by Diagnosing Intellectual Capital." Daryl Morey, Mark Maybury, and Bhavani Thuraisingham, Editors. *Knowledge Management. Classic and Contemporary Works.* (MIT Press, 2000) 376.

[168] Lyla Mehta discussed how scarcity has become naturalized as an idea that dominates human society and that serves as the basis of economics and government. She writes,

> ...notions of scarcity legitimize the need to allocate and manage property either through the means of the market or through formalizing rights regimes...Economics studies only those goods that exist in quantities insufficient to satisfy the social need for them. By contrast, all goods in abundance are classified as "non-economic."

Mehta presents a number of studies that challenge the idea that scarcity is somehow natural and not socially constructed.

> Rather than seeing scarcity as a phenomenon "out there" over which humans have no control that consequently leads to standardized responses...interpretive

approaches would be interested in looking at local-specific contingencies in culturally specific meanings and traditions. This approach would ask: how is scarcity embedded in culturally specific meanings and traditions? How do these change with time? Interpretive approaches often go hand in hand with actor-oriented approaches. Actor-oriented approaches would eschew seeing an individual as a rational actor who seeks to maximize her gain out of a scarcity situation. Instead the actor-oriented perspective to scarcity would try to understand how people actively interpret scarcity in different cultures and historical conditions based on a diverse repertoire of meanings. It would also seek to understand actions and responses to action as grounded in these meanings and beliefs. Emphasis would also be on actual social practices that emerge with the contingencies of scarcity.

Lyla Mehta. "The Scarce, Naturalization and Politicization of Scarcity." Lyla Mehta, Editor. *The Limits of Scarcity: Contesting the Politics of Allocation* (Routledge, 2013) 15. 21.

[169] Pierre Bourdieu. *Homo Academicus.* 144.

[170] My British colleague Charlotte Frost commented upon the way in which art history moves onto the web in ways that replicate standard practices that are based on the printed book. She makes the excellent point that art historians are not taking advantages of the difference digital makes to the discipline. She describes the field as being "bookish." In her chapter on "Fetishizing the Book," Frost writes on *Smart History*,

> Taking advantage of some of the database possibilities of the online realm, content is arranged via era, artist, theme and art movement. There are summaries in text and video that provide useful overviews to entire eras of artistic practice alongside others presenting more detailed readings of single works. There is a large collection of images, and links to Flickr (an image storage website) crowd-source still more, while time-lines help visualize art history's various trajectories. Over all, it is an extremely useful platform which has doubtless made the work of many teaching art historians a lot easier. Yet what I would suggest is that there is a sense in which SmartHistory – which even describes itself as a 'web

book' – perpetuates a distinctly bookish order. Many of the taxonomies it relies upon are extremely traditional (artist, art movement etc.) despite the web being such an excellent space for reorganizing material. What is the hyperlink if not a major reorientation of information? What are social sharing sites like Flickr if not the opportunity to create new categories and connections? So it is perplexing that SmartHistory does not give site users the opportunity to build their own thematic groupings, rewrite timelines, question the parameters of the discipline, or even build their own contextual projects outright. But these standards of art historical examination are part of the self-fulfilling prophecy of an archival logic that implies art must be read.

Charlotte Frost. "Is Art History too Bookish?" *Arts Future Book*: http://www.gylphi.co.uk/artsfuturebook/

[171] Elkins wrote this passage in the Preface to the Routledge edition of his 1997 book.
James Elkins. *Our Beautiful, Dry, and Distant Texts: Art History as Writing. Art History as Writing* (New York: Routledge, 2000) xx.

[172] Writing in 1988, at the height of Postmodern writing, W. McAllister Johnson stated rather colorfully,

> Of course one should be concerned with the literature that is not yet written, with subjects as yet unplumbed that could restructure for generations to come the commonplaces we so blithely mouth. Unfortunately this concern seems to require uncommon discretion when one navigates the waters between the Scylla of diverting triviality and the Charybdis of pompous barrenness common to all classical problems. These efforts are normally suitably only as scholarly exercises, as testing grounds of the moment requiring one to declare oneself according to the maturity of one's present faculties and experience…It would be seen, alas that exclusivity of source material has little to do with exegetical quality. Once committed to print, deathless prose becomes terribly mortal, not to say comic. Once given over the public like a whore, it assumes its own destiny.

W. McAllister Johnson. *Art History: Its Use and Abuse.* (Toronto: University of Toronto Press: 1988, 1990) 113.

[173] I am going to provide a somewhat lengthy quote from a report from the Pew Higher Education Roundtable in 1998, nearly twenty years ago. Since this report was written, the cost of academic journals has only increased, the budgets of academic libraries is even more strained, the dubious ways in which the supposed "worth" of a publication continued, and although the solution, Web publication of scholarly articles was recommended in 1998, the same set of problems laid out in this article continue, almost unabated. In relation to the costs to libraries (and inevitably the institution and its students), described as "old news," the Report stated,

> In chilling outline, David Shulenburger, Provost of the University of Kansas, calibrates the problem. Between 1986 and 1996, the consumer price index increased 44 percent. Over that same decade, the cost of monographs increased by 62 percent. The price of health care increased by 84 percent. And the cost of scholarly journals increased a whopping 148 percent more than three times the rate of inflation and nearly twice the rate of growth in health care costs. The price of subscriptions to online databases grew even more rapidly, in the most notorious case by over 350 percent in a single year. As David points out, "Our budget would have to increase 70 percent if we were to buy the same proportion of serials and monographs as we did in 1986. Due to inflation in price and in publications available, we would need an acquisitions budget . . . 2.5 times that of our existing acquisition budget."

The Report stated that in the academic "gift economy," scholars gave away their rights to rapacious publishers:

> Individual scholars gained an increased number of outlets for the dissemination of their work; universities and scholarly organizations found themselves relieved of a set of production activities they were not well-disposed to perform; and commercial publishers gained a new client base to augment their business. In the dance with newly expanded opportunity, the movement to commercialize the process of scholarly communication looked like a real step forward. It wasn't. The true

winners were in fact the commercial publishers. Universities found themselves taking two steps back, reeling in the grip of rising prices from an industry that shared few of their fundamental values. While members of university and college faculties regarded publication as an exchange of free goods, the handful of publishers who were coming to control access to and utilization of intellectual property saw opportunity for enlarged profits. The principle of requiring authors to assign copyright to a publisher had been standard even before commercial publishers had come to control so much of the industry. Because they do not conceive of the publication as providing direct financial benefit to themselves or their institutions, most scholars seeking the publication of their research have willingly agreed to what, on the surface, appears an inconsequential stipulation.

The Report made the point that the "publish or perish" system has fed into, if not actually created, a situation that was seen, even in 1998, as untenable, and made a number of suggestions that would perhaps solve the problems:

> The first requirement is a fundamental disentangling of the notions of quality and quantity. The habit of mind that requires "32 articles" to be included in a tenure portfolio is one that stretches the essence of a candidate's contribution so thin as to make its real value scarcely discernible. It is also a custom that encourages greater specialization of publication, thereby reinforcing the power of commercial publishing. The first step would be for faculty personnel committees to make clear that the quality of work accounts for more than the sheer number of articles and papers submitted for promotion and tenure. Were there only, say, four or five entries those which had appeared in the most highly regarded venues, representing the candidate's and the department's judgment of his or her very best work members of the committee could reasonably be expected to read in detail each publication, forming an independent judgment of its worth. Such an arrangement would help to focus the process of judging the work of single scholars in any discipline. Limiting the number of entries would also help solve the problem of

multi-authorship, when the candidate's work is subsumed within the production of a large research team; in such instances the candidate could submit articles concerning only those parts of the research project in which he or she played a central role. Paring back the emphasis on quantity would create more time for junior faculty and researchers to develop truly unique contributions.

Looking forward into a future that is still in the process of pushing its way into a world still tightly controlled, the Report concluded:

> Now is the time to get right for electronic publishing what the scholarly community got so wrong in the case of print publication. The Internet is bringing about a steady and fundamental change to the process of scholarly communication a change occasioned less in the interests of cost than of time and convenience. Most researchers are avid users of e-mail. Increasingly they post preliminary accounts of their work on private Web sites for review and comment by a circle of colleagues in the field. Within a handful of traditional disciplines, most notably physics, postings to public Web sites are also becoming a standard form of collective communication...
>
> The obvious problem with postings to the Internet is the unruly nature of a communications channel in which the attributes of tangibility, permanence, quality, and authority are all notably absent. For most researchers, the printed page connotes an accomplishment of lasting value, more so than any image on a computer screen or data consigned to a disk. However pure and incorruptible the digital environment may seem in theory, its dependency on equipment that can break down or grow obsolete gives rise to skepticism about its suitability for the permanent archiving of scientific or scholarly achievement...
>
> Electronic publication without mechanisms of peer review and certification will be all noise and precious little light. We believe that the agencies best positioned to make the Internet serve the purposes of an orderly process of scholarly communication are the scholarly and

disciplinary organizations, which have traditionally performed that role for the publication of printed research results. Many scholarly journals, despite their increasingly commercial cast, have editorial and review processes that are the responsibility of the sponsoring scholarly society or association. We believe that the World Wide Web sites of these scholarly and disciplinary organizations ought to play a major role not just in the dissemination of important work within the field but in the certification of quality as well.

From the vantage point of 2013, this Report from a Roundtable composed of almost two-dozen high-ranking university officials is quite remarkable. Clearly, the administrations understood the very real costs to higher education, but, it would seem, that, regardless of the cost to themselves and to their employers, faculty preferred to continue a system that had imposed and is still imposing very high costs upon education. Although the Report assumes that scholarly publication imparts a kind of abstract "benefit" to intellectual life, from the vantage point of the present time, it would seem that the well-preserved "publish or perish" tradition benefits the few in what can be only very personal ways.

Robert Zemsky, Senior Editor. "To Publish and Perish." *Policy Perspectives* (Special Issue, Volume 7, Number 4, March 1998):
http://www.arl.org/storage/documents/publications/to-publish-and-perish-mar98.pdf

[174] Without getting into the weeds of the complex art world, it should be noted that there is a distinction between the profession of the artist and the profession of academics in the arts, the publication of scholarly work and the publication of "art books." For an interesting article on this general topic, read
Anton Vidokle. "Art without Market, Art without Education: Political Economy of Art." *e-flux* (2013): http://www.e-flux.com/journal/art-without-market-art-without-education-political-economy-of-art/

[175] In an article calling for open-access academic publishing, John Willinsky laid out the hidden costs of old style print journals and the free labor given away by academics hopeful of future (and meager) rewards:

> Now, the assumption here is not information is, or somehow wants to be, free. Anything but. Open access begins with the fact that researchers are engaged in

expensive, labour-intensive work that often employs highly sophisticated equipment, fully equipped and staffed laboratories. Researchers fly to distant archives and remote sites; they hire teams of graduate student research assistants; they devote years to studying a single body of work. Much of this work is underwritten by public institutions, government grants, and philanthropic endowments. The very extent of this largely public investment is what sets scholarly publishing apart from the more typical commercial model. The work represented in a research article has all been paid for in advance. The article arrives at the publisher's door, having already been financed, up to that point, as a public good. The public does not expect to be repaid for this research investment, at least not through its publication.

The publisher not only does not have to pay its authors, the services of highly qualified editors and reviewers are donated, as well (with editors occasionally receiving some form of support). Publishers do cover the production cost of copyediting, layout, proofreading, printing, binding, mailing, and promotion; they are now putting up well-engineered websites for electronic editions of their journals. They bring management skills, as well as care and quality, to the journal's production. During the age of print, the finely produced journal, with a circulation that could run as low as 200-400 copies, required this mix of public and private investment. The high quality of paper, printing, and binding were not so much a luxury as a necessity to the archival quality of the journal preserving it for use by generations of scholars.

So things might have happily continued, had not the corporate interests within this limited, subsidised economy pushed journal subscription prices to the point where access to the knowledge went into a state of decline, at a time when new publishing technologies enabled researchers to take publishing back into their own hands. These new technologies have been used to demonstrate how access can be greatly increased, improving the circulation of knowledge, restoring the researcher's control of knowledge, and extending its value as a public good by making it far more widely available.

John Wilinsky. "The Nine Flavours of Open Access Scholarly Publishing." *Journal of Postgraduate Medicine* (Volume 49, Issue 3, 2003) 263-267.

[176] In writing *Books in the Digital Age: The Transformation of Academic and Higher Education Publishing in Britain and the United States*, John Thompson used Bourdieu's idea of "restricted production" or an "anti-economy" to explain the academic publishing "business:"

> The logics of publishing fields are not static because they are open to forces and pressures that stem from a variety of sources---economic pressures, technological innovations…changing social practices, etc…The logic of publishing fields is by its very nature a fuzzy logic. It is not the logic of logicians but rather a practical logic---that is, a logic that can be grasped in the practices in which and through which it is expressed. It can't be summed up by a simple formula and it is not easy to pin down and specify.

John B. Thompson. *Books in the Digital Age: The Transformation of Academic and Higher Education Publishing in Britain and the United States* (Polity, 2005) 40.

[177] Although he was writing decades ago and his observations are undoubtedly dated, W. McAllister Johnson made an interesting point about art history journals that still holds true today:

> One justified criticism of periodicals is that their research and writing is done in a vacuum, comes in when it will, and is published as one can. In a word, it lacks context. This is the mirror image of trying to put together some coherent piece of research from overly fragmented information; periodical publication asks one to insert a piece of apparent research into some historiographical and intellectual context that is never present. *This is not an inborn process; it is learned.* Scholarly mechanisms are rather like sophisticated automobiles---one opens the hood, examines the works, and begins one's career with a "very nice, I am sure, but I haven't got the faintest idea of how it all works." *Scholarship is not just working in*

> *isolation to produce something, but learning how to respond to the past and the present.*

W. McAllister Johnson. Op. cit., 74.

[178] Pierre Bourdieu wrote extensively of education and explained the concept of *noblesse de robe* and academia.
Pierre Bourdieu. "The 'Berobed' and the Invention of the State" in *The State Nobility: Elite Schools in the Field of Power* (Stanford: Stanford University Press, 1989, 1996) 377-381.

[179] John B. Thompson. Op. cit. 47.

[180] Kathleen Fitzpatrick. "Peer-to-Peer Review and the Future of Scholarly Authority." Op.cit., 127.

[181] As Bourdieu wrote,

> The structures constitutive of a particular type of environment (e.g. the material conditions of existence characteristic of a class condition) produce habitus, systems of durable, transposable dispositions, structured structures predisposed to function as structuring structures, that is, as principles of the generation and structuring of practices and representations which can be objectively "regulated" and "regular" without in any way being the product of obedience to the rules, objectively adapted to their goals without presupposing a conscious aiming at tends or an express mastery of the operations necessary to attain them and, being all this, collectively orchestrated without being the product of the orchestrating action of a conductor.

Pierre Bourdieu. "Outline of the Theory of Practice. Structures and the Habitus" reprinted in *Practicing History. New Directions in Historical Writing after the Linguistic Turn.* Edited by Gabrielle M. Spiegel (New York: Routledge, 2005) 175

[182] Brian Whitworth also noted how academic writing must conform instead of innovate:

> The modern academic system has become almost a training ground for conformity. PhD students spend 3-6

> years as apprentices under senior direction, then another 3-6 years seeking the security of a tenured appointment. At both stages, criticizing the establishment is unwise if one wants a career. It is not surprising that 6-12 years of such training produces people who toe the party line.

Ibid.: http://brianwhitworth.com/BWRF-FM-Part1.pdf

[183] As Whitworth and Friedman argued,

> In the big business of university management, department ranks, research funds, PhD scholarships and library allocations all depend on publishing (Rainer and Miller, 2005). While the nominal goal of research is to seek the truth, publishing today is the primary screening mechanism for academic appointments, grants and promotions (Katerattanakul, *et al.*, 2003). To say the goal of academic publishing is to develop, select and diffuse knowledge is naïve when scholarly journals drive all university hiring and firing (Lowry, *et al.*, 2007). When a system becomes the mechanism for power, profit and control, idealized goals like the search for truth can easily take a back seat. Authors may not personally want their work locked away in expensive journals that only endowed western universities can afford, but business exclusivity requires it. Authors may personally see others as colleagues in a cooperative research journey, but the system frames them as competition for jobs and grants. As academia becomes a business, new ideas become threats to power rather than opportunities for knowledge growth. Journals become the gatekeepers of academic power rather than cultivators of knowledge, and theories battle weapons in promotion arenas, rather than plows in knowledge fields.

Brian Whitworth and Rob Friedman. "Reinventing Academic Publishing online. Part I: Rigor, Relevance and Practice." *First Monday* (Volume 14, Number 8, 3 August 2009):
http://journals.uic.edu/ojs/index.php/fm/article/view/2609/2248

[184] Yochai Benkler. "The New Open-Source Economics." *Ted Talks* (2005): http://www.ted.com/talks/yochai_benkler_on_the_new_open_source_economics.html

See also his article, "Designing Cooperative Systems for Knowledge Production: An Initial Synthesis from Experimental Economics" in *Making and Unmaking Intellectual Property: Creative Production in Legal and Cultural Perspective*. Edited by Mario Biagioli, Peter Jaszi, Martha Woodmansee (Chicago: University of Chicago Press, 2011)

[185] Yochai Benkler. *The Wealth of Networks. How Social Production Transforms Markets and Freedom* (Yale University Press, 2006)

[186] For an extensive review of the authors and activities involved in the information economy of the Internet, see Jonathan Zittrain who makes the following observation in the conclusion to his book on "generative" culture:

> ...generativity itself is, at its core, not a technology project. It is an education project, an exercise in intellect and community, the founding concepts of the university. Our universities are in a position to take a leadership role in the Net's future...

Jonathan Zittrain. *The Future of the Internet and How to Stop It* (New Haven: Yale University Press, 2008) 245.

[187] The cost of supporting those careers of the chosen few is enormous, going far beyond the mere cost of faculty salary or of grants and fellowships, which invariably go to the same group. These scholars who are chosen to publish in academic journals are publishing in journals that no individual subscribes to. It is the libraries that must pay for those subscriptions and the annual cost of scholarship is exorbitant, paid for by student fees and rising tuitions. The expense of carrying academic journals, written by a few and read by a few, is threatening publication of scholarly work. As Puneet Opal wrote in *The Atlantic,*

> ...it is the granting agencies -- many government-funded -- that ultimately support the research endeavor, paying for researchers' salaries, research supplies and equipment, and finally the costs of publication. Given this model, you might think that accessing scientific publications would be inexpensive. But this is not the case. The publications themselves typically land in corporate-owned scientific journals that restrict access by hefty subscriptions that only major university libraries can afford. For instance, Northwestern University pays

more than $7.5 million per year for electronic subscription of journals, with the price of a single journal yearly subscription well over $1,000.

Puneet Opal. "Don't Forget the Dream of Open Access Journals Die." *The Atlantic* (March 26, 2013):
http://www.theatlantic.com/health/archive/2013/03/dont-let-the-dream-of-open-access-journals-die/274371/

[188] In point of fact, publishing in academia is not profitable and this state of non-profitability is directly related to the peer review system, which awards publication to those in academic favor rather than to those whom the wider audience wants to read. However, it is not clear that publishers who work on a profit basis are any more open-minded than their university brethren. The for-profit publishers serve up re-edited textbooks, fifty years out of date, and coffee table books. There can be no profit on scholarly books or articles unless money can be made through distribution. As Laura McKenna explained,

> Academic journals are housed at universities and are subsidized by the university, because it brings the university prestige. Academic journals are edited by faculty members. The faculty are given course release time to edit the journal and a small stipend. The university provides offices and work-study students to help with the secretarial work... The publisher is key, because he needs money to print and distribute the journal for its tiny community of readers. To make that money, the publisher sells the rights to an academic search engine company, like JSTOR. For the publisher, this venture is highly profitable because, unlike traditional publishing, the publisher does not have to pay the writer or editor. It only has to cover the costs of typesetting, printing, and distribution.

Laura McKenna. "Locked in the Ivory Tower: Why JSTOR Imprisons Academic Research." *The Atlantic* (January 20, 2012):
http://www.theatlantic.com/business/archive/2012/01/locked-in-the-ivory-tower-why-jstor-imprisons-academic-research/251649/

[190] Roger I. Geiger waded into the topic of "quality" in academic publishing:

> A second perplexing element, quality, is inherent to the advancement of knowledge. In its most basic form, new knowledge takes the form of publications, chiefly scientific papers; but another component is the formation of new scientists or scholars, the doctoral graduates of Ph.D. programs. Where knowledge is concerned, considerations of quality assume paramount importance. Universities are judged not only on the volume of knowledge they produce---the number of publications---but on the putative significance of those contributions as well…Quality can be measured more readily through the annual expenditures for sponsored research by individual universities. And quality and quantity powerfully interact…The gold standard for measuring academic quality has been the NRC-sanctioned ratings of research-doctoral programs.

This is a remarkable stretch of writing on "quality" which measures this "perplexing element" in terms of the volume and number of scholars, students and publications and how much money an institution has. Content is never mentioned. Quality is reduced to quantifiable, that which can be counted.

Roger L. Geiger. *Knowledge and Money: Research Universities and the Paradox of the Marketplace* (Stanford University Press, 2004) 148-149.

[191] Kathleen Fitzpatrick noted the inherent problem within the traditional system of peer review, a process widely viewed as corrupt and defunct but is also considered an indispensible addendum to prestige and power:

> To a surprising extent, however, scholars have resisted exploring a similar sense in which *Intellectual authority* might likewise be shifting in the contemporary world…The production of knowledge is, of course, the academy's very reason for being, and if we cling to an outdates system for the establishment and measurement of authority at the very same time that the nature of authority is shifting around us, we run the risk of becoming increasingly irrelevant to the dominant ways of knowing of contemporary culture…In the process of writing the chapter that focuses on peer review in the humanities, however, I have discovered that there has been surprisingly little scholarly exploration of the

> history and function of peer review in the humanities, in contrast to the overflow of such studies in many of the social and natural sciences...Our resistance might suggest an underlying anxiety about the outcome of the analysis, a potential concern that the time-honored procedures and standards that guide our work might be flawed...In the academy---as goes the joke about defenders of tradition in many realms---too many attitudes may be summed up in a mere eight words: "We have never done it that way before."

Kathleen Fitzpatrick. "Peer-to-Peer Review and the Future of Scholarly Authority. *Cinema Journal* (Volume 48, Number 2, Winter, 209) 124-125.

[192] There are some pioneers who defy the norm in academia. In her article "Scholars Test Web Alternative to Peer Review," Patricia Cohen quoted Dan Cohen of the Center for History and New Media at George Mason University as saying,

> "Serious scholars are asking whether the institutions of the academy — as they have existed for decades, even centuries — aren't becoming obsolete... The traditional process is not so much a gold standard but an effective accommodation to the needs of the field. It represents a settlement for a particular moment, not a perfect ideal."

Ms Cohen concluded her 2010 article by writing,

> To Mr. Cohen, the most pressing intellectual issue in the next decade is this tension between the insular, specialized world of expert scholarship and the open and free-wheeling exchange of information on the Web. "And academia," he said, "is caught in the middle."

Patricia Cohen. "For Scholars, Web Changes Sacred Rite of Peer Review." *The New York Times* (August 23, 2010): http://www.nytimes.com/2010/08/24/arts/24peer.html?pagewanted=all&_r=0

[193] A 2005 article discussed a survey of graduate students and revealed increasing pressures on publishing, such as publishing a book before going in the job market, couple with the same old restrictions. As Jamie Poster reported that one graduate student makes all of his writing available on

the Web to better facilitate collaboration...but such writing is generally regarded as extracurricular.

Jamie Poster. "Code Orange: Career Fear and Publishing." *Cinema Journal* (Volume 44, Number 3, Spring 2005) 91-92.

[194] Bourdieu wrote at length on the idea of a "gift exchange" in his critique of Claude Lévi-Strauss by replacing the structuralism of Lévi-Strauss with a Marxist analysis that unmasked the fact that the gift-giving was not disinterested by part of an reciprocal exchange. As Jeremy F. Lane explained, "For the system to function, its participants had to possess a certain partial or practical knowledge of what was at stake and which 'moves' would prove profitable or detrimental."
Jeremy F. Lane. *Pierre Bourdieu: A Critical Introduction* (Sterling, Virginia: Pluto Press, 2000) 105.

[195] Bourdieu discussed "disinterestedness" but not in the sense of a gift economy:

> Interest, in the restricted sense it is given in economic theory cannot be produced without producing its negative counterpart, disinterestedness. The class of practices whose explicit purpose is to maximize monetary profit cannot be defined as such without producing the purposeless finality of cultural or artistic practices and their products; the world of bourgeois man, with his double-entry accounting, cannot be invented without producing the pure, perfect universe of the artist and the intellectual and the gratuitous activities of art-for-art's-sake and pure theory.

Pierre Bourdieu. "The Forms of Capital" in *Economic Sociology.* Edited by Nicole Woosley Biggart (Malden, Mass.: Blackwell Publishers Inc. 2002) 281.

[196] In his book, *The State of Scholarly of Publishing: Challenges and Opportunities,* Albert N. Greco wrote,

> ...regrettably, the vast majority of all university presses require subsidies from their home university, and, even with subsidies, very few presses end up in the "black" at the end of their fiscal year. Additional areas of concern confronting these university presses include: the migration from print to the digital transmission of

> content, and few presses have the financial resources to address effectively this challenge; the Open Access movement (i.e., academics placing a book online and allowing the free downloading of this content); concern on many college campuses that continued support of a university press is becoming a luxury and not a necessity since commercial academic presses have increased their title output of important research studies; and declining unit sales.

In the same book, William W. Savage writes of what he calls "forced productivity," or the (somewhat irrational) demand that to be promoted, a university scholar must write "a book" or a body of writing between hard covers in order to get tenure or to be promoted or to be respected. Greco observed,

> Forced productivity creates both panic and pandemonium. Scholarly publishers are besieged by the detritus pouring from word processors within the halls of ivy. Competition for space on publishers' lists is so intense these days that young Ph. Ds, feeling shut out of the process and badly in need of opportunity, clamor for electronic publication, arguing that the launch of one's opus into cyberspace should count just as much as its appearance into sewn signatures. Critics reply that electronic publication may circumvent the vetting process and could not pass muster in universities where it is now de rigueur to differentiate between "referred" publications and any other kind. Some scholars (older ones, with books) even equate electronic publication with vanity publication, a taboo practice that will lead to termination of employment at reputable institutions.

Savage's account of the punishment awaiting any who dare to break the rules reveals how the rules are enforced and how the productivity is not so much "forced" but throttled.

Albert N. Greco. *The State of Scholarly of Publishing: Challenges and Opportunities* (New Brunswick, N. J.: Transaction Publishers, 2009) vii. William W. Savage. "Scribble, Scribble, Toil and Trouble: Forced Productivity in the Modern University." *The State of Scholarly of Publishing: Challenges and Opportunities* (New Brunswick, N. J.: Transaction Publishers, 2009) 4.

[197] In 1995 (the dark ages) Carol Berkenkotter wrote,

> Peer review can therefore be seen as a social mechanism through with a discipline's "experts" maintain quality control over new knowledge entering the field. Quality control is, of course, a form of social control, and those who see its utility share assumptions about the utility of the referee system...it is not too difficult for such referees to use their power as gatekeepers to prevent competitors from getting into print...As resources become even scarcer due to changes in academic institutional priorities in response to pressures from the broader culture, peer review as a system faces severe stresses. It may be, fore example, that the temptation for some referees to abuse their position as gatekeepers becomes even greater. Thus peer review can be a tough and dirty game, and is so even during "normal times" when referees have hidden agendas. But at present it's the only game in town for scholars and researchers attempting to extend new knowledge claims beyond local contexts into a field's literature. The referee system with its tradition of blind review is an integral part of the enterprise of knowledge production in the academic disciplines. It is also, as I've suggested, a site of contention and negotiation where one's skill as a rhetorician and knowledge of "rules of the game" can make a critical difference.

It is now nearly twenty years later and, despite the vast expansion of the Internet, Berkenkotter's words are still relevant today. *Le meme chose, plus le meme chose.*
Carol Berkenkotter. "The Power and the Perils of Peer Review." *Rhetoric Review* (Volume 13, Number 2, Spring, 1995) 245-249.

[198] Bill Cope and Mary Kalantzis also explained how "knowledge" is now "designed:"
> Available knowledge designs have a textual and intertextual morphology. These are the raw materials of already–represented knowledge or found knowledge objects. Designing is the stuff of agency, the things you do to know and the rhetorical representation of those things. It is also the stuff of communities of disciplinary practice. These practices involve certain kinds of knowledge representation—modes of argumentation,

forms of reporting, descriptions of methods and data, ways of supplementing extant data, linking and distinguishing concepts, and critically reflecting on old and new ideas and facts. There is no knowledge–making of scholarly relevance without the representation of that knowledge. And that representation happens in a community of practice: with collaborators who co–author or comment upon drafts, with journal editors or book publishers who review manuscripts and send them out to referees, with referees who evaluate and comment, and then the intricacies of textual revision, checking, copy–editing and publication. Knowledge contents and the social processes of knowledge representation are inseparable.

Bill Cope and Mary Kalantzis. "Sighs of Disruption: Transformations in the Knowledge System of the Academic Journal." *First Monday* (Volume 14, Number 4, 6 April 2009):
http://firstmonday.org/htbin/cgiwrap/bin/ojs/index.php/fm/article/view/2309%3D/2163

[199] In 2008, Glenn S. McGuigan and Robert D. Russell wrote about financial crisis of the Not For Profit non-business of academic publishing.

Glenn S. McGuigan and Robert D. Russell. "The Business of Academic Publishing: A Strategic Analysis of the Academic Journal Publishing Industry and its Impact Upon the Future of Scholarly Publishing." *Electronic Journal of Academic and Special Librarianship*. Volume 3, Number 3 (Winter 2008): http://southernlibrarianship.icaap.org/content/v09n03/mcguigan_g01.html

[200] In his book which discuss how private enterprise is buying and controlling and reselling what should be a public or common good, David Bollier stated,

> In ways that are variously egregious, subtle, clever and obscure, business interests are gaining ownership and control over dozens of valuable resources that the American people collectively own. The American commons include tangible assets such as public forests and minerals, intangible wealth such as copyrights and patents, critical infrastructure such as the Internet and government research, and cultural resources such as the

broadcast airwaves and public spaces. *We, as citizens, own these commons.* They include resources that we have paid for as taxpayers, and resources that we have inherited from previous generations. They are not just an inventory of marketable assets, but social institutions and cultural traditions that define us as Americans and enliven us as human beings. Public education. Community institutions. Democratic values. Wildlife and national forests. Public spaces in cities and communications media. Astonishingly, Americans are losing the right to control dozens of such commons that they own. While business and technology tend to be the forces animating this silent theft, as we shall see, our government is complicit in not adequately protecting the commons on our behalf. When it is not being seduced by what has been called the legalized bribery of campaign contributions, politicians may gamely try to defend our common assets, and occasionally succeed. But even well-meaning government leaders are often overwhelmed by the pace of technological change and the complications of consensus-building and due process. The public, for its part, is often clueless and thus politically moot in many battles over the commons. (Throughout, I will use the collective noun "commons" instead oft he more archaic term "common.") This trend raises serious questions about the future of our American commonwealth. In an age of market triumphalism and economistic thinking, does the notion of "commonwealth" – that we are a people with shared values and control over collectively owned assets – have any practical meaning? Or have we lost sight of our heritage as a commonwealth and lost control of our assets, and perhaps our democratic traditions, as private interests have quietly seized the American commons?

David Bollier. "Introduction." *Silent Theft. The Private Plunder of Our Common Weatlh.* (Routledge, 2003) 3-4.

[201] Michael Wood. *The Story of England.* Public Broadcasting System. July 2012: http://www.pbs.org/programs/michael-woods-story-england/

[202] Susan Oosthuizen described the open fields in Medieval England:

> The use of both curvilinear and rectilinear structures in the layout of fields from the prehistoric into the medieval periods suggests that at least some continuity in "traditional" forms of the *Ace* division of land between cultivators. By the post-Conquest period, such fields were characteristically sub-divided first into furlongs and then into strips.

Susan Oosthuizen. "Medieval Field Systems and Settlement Nucleation: Common or Separate Origins?" *Academia.edu*: http://www.academia.edu/1561621/Medieval_field_systems_and_settlement_nucleation_Common_or_separate_origins

[203] David Bollier. *Viral Spiral*: http://www.viralspiral.cc/sites/default/files/ViralSpiral.pdf p. 4-5.

[204] Lawrence Lessig, one of the more important supporters of Creative Commons stated in an interview:

> If we design an architecture that makes sense to developing countries; that ensures artists are paid while protecting freedoms for scientific and amateur creativity, then I think we could find that copyright is once again a well-grounded kind of regulation that everybody understands. Laws in a free society depend on people having an intuitive sense of why they exist. The fact is that the current copyright law architecture does not make sense. It is not that copyright is not important – it is critical – but that, in its current form, it fails to ensure adequate incentives and fails to protect necessary freedoms in the digital environment. It was built for a different world so let's just update it and adapt it to this world so that we can raise a generation that continues to believe in it.

Lawrence Lessig. "Interview with Lawrence Lessig." *WPO Magazine*. February 2011: http://www.wipo.int/wipo_magazine/en/2011/01/article_0002.html

[205] On the other hand, there is the traditionalist perspective. In her interesting book surveying the mind of the academic, Michèle Lamont noted that with the proliferation of journals, the publication of an article

has become less indicative of "excellence" and the fellowship (in its rarity) has become the preferred standard of judgment. Her study indicates that academic practices, especially that of peer review, works against innovation in thinking:

> Many factors in American higher education work against disciplinary and epistemological pluralism. Going against the tide in any endeavor is often difficult; it may e even more so in scholarly research, because independence of thinking is not easily maintained in systems where mentorship and sponsored mobility loom large. Innovators are often penalized if they go too far in breaking boundaries, even if by doing so they redefine conventions and pave the way for future changes. In the context of academic evaluation, there does not appear to be a clear alternative to the peer review. Moreover there seems to be agreement among the study's respondents that despite its flaws, overall this system "works." There is of course, no argument that the peer review system "works," if only in the sense that peer review functions, and so the "respondents" who think the system "works" are saying nothing of value. The question is not whether or not the peer review system as it exists should be re-thought but whether such an antiquated process can survive the weight of its own obsolescence.

Michèle Lamont. *How Professors Think: Inside the Curious World of Academic Judgment* (Cambridge: President and Fellows of Harvard College, 2009) 10.

[206] According to Lessing,

> The digital world is closer to the world of ideas than to the world of things. We, in cyberspace, that is, have built a world that is close to the world of ideas that nature (in Jefferson's words) created: stuff in cyber- space can "freely spread from one to another over the globe, for the moral and mutual instruction of man, and improvement of his condition," be- cause we have (at least originally) built cyberspace such that content is, "like fire, expansible over all space, without lessening [its] density at any point, and like the air in which we breathe, move, and have our physical being, incapable of

confinement, or exclusive appropriation." The digital world is closer to ideas than things, but still it is not quite there. It is not quite true that the stuff in cyberspace is perfectly nonrivalrous in the sense that ideas are. Capacity is a constraint; bandwidth is not un- limited.30 But these are tiny flaws that cannot justify jumping from the largely free to the perfectly controlled. There are problems of coordination and constraints of scarcity. But the solution to these problems is not necessarily systems of control or better techniques of excludability. That cyber- space has flourished as it has largely because of the commons it has built should lead us to ask whether we should tilt more to the free in organizing this space than to the controlled that organizes real space.

Lawrence Lessing. *The Future of Ideas. The Fate of the Commons in a Connected World* (New York: Random House, 2001) 115.

[207] Lessing. Ibid. 25.

[208] Brian Whitworth and Rob Friedman. "Full Access and Review: Applying Socio-technical Practice to Academia."
http://brianwhitworth.com/Fullaccess-review-2008.pdf

[209] An article posted in *The Chronicle of Higher Education* outlined some rather timid moves that academics can take to make their presence known on the Internet. "Author" Prof Hacker wrote up a summary of a recent workshop on that topic which discussed such radical moves as joining Facebook, LinkedIn, Twitter, Academia.edu and so on. Apparently the workshop saw the Internet as a professional aid for activities such as looking for a job. Prof Hacker cautiously counseled his/her colleagues:

> Thinking about how to create and maintain a Web presence might strike some academics as distasteful. After all, why should we go about marketing ourselves? Shouldn't our work stand on its own? Didn't we get an advanced degree because we were above such pettiness?

Prof Hacker. "Creating Your Web Presence: A Primer for Academics." *The Chronicle of Higher Education.* February 11, 2012:
http://chronicle.com/blogs/profhacker/creating-your-web-presence-a-primer-for-academics/30458

[210] It is almost exclusively in the field of science that the voices of protest in both Europe and America are the loudest. A promising development, the Federal Research Public Access Act, which would impact, not just science but also the humanities, proposes that if the public has paid for the research, then the public should have free access to it. Michael C. Taylor wrote,

> Let's take a look at the flow of money in the production of research. The government takes tax revenue from citizens and uses it to fund university research groups and libraries. Researchers obtain government grants and use the money to conduct experiments. They write up the results in manuscripts that are destined to become published papers. Manuscripts are submitted to journals, where they are handled by other researchers acting as unpaid volunteer editors. They co-ordinate the process of peer-review, which is done by yet other researchers, also unpaid. All these roles—author, editor, reviewer— are considered normal responsibilities of researchers, funded by grants. At this point, researchers have worked together to produce a publication-ready, peer-reviewed manuscript. But rather than posting it on the Web, where it can contribute to the world's knowledge, form a basis for future work, and earn prestige for the author, the finished manuscript is then donated gratis to a publisher: the author signs away copyright. The publisher then formats the manuscript and places the result behind a paywall. Then it sells subscriptions back to the universities where the work originated. Well-off universities will have some access to the paper (though even they are denied important rights such as text-mining). Less well-off universities have access to varying selections of journals, often not the ones their researchers need. And the taxpayers who funded all this? They get nothing at all. No access to the paper.
>
> It's pretty outrageous.

Michael Taylor. "Opinion: Academic Opinion is Broken." *The Scientist.* March 19, 2012. http://www.the-scientist.com/?articles.view/articleNo/31858/title/Opinion--Academic-Publishing-Is-Broken-/

[211] Roy Rosenzweig is one of the many twenty-first century academics to enter fully into the Internet, accepting the terms of openness. In his study of Wikipedia, Rosenzweig stated,

> Another solution is to emulate the great democratic triumph of *Wikipedia*—its demonstration that people are eager for free and accessible information resources. If historians believe that what is available free on the Web is low quality, then we have a responsibility to make better information sources available online. Why are so many of our scholarly journals locked away behind subscription gates? What about *American National Biography Online*—written by professional historians, sponsored by our scholarly societies, and supported by millions of dollars in foundation and government grants? Why is it available only to libraries that often pay thousands of dollars per year rather than to everyone on the Web as *Wikipedia* is? Shouldn't professional historians join in the massive democratization of access to knowledge reflected by *Wikipedia* and the Web in general? *American National Biography Online* may be a significantly better historical resource than *Wikipedia*, but its impact is much smaller because it is available to so few people.

Roy Rosenzweig. "Can History be Open Source? Wikipedia and the Future of the Past" from "Essay on History and New Media." Also printed in *The Journal of American History* Volume 93, Number 1 (June, 2006): 117-46 http://chnm.gmu.edu/essays-on-history-new-media/essays/?essayid=42

[212] In September 2012, Mikael Laasko and Bo-Christer Björk, writing in *BMC Medicine,* published "Anatomy of Open Access Publishing: A Study of Longitudinal Development and Internal Structure" in which the authors concluded that 17% of the scholarly research in the field of science were viewed on the Web. http://www.biomedcentral.com/1741-7015/10/124

In reporting on this study, *The Guardian* discussed changes in academic publishing:

> The academic publishing game has changed irrevocably. The change does not mean that academics have embraced the free-for-all file-sharing mentality that is

the bug-bear of the music business. Rather it reflects the deep-seated amateur ethos of scholars, who have always seen the work of producing and reviewing their research findings as an intrinsic part of the job. While the dissemination of that research relied on the printing and distribution of academic journals, the publishers' subscription model was a sensible way to manage this business. But the opportunities provided by the Web for instant distribution has fused with the principle that publicly funded research should be freely available and propelled the open access movement to the forefront of academic publishing. The escape from the physical bounds of publishing on paper should also help us to realize significantly better value for money in this core part of the research enterprise.

The rise of open access has been hampered by opposition from some publishers, who see it as a threat to a lucrative subscription model, and by some quarters of the research community fearful of jettisoning an established process of publishing in familiar journals. Scientists may have invented the Internet but some remain suspicious of its fast-moving and disruptive nature.

In fact the author reported that October 22 to 28 was the occasion for a worldwide Open Access Week.

Stephen Curry. "The Inexorable Rise of Open Access Scientific Publishing." *The Guardian.* 22 October 2012
http://www.guardian.co.uk/science/occams-corner/2012/oct/22/inexorable-rise-open-access-scientific-publishing

[213] An excellent resource for Open Access is a "bibliography" put together by Charles A. Bailey. This book is simply a list of articles and books on the topic of scholarship and publishing in an age of the Internet.
Charles A. Bailey, Jr. *Transforming Scholarly Publishing through Open Access: A Bibliography.* (Creative Commons, 2010)
Another interesting book, a pioneer in the field, was Robin P. Peer, Gregory B. Newby, Maria Santos. *Scholarly Publishing: The Electronic Frontier* (Cambridge: MIT Press, 1996, 2000). There are a number of books on this topic, oddly, many before the year 2000.

[214] In 2003 a group of scientists and intellectuals signed the Berlin Declaration on Open Access stating in part that

> Our mission of disseminating knowledge is only half complete if the information is not made widely and readily available to society. New possibilities of knowledge dissemination not only through the classical form but also and increasingly through the open access paradigm via the Internet have to be supported. We define open access as a comprehensive source of human knowledge and cultural heritage that has been approved by the scientific community. In order to realize the vision of a global and accessible representation of knowledge, the future Web has to be sustainable, interactive, and transparent. Content and software tools must be openly accessible and compatible.

Berlin Declaration on Open Access to Knowledge in the Sciences and Humanities: http://www.zim.mpg.de/openaccess-berlin/berlin_declaration.pdf

[215] Jennifer Summer wrote an interesting article about the "knowledge commons" that expressed concern about the privatization of a public good---knowledge---by corporations. She sees universities as a bastion of free knowledge exchange.
Jennifer Summer. "Keeping the Commons in Academic Culture: Protecting the Knowledge Commons from the Enclosure of the Knowledge Economy." *The Exchange University: Corporations of Academic Culture* (The University of British Columbia Press, 2008) 113.

[216] Cornelius Holtorf commented on the way in which gatekeeping keeps both disciplines and minds narrow and confined,

> Whether as a deliberate strategy or as the result of their academic education, some academics will adapt their own research topics to canonical requirements. Such behaviour is rational and understandable but it can also prevent academic innovation. Academics have internalized disciplinary canons and the need for gate-keeping to an extent that they surprisingly often agree on standard methodological and theoretical criteria, even though they may occasionally differ as to whether

or not a specific paper or proposal may fulfill sufficiently many of them.

Cornelius Holtorf. "A Comment on Hybrid Fields and Academic Gate-Keeping." *Public Archaeology: Archaeological Entnographies* (Volume 8, Number 2-3, 2009): http://www.google.com/#hl=en&gs_rn=12&gs_ri=psy-ab&gs_mss=academi%20gatekeeping&pq=pamela%20shoemaker%20gatekeeping&cp=8&gs_id=2v&xhr=t&q=academic+gatekeeping&es_nrs=true&pf=p&sclient=psy-ab&oq=academic+gatekeeping&gs_l=&pbx=1&bav=on.2,or.r_qf.&bvm=bv.46471029,d.dmQ&fp=3aad8e69494a147&biw=1196&bih=664

[217] I should note that *Thinkingshop.com* is at once a very interesting and very strange website in which it is almost impossible to find the name of the author who writes in terms of "I," but never reveals her identity. I had to search through many links to find her name.
Diane J. Bowser. "Open Access Publishing in Philosophy." *thinkingshop.com* (October 3, 2009): http://www.thinkingshop.com/2009/10/03/open-access-publishing-in-philosophy/

[218] Philip Eubanks and John D. Schaeffer wrote about academic writing in 2008 that
> Academic publication is also coy about its argumentative---ludic---character. It generally aims to refute, qualify, or expand the positions taken in other academic publications whether about the meaning of the white whale or the existence of a sub-atomic particle that lasts for billionth of a millisecond. But academics frequently describe publication as "entering the conversation" or with some other ironic descriptor. That turns successful academic writing into a complex game indeed---an art or craft in which arguments are forwarded, but more than just argumentative imperatives must be attended to...Consider the plethora of constraints to which the academic writer must conform. The academic writer must make claims and prove them according to the conventions of the discipline. The writer must marshal supporting information and arguments and present them in an approved format. The level of writing must be congruent with that of other publications in the field. Even if the writer profoundly disagrees with another position, it is an implicit rule that the opponent's professional be respected. Abiding by these conventions

> creates a certain tone, the tone of the competent, often dispassionate, expert who is attempting to expand a fund of knowledge. Someone who can create this tone may indeed be playing the game of academic publication.

Philip Eubanks and John D. Schaeffer. "A Kind Word for Bullshit: The Problem of Academic Writing." *College Composition and Communication* (Volume 59, Number 3, February 2008) 372-288.

[219] Eric von Hippel. Op. cit., 166.

[220] Benkler explained how the old system of exclusive ownership is being challenged in today's world where information can circulate freely---and therefore should be free:

> From the perspective of a society's overall welfare, the most efficient thing would be for those who possess information to give it away for free—or rather, for the cost of communicating it and no more. On any given day, enforcing copyright law leads to inefficient underutilization of copyrighted information. However, looking at the problem of information production over time, the standard defense of exclusive rights like copyright expects firms and people not to produce if they know that their products will be available for anyone to take for free. In order to harness the efforts of individuals and firms that want to make money, we are willing to trade off some static inefficiency to achieve dynamic efficiency. That is, we are willing to have some inefficient lack of access to information every day, in exchange for getting more people involved in information production over time. Authors and inventors or, more commonly, companies that contract with musicians and filmmakers, scientists, and engineers, will invest in research and create cultural goods because they expect to sell their information products. Over time, this incentive effect will give us more innovation and creativity, which will outweigh the inefficiency at any given moment caused by selling the information at above its marginal cost. This defense of exclusive rights is limited by the extent to which it correctly describes the motivations of information producers and the business models open to them to appropriate the benefits of their in- vestments.

> If some information producers do not need to capture the economic benefits of their particular information outputs, or if some businesses can capture the economic value of their information production by means other than exclusive control over their products, then the justification for regulating access by granting copyrights or patents is weakened.

Yochi Benkler. *The Wealth of Networks.* Op. cit., 37.

[221] The story of Aaron Swartz, dedicated to open access, is a tragic one and a testament to the tragic collision between those dedicated to the free distribution of knowledge and those who would control knowledge. That someone so young should have been threatened with thirty-five years in prison for downloading more than his "share" of JSTOR articles is nothing short of moral criminality and a blot on the reputation of MIT and the Attorney General of Massachusetts. Among the many, many articles on the unethical pursuit of a young and fragile person, Peter Singer and Agata Sagan wrote in *The New York Review of Books,*

> The fact that JSTOR has made millions of documents freely available, after Swartz had downloaded them, shows that his actions have had what many people—perhaps to some extent even JSTOR, which after all is a non-profit organization dedicated to increasing access to scholarly publications—believe to be a public benefit. Thousands of researchers are currently putting all of their downloaded PDF files online, often in breach of copyright, as a tribute to Swartz. There is no doubt that we should improve access to scientific resources, and the Internet makes it almost inevitable that this will happen. The only question is when. As Lawrence Lessig argues, this is knowledge paid for in large part by our taxes. More important still, in the long run, will be raising the level of general access to information throughout the world. The price now asked for a single journal article is equivalent to a month's earnings in many countries. The Internet makes the ancient dream of a universal library possible. Why should not everyone, anywhere in the world, be able to use, without charge, all the available knowledge that humans have created?

Peter Singer and Agata Sagan. ""The Death of Aaron Swartz." *The New York Review of Books.* January 18, 2013:
http://www.nybooks.com/blogs/nyrblog/2013/jan/18/death-aaron-swartz/

[222] Over time I have come to suspect that the government (and MIT, where Swartz had access to JSTOR) confused "hacking" with the very well documented and on-going efforts to free knowledge from corporate control.
Sam Gustin. "Aaron Swartz's Father Calls for U. S. Legal Reforms Ahead of MIT Report." *Time. Business & Money* (May 10, 2013):
http://business.time.com/2013/05/10/aaron-swartzs-father-calls-for-u-s-legal-reforms-ahead-of-mit-report/

[223] In 2012 the "Faculty Advisory Council Memorandum on Journal Pricing" advised the faculty of Harvard University to take steps to protest and change the restrictive practices of databases:

> We write to communicate an untenable situation facing the Harvard Library. Many large journal publishers have made the scholarly communication environment fiscally unsustainable and academically restrictive. This situation is exacerbated by efforts of certain publishers (called "providers") to acquire, bundle, and increase the pricing on journals.

The Faculty Advisory Council. "Faculty Advisory Council Memorandum on Journal Pricing." April 17, 2012:
http://isites.harvard.edu/icb/icb.do?keyword=k77982&tabgroupid=icb.tabgroup143448

[224] For a brief and useful definition of "Open Access," see Peter Suber's "Open Access Overview:"
http://www.earlham.edu/~peters/fos/overview.htm
His book *Open Access* was published by MIT Press in June of 2012 but will become OA by June 2013.

[225] In fact academics organized an online tribute to Swartz a few days after his death.
Andreas Jauregui. "Academics Tweet Tribute to Aaron Swartz, Share Research with Internet in Honor of Activist." *The Huffington Post.* January 15, 2013: http://www.huffingtonpost.com/2013/01/13/academics-tweet-tribute-aaron-swartz_n_2468272.html

[226] Heather Joseph. "The Impact of Open Access on Research and Scholarship. Reflections on the Berlin 9 Open Access Conference." *College & Research Libraries News.* 2012. http://crln.acrl.org/content/73/2/83.full

[227] In his acclaimed book, *Outliers*, Malcolm Gladwell wrote of Steve Jobs and Bill Gates in terms of their birth year, 1955, a year that catapulted them into a culture of computers that they were just the right age to respond to. In his biography of Steve Jobs, Walter Isaacson also described the culture of innovation in Northern California, a culture that paralleled the counterculture of the sixties and seventies.
Malcolm Gladwell. *Outliers: The Story of Success* (Hachette Digital, Inc. 2008)
Walter Issacson. *Steve Jobs* (Simon Schuster, 2011)

[228] There is little question that the "academic culture" is not the ivory tower existence of yore. An Australian publication, *The Conversation* wrote about "Cracks in the Ivory Tower: Is Academic's Culture Sustainable?"

> In the past, metrics of quantity allowed us to assess the performance of researchers, but now they have become an end in their own right. Ironically, once people deliberately pursue key indicators of performance, these indicators become less useful as independent yardsticks of what they were originally designed to measure. Only a few years ago, researchers who published ten papers a year were regarded as highly productive. Now, leading researchers in our field publish 20, 30, or in extreme cases, over 40 papers a year, and this is a growing trend. To feed such a volume of papers necessitates large and very well-funded research groups or consortia. So, since grant income is itself a key performance indicator in its own right, funding goes to the biggest groups, keeping them big or growing them even further.

Euan Ritchie and Joern Fischer. "Cracks in the Ivory Tower: Is Academic's Culture Sustainable?" *The Conversation* (August 23, 2012): http://theconversation.com/cracks-in-the-ivory-tower-is-academias-culture-sustainable-8294

[229] An assessment of the pressure to perish on the quality of research written in 2005 did not discuss who technology might change academic

publishing. The authors wrote as if the Internet did not exist and as if a new generation of academics were not increasingly dubious about traditional practices. The authors discussed the negative results of the demands that all of the faculty publish in one of the few acceptable journals, i.e. research was unadventurous but methodologically sound. In other words, "research" was being done not for the sake of furthering intellectual discourse but for the purposes of maximizing one's chance of getting published. Sadly, there was no mention of the mathematical impossibility of achieving such demands, although there was a realization that the system was rewarding mediocre thinking. As Mark de Rond and Alan N. Miller stated,

> Surprisingly few serious works (outside of the popular press) have investigated this phenomenon empirically, despite its familiarity to those "on the inside." We do not dispute researching and writing as a vital component of academic life. We fully endorse it. Nor are we concerned with the anxieties that come with a career involving research per se. Anxiety might be rather wholesome in fueling our efforts to write, never quite sure whether our articles will be sufficiently competitive to fend off rival articles en route to elite journals. We do worry about strangleholds on what it takes to gain promotion, tenure, and mobility, as a consequence of institutional demands and, more subtly, the persistence of mainstream criteria to defining so-called good research. We also worry about barriers to innovation in publishing because of deeply engrained commitments to so-called normal science research.

Once again, we are confronted with the acknowledgment of the fact that the life-threatening professional practice of terrorizing junior faculty is rarely written about in a serious manner.

Mark de Rond and Alan N. Miller. "Publish or Perish. Bane or Boon of Academic Life?" *Journal of Management Inquiry* (Volume 14, Number 4, December 2005): http://laisumedu.org/DESIN_Ibarra/salon/2007p/UAMX-teoria/Rond-01.pdf

[230] Most of the writing on publish or perish has been done in the field of science. In contrast to the humanities, where scholars are not paid and do not pay to have their work published, scientists pay to have their works published---a sort of cost-of-processing fee, some of which are quite high,

well over $1000 in some instances. That said, the main result of publish or perish has been a flood of unremarkable writing, inspired by anxiety and need to be in print. Faculty are "ranked" in terms of how many times their work is cited, meaning that the more people who read the study, the more influential it is. The scientific community is supported by government grants, which would bend the kind of research being done towards government needs rather than free exploration of the field. In an open letter to *The Chronicle of Higher Education,* a quartet of scientists decried the proliferation of low quality research.

> Our suggestions would change evaluation practices in committee rooms, editorial offices, and library purchasing meetings. Hiring committees would favor candidates with high citation scores, not bulky publications. Libraries would drop journals that don't register impact. Journals would change practices so that the materials they publish would make meaningful contributions and have the needed, detailed backup available online. Finally, researchers themselves would devote more attention to fewer and better papers actually published, and more journals might be more discriminating. Best of all, our suggested changes would allow academe to revert to its proper focus on quality research and rededicate itself to the sober pursuit of knowledge. And it would end the dispiriting paper chase that turns fledgling inquirers into careerists and established figures into grouches.

Mark Bauerlein, Mohamed Gad-el-Hak, Wayne Grody, Bill McKelvey, and Stanley W. Trimble. *The Chronicle of Higher Education* (June 13, 2010): http://scholar.google.com/scholar?start=20&q=academic+culture%2Bpublish+or+perish&hl=en&as_sdt=0,5&as_vis=1

[231] Many of us remain connected to print journalism and are restricted to topical exhibitions and are limited to a certain number of words. The reasons for maintaining an old format based on print limitations, even when the work goes on line, is to fairly compensate the writers, i.e. a certain amount of money for a certain number of words. But for most of us, this kind of writing is but one of our literary outlets.

[232] David Glance argued that "The Long Tail" model should also be adopted by academia:

> It turns out that in universities, academic publication also follows a long tail distribution. A relatively few academics produce a lot of work each year and the majority (80 per cent) produce very much less, perhaps one or two outputs a year. As a consequence of government funding approaches and global university ranking schemes, universities have been encouraged to look at the quantity of overall output from their institutions. This has caused some universities to focus on the "short head" part of the distribution, imagining how good it would be to expand that section by having every academic be a "hit" and move into the head of the distribution. By focusing on the head of the distribution however, they have missed another approach that, like Amazon, Apple and other online industries focuses on the long tail.

David Glance. "The Long Tail of Academic Publishing and Why it isn't Such a Bad Thing." *The London School of Economics and Political Science.* August 22, 2012.
http://blogs.lse.ac.uk/impactofsocialsciences/2012/08/22/the-long-tail-of-academic-publishing-and-why-that-isnt-a-bad-thing/

[233] Although his article in *Wired* was about "The Long Tail" of music, Anderson paused to consider books and stated,

> What's really amazing about the Long Tail is the sheer size of it. Combine enough nonhits on the Long Tail and you've got a market bigger than the hits. Take books: The average Barnes & Noble carries 130,000 titles. Yet more than half of Amazon's book sales come from *outside* its top 130,000 titles. Consider the implication: If the Amazon statistics are any guide, the market for books that are not even sold in the average bookstore is larger than the market for those that are (see "Anatomy of the Long Tail"). In other words, the potential book market may be twice as big as it appears to be, if only we can get over the economics of scarcity. Venture capitalist and former music industry consultant Kevin Laws puts it this way: "The biggest money is in the smallest sales."

Chris Anderson. "The Long Tail." *Wired Magazine.* October 2004.

http://www.wired.com/wired/archive/12.10/tail.html
Anderson turned the article into a book *The Long Tail: Why the Future of Business is Selling Less of More* (New York: Hyperion. 2006)

[234] K. A. Wallace wrote a very interesting article on The Long Tail and its use in academia. As Wallace wrote,

> Traditionally, academics have focused on the research or "prestige" values of their work. Before the emergence of digital media, the market for academic work in the humanities and social sciences was small, providing little incentive for authors to think about monetary gain. In principle, anyone could have purchased a scholarly article. But in practice it was unlikely that anyone outside of academia would do so. Unless one was an expert with an understanding of and access to scholarly and research resources, the means of developing an interest in a topic did not exist, and the sources themselves were scarce and expensive. Moreover, unlike in the sciences, in the humanities and social sciences there was usually no commercial application from which profit could be made. But online search engines and digital production, by allowing for cheap storage and reproduction, open up a huge potential audience and market. Once scholarly articles have been "produced," the costs of maintaining and delivering digital inventory are minuscule compared to the costs of maintaining print inventory, as Anderson pointed out in his "long tail" analysis, and there is potential for profit even from infrequently purchased items. But who would have an interest in obscure or difficult scholarly publications in the humanities or social sciences? I do not think we know. What we do know is that if millions, and perhaps eventually billions, of people have access to online search engines and digital media, as Michael Jensen, director of strategic Web communications at the National Academies and National Academies Press, pointed out in his article "The Deep Niche," there could be many "niche" markets that simply could not have existed before.

One of the interesting issues that opening the niche market to academics is that of who profits? In the ideal world, academics, who never get paid for any of their work, as reviewers or as writers, would get some long overdue remuneration for their contributions. However, in the real world, the vast majority of their publications are enclosed behind the Iron Curtain of subscriber only databases.

K. A. Wallace. "Who Profits When You Publish?" *WWW. AAUP.org* (July-August 2008): http://www.kathwallace.com/whoprofitswallace.pdf

[235] For a discussion of The Long Tail from a business perspective, complete with math, charts and graphs, see
Anita Elberse and Felix Oberholzer-Gee. "Superstars and Underdogs: An Examination of the Long Tail Phenomenon in Video Sales." *Harvard Business School Working Paper Series, Nos. 07-015.* 2007:
http://www.aeaweb.org/annual_mtg_papers/2007/0107_1015_1002.pdf

[236] As Anderson explained,

> Chart Rhapsody's monthly statistics and you get a "power law" demand curve that looks much like any record store's, with huge appeal for the top tracks, tailing off quickly for less popular ones. But a really interesting thing happens once you dig below the top 40,000 tracks, which is about the amount of the fluid inventory (the albums carried that will eventually be sold) of the average real-world record store. Here, the Wal-Marts of the world go to zero - either they don't carry any more CDs, or the few potential local takers for such fringy fare never find it or never even enter the store. The Rhapsody demand, however, keeps going. Not only is every one of Rhapsody's top 100,000 tracks streamed at least once each month, the same is true for its top 200,000, top 300,000, and top 400,000. As fast as Rhapsody adds tracks to its library, those songs find an audience, even if it's just a few people a month, somewhere in the country. This is the Long Tail. You can find everything out there on the Long Tail. There's the back catalog, older albums still fondly remembered by longtime fans or rediscovered by new ones. There are live tracks, B-sides, remixes, even (gasp) covers. There are niches by the thousands, genre within genre within genre: Imagine an entire Tower Records devoted to '80s hair bands or ambient dub. There are foreign bands, once priced out of reach in the Import aisle, and obscure bands on even more obscure labels, many of which don't have the distribution clout to

get into Tower at all.

Anderson. Op.cit, 2.

[237] In 2008 with the idea of Open Access, allowing free distribution of scholarly work, the Harvard faculty voted to publish any scholarly articles by faculty on their website. The move was an interesting one as it opened more questions: who really "owned" the work? The University or the scholar? Although the copyright ostensibly belonged to the writer, however, a legal scholar Eric Priest had his doubts. Writing in 2012, Priest commented,

> By invoking copyright law terminology in permission mandates, schools might intend that they have the legal effect of transferring nonexclusive rights to the school, thereby clarifying and fortifying the school's rights to reproduce and publicly disseminate faculty works. However, the legal effect of these mandates is uncertain…

Eric Priest. "Copyright and the Harvard Open Access Mandate." *Northwestern Journal of Technology & Intellectual Property.* Social Science Research Network (August 1, 2012): http://papers.ssrn.com/sol3/papers.cfm?abstract_id=1890467

[238] Interview with Chris Anderson. "Chris Anderson. The Long Tail." *Blogging Heroes:* http://www.longtail.com/bloggingheroes.pdf

[239] The Vly House. "The iTunes Business Model and its Widespread Effects." *Culture and Society.* January 28, 2011 http://www.thevlyhouse.com/2011/01/the-itunes-business-model-and-its-widespread-effects/

[240] About ten years ago, James Elkins observed the way in which art criticism was being produced and complained that there was too much and hence there was a "crisis" in the field: more writing meant less impact,

> Daily newspapers are collected by local and national libraries, but newspaper art criticism is not a subject term in any database I know, so art criticism published in newspapers quickly becomes difficult to access. In a sense, then, art criticism is very healthy indeed. So healthy that it is outstripping its readers—there is more

> of it around than anyone can read. Even in mid-size cities,
> art historians can't read everything that appears in
> newspapers or is printed by museums or galleries. Yet at
> the same time art criticism is very nearly dead, if health is
> measured by the number of people who take it seriously,
> or by its interaction with neighboring kinds of writing
> such as art history, art education, or aesthetics. Art
> criticism is massively produced, and massively ignored.

Referring back to a 2001 conference on art criticism, Elkins summarized the conclusions, such as the assertion that the work of a few people serve as the model for the practice. Because the role of the Internet in distributing art criticism was not on the horizon, Elkins and his fellow professionals did not think of the intellectual consequences of narrowing the scope of writing to that of a select few. But to the credit of the writer, he notes that "those values" might not suit the 21st century.

> All that is the foundation of what "serious criticism"
> continues to mean. Since 1976, it has also been
> exemplified by *October,* and by essays written by Thomas
> Crow, Thomas McEvilley, and a score of others in
> different venues. Calls for a return to criticism that is
> serious, complex, and rigorous are indebted to the model
> provided by *Artforum* and its descendents. That means,
> in turn, that it is important to ask whether it makes sense
> to revive those particular senses of commitment,
> verifiability, and intellectualism. It seems to me the only
> defensible answer is that such values are no longer a
> good fit for art at the beginning of the twenty-first
> century. Metaphors of intellectual *labor,* of difficulty, of
> challenge recur in *Artforum* discussions, beginning with
> Greenberg: when it is good the work is dry, hard,
> obdurate and irrefragible... it is not easy to imagine how
> those values can be transposed to the present, and even
> if they were, it is not easy to picture how useful they
> would be.

Perhaps it would be nit-picking on my part to point out that the very paragraph that looks back nostalgically to a golden age of "intellectualism" has two spelling errors. However, four years later the thirty-one page pamphlet was replaced by book where the spelling errors are corrected.

James Elkins. "What Happened to Art Criticism?" Pamphlet, 2004: http://criticaycontracritica.uniandes.edu.co/textossimposio/ElkinsWhathappened.pdf
The State of Art Criticism (Routledge, 2008) 85.

[241] Roland Barthes. "The Death of the Author." *Image, Music, Text* (1977): http://evans-experientialism.freewebspace.com/barthes06.htm

[242] I borrow the idea from Roland Barthes, knowing that these terms were originally used in the context of images---photography to be precise. But Web reading is visual—one looks for, scans, and is caught, or as Barthes might say, "wounded" by something that is like, again as Barthes would say, "punctuation." According to Barthes,

> *Studium*... a kind of general, enthusiastic commitment, of course, but without special acuity. It is by *studium* that I am interested in so many photographs, for it is culturally that I participate in the figures, the faces, the gestures, the settings, the actions" "The second element will break (or punctuate) the *studium*... this element which rises from the scene, shoots out of it like an arrow, and pierces me. A Latin word exists to designate this wound, this prick, this mark made by a pointed instrument: the word suits me all the better in that it also refers to the notion of punctuation, and because the photographs I am speaking of are in effect punctuated, sometimes event speckled with this sensitive points... I shall therefore call *punctum*; for *punctum* is also: sting, speck, cut, little hole - and also a cast of the dice. A photograph's *punctum* is that accident which pricks me (but also bruises me, is poignant to me).

Roland Barthes. *Camera Lucida: Reflections on Photography*. Translated by Richard Howard (McMillian, 1982) 27.

[243] As Graham Allen wrote,

> Writing is radical for Barthes when it interrogates the world, rather than when it gives us answers which appear to explain the world and justify it. Art is radical, for Barthes, when through its questions it exposes, as in the theater or Brecht, the meanings bourgeois culture would have us accept as true and natural. The practice of

questioning the world makes radical writing a form of criticism.

Graham Allen. *Roland Barthes* (Routledge, 2003) 6.

[244] Eugene Garfield traced the origin of the phrase, "publish or perish," back to the 1940s where it was in common usage. As Garfield wrote in this short article,

> ...*The Academic Man: A Study in the Sociology of a Profession*, a 1942 book by Logan Wilson (New York, Oxford University Press, reprinted in 1964 by Octagon Books, New York, and in 1992 and 1995 by Transaction Publishers, New Brunswick, N.J.). In a chapter on prestige and the research function, Wilson stated: "The prevailing pragmatism forced upon the academic group is that one must write something and get it into print. Situational imperatives dictate a 'publish or perish' credo within the ranks" (p. 197). However, Wilson did not provide a reference and-again-the telltale quotation marks raise a question whether he was citing or coining the phrase. Since Wilson was a sociologist, I suspected he might be known to Robert K. Merton, professor, emeritus, at Columbia University, the eminent sociologist of science whom I also consulted in the effort to trace the elusive origin of the phrase. Merton is coeditor with David Sills of *The Macmillan Book of Social Science Quotations: Who Said What, When, and Where* (New York, Macmillan, 1992). You can imagine my surprise upon learning that Wilson had been Merton's student at Harvard University. He later became president of the University of Texas and, subsequently, president of the American Council on Education. Merton and others familiar with pre-war academe believe that "publish or perish" was a term in fairly common usage at the time.

Eugene Garfield. "What is the Primordial Reference for The Phrase 'Publish or Perish'?" *The Scientist* (Volume 10, Number 12, June 10, 1996): http://www.garfield.library.upenn.edu/commentaries/tsv10(12)p11y1996 0610.pdf

[245] In an article that examines the current state of academic publishing in contrast to what it could be, Bard professor, Walter Russell Mead, wrote,

With their characteristic moral blindness and ignorance of markets, many academics reflexively blame the "greed" of publishers, and of course publishers are no more likely to turn up their noses at the occasional obscene profit than any other corporations. But in fairness to the publishers, it is worth noting that most academic research is a vanity publishing project: nobody reads what is published except for the authors and a small circle of friends. (That is not necessarily an indication that the article is worthless; it is merely an observation that for all but a tiny handful of academic journal articles the audience is miniscule.) The editorial process at these journals is extremely cumbersome and expensive, and publishing articles with lots of footnotes and fancy format issues takes a lot of time and money to do. In the vanity press world, the authors pay directly; in the quasi-vanity world of academic publishing, the faculty pay indirectly through sky high university subscription and access fees. Without very large subsidies, however they are packaged, the whole enormous edifice would crash to the ground because, with the exception of a tiny sliver of work that is truly significant to large numbers of readers and researchers, the whole enterprise of academic publishing is, economically speaking, unsound.

Walter Russell Mead. "Publish or Perish or Pay Through the Nose." *The American Interest* (April 28, 2012): http://blogs.the-american-interest.com/wrm/2012/04/28/publish-rubbish-or-perish-and-pay-through-the-nose/

[246] Another highly detailed paper from Hong Kong with charts, graphs, equations and so on attempted to track number of citations per publication came up with the rather unexpected conclusion that "we do not have enough time to read all the papers being published on the research problems we are working on."
Dah Ming Chiu and Tom Z. J. Fu. "'Publish or Perish' in the Internet Age. A Study of Publication Statistics in Computer Networking Research" (2010): http://home.ie.cuhk.edu.hk/~dmchiu/ccr_paper.pdf

[247] It is rather sad to read an article written ten years ago on the on-going and deteriorating position of scholars who are told to publish under the old rules as the old system is vanishing.

> Young scholars have been caught in a double squeeze. On one side are the struggling university presses, which are losing their university subsidies at the same time they're being pressured to make a profit. Originally established solely to publish dissertations, more and more of these presses are picking up books that have been rejected by commercial publishers, who prefer to focus on potential blockbusters. Indeed, many university presses have stopped publishing books on certain subjects that aren't big sellers...

Dinitia Smith. "Hoping the Web Will Rescue Young Professors; In the Publish-or-Perish World, Can They Live on the Internet?" *The New York Times* (June 12, 1999): http://www.nytimes.com/1999/06/12/arts/hoping-web-will-rescue-young-professors-publish-perish-world-can-they-live.html?pagewanted=all&src=pm

[248] Bourdieu continued,

> Symbolic power, whose form par excellence is the power to make groups (groups that are already established and have to be consecrated or groups that have yet to be constituted such as the Marxian proletariat), rests on two conditions. Firstly, as any form of performative discourse, symbolic power has to be based on the possession of symbolic capital. The power to impose upon other minds a vision, old or new, of social divisions depends on the social authority acquired in previous struggles. Symbolic capital is a credit; it is the power granted to those who have obtained sufficient recognition to be in a position to impose recognition. In this way, the power of constitution, a power to make a new group, through mobilization, or to make it exist by proxy, by speaking on its behalf as an authorized spokesperson, can be obtained only as the outcome of a long process of institutionalization, at the end of which a representative is instituted, who receives from the group the power to make the group. Secondly, symbolic efficacy depends on the degree to which the vision proposed is founded in reality.

Pierre Bourdieu. "Social Space and Symbolic Power." *Sociological Theory,* Volume 7, umber 1 (Spring, 1989) 14-25.

[249] In 2010, *The New Yorker* described, in contrast to the e-book, the traditional and not very profitable economic model used by traditional publishers. According to Ken Auletta,

> Traditionally, publishers have sold books to stores, with the wholesale price for hardcovers set at fifty per cent of the cover price. Authors are paid royalties at a rate of about fifteen per cent of the cover price. A simplified version of a publisher's costs might run as follows. On a new, twenty-six-dollar hardcover, the publisher typically receives thirteen dollars. Authors are paid royalties at a $3.90. Perhaps $1.80 goes to the costs of paper, printing, and binding, a dollar to marketing, and $1.70 to distribution. The remaining $4.60 must pay for rent, editors, a sales force, and any write-offs of unearned author advances. Bookstores return about thirty-five per cent of the hardcovers they buy, and publishers write off the cost of producing those books. Profit margins are slim.

Ken Auletta. "Publish or Perish." *The New Yorker.* April 26, 2010. http://www.newyorker.com/reporting/2010/04/26/100426fa_fact_auletta #ixzz2DBNL7trm

[250] Although he was writing about traditional news journalism, Paul Grabowicz described how "pull" journalism works,

> Pulling people to news Websites serve two important functions: More in-depth stories and richer content can be published on a Website than in the relatively short snippets of information distributed to people via mobile devices, on YouTube and Flickr, or through blogs and micro-blog postings. Providing deeper content fulfills the public service function of journalism and can help form online communities at news Websites where people can gather to discuss issues of importance to their communities, both geographic and topical. Attracting a loyal audience of repeat users to a news Website offers a way to monetize journalistic content by selling that dedicated audience to advertisers. Creating a viable

business model for online content has been a particular challenge for news organizations, with Web site advertising rates, as measured by CPM's or costs per thousand views/impressions, usually a fraction of what can be charged for a print or broadcast product.

Paul Grabowicz. "The Transition to Digital Journalism." *Knight Digital Media Center.* Updated November 2012.
http://multimedia.journalism.berkeley.edu/tutorials/digital-transform/Websites/

[251] There are already responses to the problem of the expense of subscriptions to academic sites. In a June 2012 article on "Crisis in Academic Publishing," Joanie Lavoie and Dominique Bérubé wrote,

> "In the early 90s, a major event occurred: the creation of ArXiv, a platform for physicists to submit preprints of their articles. The original goal of this project was not to circumvent journals because of their astronomical prices, but rather, to accelerate the dissemination of knowledge, which for traditional journals, can stretch out over one or even two years. In 2012, ArXiv hosts articles from many disciplines and occupies an important place in the scientific world," said Vincent Larivière, a professor at Université de Montréal's School of Library and Information Sciences... "All researchers want to publish in high-impact journals because it influences their careers," Larivière said. "Publishing in a prestigious journal can mean getting a particular grant or position. To be considered an important researcher, one simply cannot publish outside these journals." However, this is less true today, notes Larivière}, who, with colleagues George Lozano and Yves Gingras, compared impact factor with citation numbers for millions of articles published between 1902 and 2009. "The most cited articles are published less exclusively in high-impact journals. In other words, major findings are no longer reported in only elite journals. And this decline began in the early 90s... in short, it's power of the Web."

Joanie Lavoie and Dominique Bérubé. "Crisis in Academic Publishing." *Phys.Org*. June 2012: http://phys.org/news/2012-06-crisis-academic-publishing.html#jCp

[252] One of the greatest mistakes that a publisher or writer on the Web can make is to believe that it is possible to simply move print-style material from paper pages to a screen in cyber space. The physical fact of seeing, looking and reading is different on the Web. The way the text looks on the computer screen is transformed from a bounded text in a book and becomes an expanse of undifferentiated gray, which is no longer acceptable to readers.

During a visit to JSTOR, a site that has the worst search engine in the known world, I selected an article from 1978, "A Socialist Critique of Art History in the U.S.A." by Edmund Burke Feldman as an article that would be perfectly fine for us but that would not attract today's internet reader:

> For a concise critique of culture I can do no better than to quote Arnold Hauser's listing of the features of the crisis of Western societies: "Economic and social disintegration, the mechanization of life, the reification of culture, the alienation of the individual, the institutionalisation of human relations, the atomisation of functions, and the feeling of general insecurity. These features are "symptom," according to Hauser, which means that they belong to a complex of causes and effects, some of which are immediate and some of which are remote so far as any particular cultural observation is concerned. It would not be difficult to gain a consensus as to the pervasive existence of the traits Hauser cites. Disagreement might arise, however, as to their status as symptoms, their relative weight and their shifting character as cause and effect. From a general socialist perspective, Hauser's symptoms are secondary manifestations of fundamental economic and social relationships. These manifestations may not be uniform in time and space; still it is recognized that they have a connection with late capitalism that is more thorough and consistent than the connections that might be adduced to such other prominent features of these societies such as automation, technology, atheism, cultural relativism, neo-tribalism or bureaucratic centralization.

Edmund Burke Feldman. "A Socialist Critique of Art History." *Leonardo.* Volume 11, No. 1 (Winter 1978) 22-23.

For the reader who is searching for a topic or a thesis or a reason why the article was written, the question is where are the key words? With no immediate announcement of the content, the reader is immediately discouraged and wonders in passing before clicking on to the next entry: who is Hauser? One can argue that if the reader does not know the Marxist origin for the idea of " symptoms," then this individual is not the audience the writer imagined. And this is an excellent point, as long as the article was confined to the professional journal *Leonardo* but on the Web, unimaginable readers may come and the writer has to pause and explain who Arnold Hauser was, who Karl Marx was, what is the difference between a Marxist "symptom" and a Freudian "symptom" and what is "social art history" and "critique" and somehow be interesting enough to capture the reader's attention and to convince him or her that yes, there is information here, keep reading. And you have about three seconds to do all that, through key words that can be readily picked out by the reader.

[253] Science fiction writer, William Gibson, who wrote of the "Matrix," which controlled all of the world's telephones, coined the term "cyberspace". In their book on Internet history, Asa Briggs and Peter Cook also cite J. G. Ballard and William Burroughs and mention the idea of cyberspace in the 1982 film, *Tron.*
Asa Briggs and Peter Burke. *Social History of the Media: From Gutenberg to the Internet* (Polity Press, 2009) 277.

[254] Writing in the *Berkeley Planning Journal,* Ruth Miller stated that

> Though the opportunity to self-publish is universally available, many researchers prefer to publish in the high-cost academic journals distributed by Elsevier and others. Academia often judges the quality of research by the prestige of the journal that publishes it. An author's work is 36 to 200 percent more likely to be cited if is available online (Hill 2012), but online publishing is not yet regarded as serious enough to establish an academic career. This bias to tradition gives publishers an effective monopoly. The scholarly community depends upon the ability to disseminate research and read that of others, and so researchers and librarians decry high subscription fees to be a necessary evil.

Ruth Miller. "Insurgency in Academic Publishing." *Berkeley Planning Journal.* 25(1)(2012) http://ced.berkeley.edu/bpj/2012/05/insurgency-in-academic-publishing/

[255] The old models will not go down without a fight and will, undoubtedly find a way to monopolize the market. And those who want to participate in this paradigm will rejoice in its ultimate survival. In *The Journal of Electronic Publishing,* Joseph J. Esposito defended the Old Ways:

> The lesson to be drawn from HighWire is that the NFP sector can devise useful, practical strategies for improving the state of scholarly communications without doing anything as extreme as a repudiation of copyright or a single-minded focus on Open Access. The commercial sector was not overturned by the HighWire strategy; rather, commercial publishers found themselves challenged and their influence moderated: competition can be a very good thing. HighWire allowed the NFPs to fight back. Intriguingly, HighWire now includes commercial entities (e.g., Sage) among its clients.

Joseph J. Esposito. "The Wisdom of Oz: The Role of the University Press in Scholarly Communications." *The Journal of Electronic Publishing.* Volume 10, Issue 1, Winter 2007.
http://quod.lib.umich.edu/cgi/t/text/text-idx?c=jep;cc=jep;view=text;rgn=main;idno=3336451.0010.103

[256] A great deal has been written about the recalcitrance of the academic publishers to respond to the Perfect Storm of the rising costs of publishing and the shrinking budgets of academic libraries. As Peter Brantley wrote in February 2012,

> Fixed price determination, even if premised on a one-time acquisition, also has the unremarkable but unpleasant effect of reducing competitive pressures in the book marketplace. There are a great many monographs published today by university presses that find very small outlets, partially as a result of library budgets that are **squeezed** by the costs of electronic journal and database licensing. Many libraries are backing away from full-list university press acquisition policies, and a growing number are **banding together** in shared print and e-acquisition agreements that spread

purchasing costs across multiple institutions. Perversely, instead of responding to this decrease in demand, many UPs remain bound up in the academic promotion and tenure process, which for humanities and social science disciplines often requires a published monograph derived from one's doctoral thesis or dissertation. The growing interest in **open peer review** and open access publishing for both monographs and serials suggests, however, that a great deal of existing scholarly output could be redirected into more informal, web-based platforms. Ranging from self-published material deposited into university repositories, to scholarly association-backed peer-review platforms, there are a growing number of ways for web-based systems to publish materials that do not need to be "rolled up" into more formal manifestations, such as a traditionally published manuscripts or journal articles. There is a considerable amount of potential savings lurking here.

Peter Brantley. "Academic E-Books: innovation and Transition." *Publishers' Weekly*. February 3, 2012. http://www.publishersweekly.com/pw/by-topic/digital/content-and-e-books/article/50486-academic-e-books-innovation-and-transition.html

Another interesting book on this topic is by one already mentioned: John B. Thompson. *Books in the Digital Age: The Transformation of Academic and Higher Education. Publishing in Britain and the United States* (Polity, 2005). However, this book, like so many books and articles on this subject focuses on the publishers and not on the writers.

[257] The British have been far move active in exploring this problem of scholarly publication and one of the recent books on this topic was written by John B. Thompson who examines the world of academic publishing from an economic perspective. Without going into the question of how economic considerations impact scholars and their careers, this book implies that future jobs and promotions may owe less to whether of not one has written a worthy volume but whether or not a publisher thinks a book is marketable or not. Thompson stated,

> ...academic publishing firms have been in the throes of a profound transformation for more than a decade, and the impact of this transformation is still being played out

in the day-to-day running of these organizations. The traditional culture of academic publishing, which was concerned above all with building a list of high-quality scholarly books in a broad range of subject areas, has increasingly given way to a more market-conscious culture. Questions of quality have certainly not been brushed aside---the suggestion that quality has been sacrificed on the altar of the market would be an oversimplification of the dynamic of this field. But questions of quality have been supplemented in myriad ways by considerations of the sales potential and financial viability of new book projects.

John B. Thompson. Ibid. 137.

[258] As early as 2007, the decline of traditional readers was well underway. Caleb Crain reported,

> The most striking results were generational. In general, older Dutch people read more. It would be natural to infer from this that each generation reads more as it ages, and, indeed, the researchers found something like this to be the case for earlier generations. But, with later ones, the age-related growth in reading dwindled. The turning point seems to have come with the generation born in the nineteen-forties. By 1995, a Dutch college graduate born after 1969 was likely to spend fewer hours reading each week than a little-educated person born before 1950. As far as reading habits were concerned, academic credentials mattered less than whether a person had been raised in the era of television. The N.E.A., in its twenty years of data, has found a similar pattern. Between 1982 and 2002, the percentage of Americans who read literature declined not only in every age group but in every generation—even in those moving from youth into middle age, which is often considered the most fertile time of life for reading. We are reading less as we age, and we are reading less than people who were our age ten or twenty years ago.

Caleb Crain. "Twilight of the Books." *The New Yorker*. December 24, 2007. http://www.newyorker.com/arts/critics/atlarge/2007/12/24/071224crat_atlarge_crain#ixzz2DBUAZ4nx

[259] As Nicholas Carr wrote in a now famous article, "Is Google Making Us Stupid?"

> For me, as for others, the Net is becoming a universal medium, the conduit for most of the information that flows through my eyes and ears and into my mind. The advantages of having immediate access to such an incredibly rich store of information are many, and they've been widely described and duly applauded. "The perfect recall of silicon memory," *Wired*'s Clive Thompson has written, "can be an enormous boon to thinking." But that boon comes at a price. As the media theorist Marshall McLuhan pointed out in the 1960s, media are not just passive channels of information. They supply the stuff of thought, but they also shape the process of thought. And what the Net seems to be doing is chipping away my capacity for concentration and contemplation. My mind now expects to take in information the way the Net distributes it: in a swiftly moving stream of particles. Once I was a scuba diver in the sea of words. Now I zip along the surface like a guy on a Jet Ski.

Nicholas Carr. "Is Google Making Us Stupid?" *The Atlantic*. July-August 2008. http://www.theatlantic.com/magazine/archive/2008/07/is-google-making-us-stupid/306868/

[260] One of the first articles written on "reading formations" was, of course, by Tony Bennett who stated,

> In the case of canonized texts, there is a considerable degree of coincidence between the discourses of academic criticism and the reading formations that productively activate texts. In as much as, for most readers, some form of acquaintance with these discourses constitutes a necessary apprenticeship for reading, this coincidence constitutes the means by which readers are socialized into the literary community. In the case of popular fictions, however, no such coincidence exists. Academic criticisms of all varieties have dissected

popular texts, analyzed their relations, and made suppositions abut their effects on readers. Yet all this has taken place without interrogating the necessary disparity that exists between the discourses of criticism and the reading formations that circulate outside the academy and effectively organize popular reading.

Tony Bennett. "Texts, Readers, Reading Formations." *The Bulleting of the Midwest Modern Language Association.* Volume 16, Number 1 (Spring, 1983) 3-17.
Several years later, Bennett elaborated upon his now-famous concept:

> The concept of reading formation, then, is an attempt to weave a way between these two approaches to the study of reading by conceiving the intratextual determinations of reading as being overdetermined by the operation of determinations, which, while they cannot be derived from the text concerned, are not reducible to an extratextual social context either. It is an attempt to identify the determinations that, in operating on both texts and readers, mediate the relations between text and context, connecting the two and providing the mechanisms through which they productively interact in representing context, not as a set of extradiscursive relations, but as a set of intertextual and discursive relations that produce readers for texts and texts for readers. This is to question conventional conceptions of texts, readers, and contexts as separable elements, fixed in their relations to one another, by suggesting that they are variable functions within a discursively ordered set of relations. Different reading formations, that is to say, produce their own texts, their own readers, and their own contexts.

Tony Bennett. "Texts in History: The Determinations of Readings and Their Texts." *The Journal of the Midwest Modern Language Association.* Volume 18, Number 1 (Spring, 1985) 8.

[261] One of the most interesting commentaries on the monopoly capitalism practiced by supposedly not for profit subscriptions services to libraries was written by the British journalist, George Monblot who charged,

> More importantly, universities are locked into buying their products. Academic papers are published in only one place, and they have to be read by researchers trying to keep up with their subject. Demand is inelastic and competition non-existent, because different journals can't publish the same material. In many cases the publishers oblige the libraries to buy a large package of journals, whether or not they want them all.

George Monblot."Academic Publishers Make Murdoch Look Like a Socialist." *The Guardian.* 29 August 2011.
http://m.guardian.co.uk/commentisfree/2011/aug/29/academic-publishers-murdoch-socialist?cat=commentisfree&type=article

[262] Tony Bennett. Op. cit. "Texts, Readers, Reading Formations."

[263] Writing in *The Chronicle of Higher Education,* Hugh Gusterson suggested that the way to change the rules of a game that favors the publishers over the academics is to "just say no." However, Gusterson does not mean opting out, he means getting paid:

> If academic work is to be commodified and turned into a source of profit for shareholders and for the 1 percent of the publishing world, then we should give up our archaic notions of unpaid craft labor and insist on professional compensation for our expertise, just as doctors, lawyers, and accountants do.

Hugh Gusterson. "Want to Change Academic Publishing? Just Say No." *The Chronicle of Higher Education.* September 23, 2012.
http://chronicle.com/article/Want-to-Change-Academic/134546/

[264] The Internet is just beginning to receive serious study in terms of history and theory but one interesting analysis of Web aesthetics can be found in Megan Sapnar Ankerson. "Web Insdustries, Economies, Aesthetics: Mapping the Look of the Web in the Dot-Com Era." in Niels Brügger. *Web History* (New York: Peter Lang Publishing Company, 2010) 173-194.

However this study does not go beyond the year 2000 and thus the current trends in web design today are not covered.

[265] To date a number of institutions have past resolutions to support Open Access in order to share content. The Oberlin Group has posted a current list of the participants.
The Oberlin Group, A Consortium of Liberal Arts College Libraries:
http://www.oberlingroup.org/node/14078

[266] Roger C. Schonfeld. *JSTOR. A History.* (Princeton University Press, 2003) This book does not go beyond 2001 and therefore could not have taken into account the evolving twenty-first century expectations of a Web-savvy user base. These users are put off by the primitive scanning of existing articles, which were designed for paper pages and not for screen scanning or scrolling. Potential readers are also discouraged by the need for a password and even for those most determined to "get into" JSTOR, the problem of access continues with the very unhelpful search engine of the site. For the reader/researcher, used to the efficiencies of Google, it is clear that JSTOR is based on an older model, dating back to the early nineties, which was, in turn based on library (printed publications) models. JSTOR is simply not designed or laid out for the modern Internet and hence loses the majority of its users due to the sheer inconveniences that thwart the potential consumer. In addition to the deficiencies of the "search engine," the articles contained in JSTOR have not been written for the twenty-first century reader. In an age where the author has exactly three seconds to grab the attention of the demanding reader, most of these articles do not state the topic for several pages. Few researchers of today have the patience for long unbroken paragraphs of tiny print, peppered with un explained jargon, which have the effect of excluding the reader and discouraging all but the most dedicated scholar who will be the only one willing to click onward to the next page.

[267] In just the past few years, in the wake of the Web, I would guess, academic publishing has acquired such a bad reputation, that even Aljazeera got in on the criticism, reporting that

> Discussions of open access publishing have centered on whether research should be made free to the public. But this question sets up a false dichotomy between "the public" and "the scholar". Many people fall into a grey zone, the boundaries of which are determined by institutional affiliation and personal wealth. This category includes independent scholars, journalists, public officials, writers, scientists and others who are experts in their fields yet are unwilling or unable to pay for academic work. This denial of resources is a loss to those who

value scholarly inquiry. But it is also a loss for the academics themselves, whose ability to stay employed rests on their willingness to limit the circulation of knowledge. In academia, the ability to prohibit scholarship is considered more meaningful than the ability to produce it.

Sarah Kendzior. "Academic Paywalls Mean Publish or Perish." *Aljazeera* (October 2012): http://www.aljazeera.com/indepth/opinion/2012/10/201210175587855 51.html

[268] Dirk Lewandowski and Philipp Mayr. "Exploring the Academic Invisible Web:" http://arxiv.org/pdf/cs/0702103.pdf

Their paper was posted on a science website connected the Cornell University Library, arxiv.org, which is an open access database.

[269] Writing in 2011, performing arts critic, Michael Kaiser expressed concern about the decline of support for criticism and the impact of critics:

> This has happened for three reasons. First, far fewer people are getting their news from print media. There is a reason the newspaper industry is in trouble. Advertisers are spending less in print media because fewer people are reading hard copy newspapers. And for those arts projects aimed at younger audiences, hard copy newspapers are no longer a central element of a marketing strategy. Younger people get virtually all of their information online, through news web sites, social media and chat rooms. And older people are increasingly getting their information online as well. Second, because serious arts coverage has been deemed an unnecessary expense by many news media outlets looking to pare costs, there are fewer critics and less space devoted to serious arts criticism. Even the *New York Times*' arts section is dominated now by features and reviews of popular entertainment -- television, movies and pop music -- rather than serious opera, dance, music or theater. And third, the growing influence of blogs, chat rooms and message boards devoted to the arts has given the local professional critic a slew of competitors... Many

arts institutions even allow their audience members to write their own critiques on the organizational website. This is a scary trend.

Michael Kaiser. "The Death of Criticism or Everyone is a Critic." *Huffpost Arts & Culture* (November 14, 2011):
http://www.huffingtonpost.com/michael-kaiser/the-death-of-criticism-or_b_1092125.html

[270] In 2012, Sarah McKenna outlined the process whereby JSTOR gets paid and everyone else has to pay for JSTOR, which is accessible for "free" to only the privileged few (who pay fees for this access):

> Having bought the rights to the academic research, JSTOR digitizes the material and sells the content back to the university libraries. To recoup their costs of leasing the information from the publishers, the academic search engines use a subscription model to restrict the content to those who can pay the hefty price tag. A substantial part of the university library budget is devoted towards subscriptions to those databases. The UC San Diego Libraries report that 65% of their total budget goes towards getting access to JSTOR and other databases. To get access to the Arts and Sciences collection at JSTOR -- only one of the many databases and collections of information -- university libraries must pay a one time charge of $45,000 and then $8,500 every year after that.
>
> Step back and think about this picture. Universities that created this academic content for free must pay to read it. Step back even further. The public -- which has indirectly funded this research with federal and state taxes that support our higher education system -- has virtually no access to this material, since neighborhood libraries cannot afford to pay those subscription costs. Newspapers and think tanks, which could help extend research into the public sphere, are denied free access to the material. Faculty members are rightly bitter that their years of work reaches an audience of a handful, while every year, 150 million attempts to read JSTOR content are denied every year.

Laura McKenna Laura McKenna. Ibid.

Nancy Sims, Copyright Program Librarian, University of Minnesota Libraries wrote an article, "Academic Publishing is Full of Problems; Let's Get Them Right," disagreeing with the details if not the main points of McKenna's article:
http://blog.lib.umn.edu/copyrightlibn/2012/01/factcheckingtheatlantic.html

[271] Kendizor also quoted Kathleen Fitzpatrick, the Director of Scholarly Communication at the Modern Language Association as saying,

> The more difficult it is to get an article into a journal, the higher the perceived value of having done so. But this sense of prestige too easily shades over into a sense that the more exclusively a publication is *distributed*, the higher its value.

Op.cit. Kenzidor.

[272] *The Economist* recently published an article on the extraordinary cost of academic publishing and the extreme expense of the journals:

> Publishing obscure academic journals is that rare thing in the media industry: a license to print money. An annual subscription to *Tetrahedron*, a chemistry journal, will cost your university library $20,269; a year of the *Journal of Mathematical Sciences* will set you back $20,100. In 2011 Elsevier, the biggest academic-journal publisher, made a profit of £768m ($1.2 billion) on revenues of £2.1 billion. Such margins (37%, up from 36% in 2010) are possible because the journals' content is largely provided free by researchers, and the academics who peer-review their papers are usually unpaid volunteers. The journals are then sold to the very universities that provide the free content and labor. For publicly funded research, the result is that the academics and taxpayers who were responsible for its creation have to pay to read it. This is not merely absurd and unjust; it also hampers education and research.

---"Open Sesame. When Research is Funded by Taxpayers or by Charities, the Results should be Available to All Without Charge." *The Economist.* April 14, 2012. http://www.economist.com/node/21552574
This article is a reprint, without giving credit, of the original article April 12th by John Noughton in *The Guardian:* "Academic Publishing Doesn't Add Up." http://www.guardian.co.uk/technology/2012/apr/22/academic-publishing-monopoly-challenged
This article attracted a great deal of attention. That same month, Tom Worstall of *Forbes* chimed in "The Coming Collapse of the Academic Publishing Model."
http://www.forbes.com/sites/timworstall/2012/04/10/the-coming-collapse-of-the-academic-publishing-model/

[273] In 2006, ancient times in cyber years, the *Art Journal* published a special issue, containing a "forum" on "Publishing Paradigms in Art History." Despite the presence of an article entitled, "Art History and the Digital World," neither the websites of the kind discussed in this paper nor the kind of web resources available today could be envisioned. Two of the publications were conversations and the lead article was an overview. The internet was seen as a resource that would serve the needs of traditional art history in a marginal fashion, while the traditional world of book publishing, regardless of the cost to the environment (mentioned by one discussant) would continue, unchanged by the web.

Catherine M. Soussloff. "Publishing Paradigms in Art History." *Art Journal* (pp. 36-40): Stable URL: http://www.jstor.org/stable/20068496

Art History and Its Publishers (pp. 41-50)
Michael Ann Holly, Mark Ledbury, Douglas Armato, Susan Bielstein, Andrew Brown, Roger Conover, Vivian Constantinopoulos, Stephanie Fay, Herman Pabbruwe, Catherine M. Soussloff and Ken Wissoker
Stable URL: http://www.jstor.org/stable/20068497

Murtha Baca and William Tronzo. "Art History and the Digital World." *Art Journal* (pp. 51-55): Stable URL: http://www.jstor.org/stable/20068498

[274] Contemplating her "second book" for tenure, Assistant Professor, Dennis Horn wrote of writing styles she admired a

> "...style that is at once approachable and deep...These are authors I want to emulate, not the stilted jargon-laden stuff of mainstream political science or theory. I wonder when this change happens – when do we gain

the confidence of finding our own voices, or feel free to write this way? I think it must happen – it's the only way we as academics can be relevant. We have to stop writing for our advisers and our colleagues. The opaque language and tortured rhetoric of the academy should no longer be the norm.

Denise Horn. "Academic Publishing. This is not a Dissertation." *The Guardian* (30 January 2012): http://www.guardian.co.uk/higher-education-network/blog/2012/jan/30/academic-publishing-not-dissertation

[275] As far back as 1992, Brian Martin succulently explained why jargon had to exist:

> If a discipline is to effectively control its intellectual turf, it cannot afford to be too easy to understand by outsiders. Jargon may serve as a convenient medium for practitioners, but it simultaneously serves as a way of excluding interlopers, namely those who have not served their time in study and research. Suppose you have a bright idea about a subject that is not your specialty. The idea is the easy part. Getting it taken seriously in a different field is difficult. To get published in an academic journal, it is necessary to know the literature in the field. You've got a lot of study ahead to get on top of it. You must cite appropriate references and be familiar enough with the jargon to write comfortably in it. Referees can pick up an outsider readily enough, and a few false steps are enough for a rejection. Although your idea might be a good one, that's not enough. After all, if every outsider with a bright idea were allowed to be published, what would be the point of all that long training? Jargon serves to police the boundaries of disciplines and specialties. It's like a toll collected from those who attempt to cross an intellectual border, a toll collected in the currency of intellectual labour. Jargon, on top of credentials, ensures that migration between disciplines is kept to a low level. Jargon serves another purpose too. It separates academic work from the so-called "general public." Academics may battle among themselves over knowledge, but they have a common interest in maintaining the status of academic knowledge in the eyes of outsiders. If what academics do is too easy to

understand, then it becomes harder to justify comfortable salaries and conditions. This helps explain why most academics consider research to be more prestigious than teaching. Research is the creation of new knowledge, which adds to the lustre of the discipline. Most research helps maintain and raise the barriers against understanding by outsiders.

Brian White. "Why Academic Jargon Thrives." Published as "Secret Passwords at the Gate of Knowledge." *The Australian* (September 23, 1992) 16: http://www.bmartin.cc/pubs/92aust09.html

[276] Writing shortly after the death of Aaron Swartz, Maria Bustillos wrote,

> Another thing to consider is that academic writers are paid through salaries and grants; they aren't paid (not directly, anyway) for the publication of their work. The whole system of compensation for academic content is very different from commercial publishing. When you pay for a JSTOR article online, none of the money goes to the author, it goes to the publisher.

Although JSTOR claims to be non-profit, it is not. "Non-profit" is a tax designation, not an actual financial situation.
Maria Bustillos. "Was Aaron Swartz Stealing?" *The Awl* (August 3, 2011): http://www.theawl.com/2011/08/was-aaron-swartz-stealing

[277] Julian Fisher an M.D. is one of the many scientists disgusted with the behavior of corporate databases wrote of the cost of obtaining information that should be freely available,

> What are the costs in this new Internet age? As you might suspect, they have plummeted (an article I wrote several years ago here is helpful), to roughly 1/100 of what they were if you produce the article as an electronic document only rather than in print. Print is no longer necessary or even desired. Why, then, the $30-$50 financial firewall that you need to pay to see the article I want to show you? In part, tradition. In part, publishers keep doing what they do and the scholars do not complain much, since their subscriptions come through their grants or university libraries. But the

> libraries complain, individuals like all of you reading this should complain, and everyone in the developing world complains.

Julian Fisher, M.D. "Read This Academic Journal Article, but Prepare to Pay." *The Atlantic* (February 222, 2011): http://www.theatlantic.com/national/archive/2011/02/read-this-academic-journal-article-but-prepare-to-pay/71536/

[278] Laura Mckenna wrote of how JSTOR doesn't function for those outside designated institutions,

> Step back and think about this picture. Universities that created this academic content for free must pay to read it. Step back even further. The public -- which has indirectly funded this research with federal and state taxes that support our higher education system -- has virtually no access to this material, since neighborhood libraries cannot afford to pay those subscription costs. Newspapers and think tanks, which could help extend research into the public sphere, are denied free access to the material. Faculty members are rightly bitter that their years of work reaches an audience of a handful, while every year, 150 million attempts to read JSTOR content are denied every year.

Laura Mckenna. Op. cit.

[279] Tadween Editors reported that

> Most, if not all, researchers and university-level students are familiar with JSTOR. As a digital library of academic articles and books as well as primary sources, JSTOR is an essential portal for those conducting academic research. But access to JSTOR has been limited to libraries able to pay the hefty subscription fees, which could cost as much as $50,000 for a four-year institution (experiment with JSTOR's price calculator by clicking here). Thus while access to JSTOR and other academic libraries is afforded to some university students, some university libraries are having to forgo their subscriptions due to budget cuts. Individuals have the ability to purchase articles without a subscription; however, the price range for articles varies

depending on which journal or publication they are being purchased from.

Tadween Editors. "Despite New Program Promising Open Access, JSTOR Prices Remain a Concern. *Tadween Pubublishing* (January 22, 2013): http://tadweenpublishing.com/blogs/news/7215458-despite-new-program-promising-open-access-jstor-prices-remain-a-concern

[280] James Panero wrote of the changes faced by traditional art writers in the face of the digital challenges:

> It may be no coincidence that the writers and critics who have found success online have rarely been from the print world. The skill-set is quite different. On one side, you have the practitioners of a lost artisanal craft, like the carvers of scrimshaw or those who ferment small batch raw-milk cheese; the speed of the internet is anathema to their deliberative process. On the other, you have graphomanic-insomniac, egomaniacal headcases with something to prove and nothing to lose. My friends excepted. Aside from unfamiliarity, there is resentment among the old print crew for new media. The very technologies that print writers must employ to keep themselves in the conversation are the same ones that seem to be putting them out of business. Once writers for high-flight glossy publications could expect a dollar or more a word. Perhaps we dreamed of filing remembrances of literary friends from a cozy cottage in Normandy. Today we are considered fortunate if we get to pull the oars at *The Huffington Post* for some stale breadcrumbs and the pleasure of the lash. And while print fiddles, criticism burns, at least for those critics who hope to practice their craft in traditional publications for traditional pay. Read about any newspaper or magazine purge, and serious critical writers are always the first to go.

James Panero. "My Jerry Saltz Problem." *The New Criterion* (December 2010): http://www.newcriterion.com/articles.cfm/My-Jerry-Saltz-problem-6502

[281] In fact the sheer proliferation of art exhibitions on the international art scene have reduced art critics to cranking out low-level short-winded commentary, writing at the beck and call of the latest exhibition. The problem of value judgments by the critic becoming co-opted for the market is presented as a crisis.
Jeff Khonsary. *Judgment and Contemporary Art Criticism: Folio Series A* (Fillip Editions/Artspeak, 2010)

[282] This past April, not even a year ago, Simon Owens wrote about the fact that

> Harvard's Faculty Advisory Council sent a letter to the faculty concerning what it alleged was a crisis with its scholarly journal subscriptions… Though the letter's short-term impact was to inform the non-academic world of the growing tension between research libraries and journal publishers, many in the industry say its long-term effect lies in its list of recommendations for how to ameliorate the situation. Harvard implores its top researchers to "consider submitting articles to open-access journals" and to "consider resigning" from the editorial boards of journals that don't provide open-access offerings. Because an open-access journal allows anyone to easily and without cost read any of its published material, a large-scale migration to the platform would ease many of the financial burdens posed by subscription journals.

The letter read, in part, according to Owens,

> The letter reported an "untenable situation facing the Harvard Library" in which "many large journal publishers have made the scholarly communication environment fiscally unsustainable and academically restrictive." The letter revealed that Harvard is paying $3.75 million annually in journal subscriptions and that they make up "10% of all collection costs for everything the Library acquires." A few of the journals, it says, cost upward of $40,000 a year--each. "Prices for online content from two providers have increased by about 145% over the past six years, which far exceeds not only the consumer price index, but also the higher education and the library price indices." Its conclusion: "Major periodical subscriptions,

especially to electronic journals published by historically key providers, cannot be sustained." To underscore the weight of what Harvard had just done by releasing this letter, one blogger headlined his post, and "The wealthiest university on Earth can't afford its academic journal subscriptions."

Simon Owens. "Is the Academic Publishing industry on the Verge of Disruption?" *U.S. News Weekly.* July 23, 2012.
http://www.usnews.com/news/articles/2012/07/23/is-the-academic-publishing-industry-on-the-verge-of-disruption

[283] A brief description of a seminar on art criticism that took place in Holland in 2009, the organizers asked the question: "Can Art Criticism Survive the Digital Age?" As Bruce Sterling wrote,

> The digital revolution has profound effects on the status of art criticism. With newspapers and other printed media in decline, the traditional platform for critical reflection on art has shrunk or shifted towards electronic (web-based) media. At the same time the presence of art criticism on the internet is mostly limited to the "blog" – a format that celebrates an impressionistic, subjective and often populistic point of view. More substantial forms of web-based criticism are still rare to be found.

Bruce Sterling. "As Art Critics Face Sudden Planetary Extinction." *Beyond the Beyond* (November 18, 2009):
http://www.wired.com/beyond_the_beyond/2009/11/as-art-critics-face-sudden-planetary-extinction/

[284] For the recent Ai Weiwei exhibition at the Hirshorn, art writer, Anne Midgette was given a hefty 1631 words by *The Washington Post* to review "According to What?" That said, neither the *Post* nor the Hirshorn took advantage of the technology of the Internet by providing a guided video tour or the installations in the exhibition. Independent art critics with cell phone cameras can, given permission by the museum, could do this obvious and needed service to those who cannot attend.

Anne Midgette. "Ai Weiwei: Separating the Dissident from the Artist." *The Washington Post.* October 2012.
http://www.washingtonpost.com/entertainment/museums/separating-

the-dissident-from-the-artist/2012/10/04/4165e77c-0caa-11e2-bd1a-b868e65d57eb_story.html

[285] Marek Bartelik joined in the conversation of the "crisis" of art criticism,

> To return to the alleged death of art criticism, which is the subject of my sketchy reflections here, I would define today's "crisis" as a slow and open-ended testing time, rather than a fast and conclusive emergency event or an exit. Artists still make art, we are still writing about it. I would like to conclude by paraphrasing how the Paris-based Romanian writer Dumitru Tsepeneag commented on the statements regarding the "end of literature" during a panel discussion held at the New York Public Library on November 16, 2012: *"A procession of small men climbs a hill, one following another. The first man reaches the edge of a cliff but keeps walking; others follow him. A question: Why do the men follow the first one if they know that it is impossible to walk in the air, that going over the cliff means dying? The answer: Because they do not know that we have reached the end of [art criticism]."*

Marek Bartelik. "Is There a Crisis in Art Criticism? Response from Marek Bartelik." *The Brooklyn Rail. Critical Perspectives on Arts, Politics, and Culture* (December 10, 2012):
http://www.brooklynrail.org/2012/12/artseen/ldquois-there-a-crisis-in-art-criticismrdquo-response-from-marek-bartelik

[286] It should also be pointed out that as long as women remain bound to the traditional routes of publication, they continue to be disadvantaged in the colleges and universities. Despite the increasing numbers of women on faculties, they publish less than their male counterparts, at least that was perspective of a 2012 article in *The Chronicle of Higher Education*. The article noted the fact that women published a quarter of their male counterparts but got bogged down in whether or not women as authors were listed first or second, while ignoring the huge disparity which was attributed to women being distracted by family. Author Robin Wilson reported,

> ...studies show that women spend less time on research and more time on teaching and committee work. And it is often research and publishing, which require sustained

attention, that suffer when women devote time to caring for young children.

As more women earn Ph.D.'s and take faculty jobs, though, and as the gap between the number of women and men in academe narrows, scholars have begun thinking about whether anything can or should be done about gender-based differences that remain in publishing, hiring, promotion, and pay. Do those differences result from choices women make, scholars wonder, or from discrimination?

Surely, if one understands that publication equals symbolic power which translates into real power, then one would have to consider gender discrimination as a possibility.

Robin Wilson. "The Hard Numbers Behind Scholarly Publishing's Gender Gap." *The Chronicle of Higher Education*. October 22, 2012: http://chronicle.com/article/The-Hard-Numbers-Behind/135236/

[287] An Australian scholar, Dave Glance, wrote about the Long Tail in relation to academia,

> The long tail in academic terms represents a whole range of people who produce a modest amount of research around an almost equally large number of research topics. The benefits of this are that the range of research that is carried out by a university is broad and diverse. This should factor into the overall quality of the teaching that the university carries out, which is also usually broad in coverage. It also factors into the potential impact and social engagement ability that the university is able to bring to bear. From the perspective of a university worried about performance in ranking or government assessment exercises, the issue is not having a tail in the first place but that the tail is not sufficiently long and is related to the number of staff that are employed. The answer here is not how to get rid of people in the tail or somehow to convert them into superstar performers, but to extend the tail by various means. Two ways of doing this are already employed by most universities although they probably don't realise how important they are. The

first involves increasing collaboration with other academics in other universities. The second is by increasing the number of people who can publish, use the university by-line and not cost anything, e.g. visitors and other adjunct appointments.

Dave Glance. "The Long Tail of Academic Publishing and Why it isn't a Bad Thing." *The Conversation* (July 8, 2012): http://theconversation.com/the-long-tail-of-academic-publishing-and-why-it-isnt-a-bad-thing-8126

[288] Thomas H. P. Gould wrote a very interesting chapter on academia and The Long Tail idea. He speculated on the future of publishing based combining The Long Tail with Open Access:

> …new journals have been generated as solely online journals by off-campus nongovernmental organizations (NGO), on-campus interest groups, university committees, academic departments, and individual researchers. This shift defines more than just a change in journal ownership, but a significant redefinition in the culture of publishing. Given the new economics of online publishing, a new journal will not need to appeal to a broad base of academia to generate a sufficient number of "readers" or to require subscriptions. Taken as a pattern of publishing, these new journals might fall more to the right side of Anderson's Long Tail---small readership, low cost, and self-defined. This trend is driven, at least in part, by the increasing number of articles generated by an increasing number of researchers worldwide.

Gould then discussed what would happen now one of the criteria for "quality," then number of citations is no longer relevant.

> This "impact" factor citation rating method comes with its own set of problems not mentioned in previous research. Given the likelihood that researchers will gravitate more and more toward open access publications to find research information, citation rates of articles published within anything other than fully open access journals are likely to fall, not because these journals are of lesser quality, but simply based on ease

of access. Thus, citation of a journal would not reflect on the value of the journal itself, but whether it is an open access or even slightly closed publication. Add to this that the vast amount of research is unavailable online, specifically works published prior to 1980.

After discussing traditional peer review (described as "biased," "inept," "scorned," "elitist," "racist," "rotten," and prone to "competition," and "jealousy") and citing numerous studies that have exposed the inherent flaws in the system, Gould concluded the chapter by writing about the future of peer review and online independent journals,

> Two forces drive this shift to online publishing. First, the economics of posting versus printing are clear and persuasive to any agency or group funding a journal. But second and equally persuasive, is the preference that academics---especially younger academics---have shown for online accessible research. In fact, it is this younger researcher who is making it clear that all research must be accessible without even a hint of requiring a modest registration or logon. Tenure committees are struggling to establish new standards as well as evaluate new born-online journals. By and large---at least within mass communication faculty---less than one in six professors believes his school tenure committee places any value on publishing that appears in an online-only journal. As the rules shift in both journal evaluation and status, and in the peer-reviews process itself, research appearing online (and only online) will become more acceptable.

Thomas H. P. Gould. *Creating the Academic Commons: Guidelines for Learning, Teaching, and Research* (Plymouth, Scarecrow Press, 2011) 132, 137, 150.

[289] William Grimes reported in 1996 (!) of the crisis that apparently was allowed to continue discussed in a seminar called "Invisible Ink: Art Criticism and a Vanishing Public." The title of the seminar referred to an essay written by Donald Kuspit, which was later printed in *Redeeming Art: Critical Reveries* (Skyhorse Publishing, 2000). This book is not available in a digital form and hence will not be read.

William Grimes. "Art Critics are Critical of Each Other's Criticism." *The New York Times* (May 18, 1996):

http://www.nytimes.com/1996/05/18/arts/art-critics-are-critical-of-each-other-s-criticism.html

[290] *Culturebot* a really good Web publication presented an interesting article on the 21st century critic by theater arts writer, Andy Horwitz,

> At this point I would like to re-emphasize the importance of the critical voice. As mentioned previously, since the beginning *Culturebot* has consciously worked to cultivate a critical voice that embraces the subjectivity and informality of the Internet while aspiring towards intellectual rigor. That being said, we do not aspire to be academics. The function of the 21st Century critic is not only to mediate between artist and audience but between academic and audience as well. At the moment the bulk of thoughtful writing about contemporary performance happens in academic settings or esoteric industry publications. It is frequently jargon-laden and obscure, alienating all but the most deeply invested of audience members. Theory, of course, is a vital and essential component of a healthy arts ecosystem, but the biggest challenge facing contemporary performance today is not a lack of people with Masters degrees and Doctorates exploring theory but rather a perceived lack of relevance and a noticeable lack of audience. The Performing Arts in America generally is suffering from audience attrition and the perception of irrelevance due, in no small part, to wider cultural assumptions around what the performing arts are and who they are for. We are now presented with the extraordinary opportunity to look deeply into the origins and potential of live performance, revisit our assumptions about spectatorship and rebuild the arts institution.

Andy Horwitz. "Reframing the Crisis for the 21st Century" Dramaturgy, Advocacy and Engagement. *Culturebot* (September 5, 2012): http://www.culturebot.org/2012/09/13258/re-framing-the-critic-for-the-21st-century-dramaturgy-advocacy-and-engagement/

[291] One of the more recent books on Mallarmé is by Roger Pearson. *Stéphane Mallarmé* (Reaktion Books Ltd, 2010)

[292] Rosemary Lloyd discussed Mallarmé's circle of friends and explained how the Parisian writers wrote about and supported each other. Rosemary Lloyd. *Mallarmé: The Poet and His Circle* (Cornell University Press, 1999)

[293] In starting her book on neo-Impressionism, Martha Ward noted that in the late twentieth century, postmodernist theory and the feminist critique of the gender exclusionary nature of the *avant-garde* seemed to bring about the demise of the *avant-garde*. However, Ward continued,

> ...now is a time when specific avant-gardes can be reexamined for the ways in which they were, in fact, embedded in the conditions of particular and localized historical moments and produced as much by a loss of a sense of purpose as by a newly discovered mission of progress.

Martha Ward. *Pissarro, Neo-Impressionism, and the Spaces of the Avant-Garde* (Chicago: The University of Chicago Press, 1996) 2.

[294] The enmity of Gérôme towards Manet in the name of tradition and the importance of following the rules of the Salon were discussed by Claudia Mitchell in "The Damaged Mirror. Gérôme's Narrative Technique and the Fractures of French History." *Reconsidering Gérôme.* Edited by Scott Allan and Mary Morton (J. Paul Getty Trust, 2010) 92 -105.

[295] As Roberta Smith commented on the fascination of the Impressionist with fashion, which was in and of itself, an *avant-garde* "painter of modern life" stance:

> The tension between the innovative and the staid — the Impressionists using clothes as occasions to explore paint; the loyal opposition focusing on them as things in themselves — is the show's main engine. The artists from both sides of the aisle knew, borrowed from and competed with one another, formulating together a new combination of genre painting and portraiture, catching their subjects in the moment, yet often in a full-length, slightly larger-than-life scale.

Roberta Smith. "The Cross-Dressing of Art and Couture. Impressionism, Fashion and Modernity at the Met." (February 21, 2013) *The New York*

Times http://www.nytimes.com/2013/02/22/arts/design/impressionism-fashion-and-modernity-at-the-met.html?pagewanted=all

The recent exhibition of Impressionism and Fashion, organized between France and America situates the vanguard aspects of Impressionism in the popular culture, as exemplified by fashion.
Sylvie Thomas. "Impressionism and Fashion, a Joint French and US Exhibition (September 2012)" *France Diplomatie* : http://www.diplomatie.gouv.fr/en/country-files/united-states/events-3285/article/impressionism-and-fashion-a-joint-17601

[296] Occasionally a book on art criticism emerges and one of the more recent is a collection of essays on the "crisis" in the field. Michael Shreyach, the lead essayist, asserted,

> An assertion: the central aim of art criticism is conservative: it means to preserve, even to perpetuate, the latent or manifest possibilities of understanding that threaten to disappear from historical encounters. But not in any naïve way: an appeal to preserve "original" or "authentic" experience is bound to the perspective of the writer, whose inventive task it is to convert that experience into one with value for those with other perspectives, in the present. This is a performatiave task, the significance of which should be judged not only by how adequately the writer attends to his or her objects, or how well the piece of writing conforms to the conventions governing the production and publication of art criticism.

It is interesting to note that the paragraph, written very recently, assumes that art criticism is secondary to works of art and that the text must "conform" to the "governing" of "the production and publication of art criticism." Shreyach then quoted James Elkins from an earlier book of 2003, *What Happened to Art Criticism?* in which Elkins argued that too much art criticism is being written.
Michael Shreyach. *The State of Art Criticism* (Routledge, 2008) 6.

[297] In the winter of 2012, columnist Christian Viveros-Faune wrote,

> There is an epistemic crisis of historical proportions everywhere, so of course this affects art and art criticism. We went from an age of postmodern relativism to

recently recognizing that particularly Nietzschean strain of anti-universalist thinking for what it is: cultural conservatism in a countercultural garb. In the words of Fredric Jameson, postmodernism *is* the cultural logic of late capitalism. Crisis, therefore, is bound to be one of the chief experiences communicated by criticism today, both in art and in its own, far more fragile practice. I don't believe judgment should be the primary value of art criticism, but it remains—like writing itself or informed thought—a sine qua non for the entire discipline. Thirty years of cultural relativism have not necessarily begotten a more equanimous, less tendentious kind of criticism. Instead, it's produced both a kind of judgment that shelters beneath a hermetic crust of jargon and unintelligibility, and a more generalized atrophying of critical faculties. It's a good critic's job to address those and other manifestations of the crisis in criticism and in art, while always keeping an eye peeled to culture's larger narratives. Just like in our present day, they are always related.

Christian Viveros-Faune. "Re: Art Criticism Today." *The Brooklyn Rail. Critical Perspectives on Arts, Politics, and Culture* (December 10, 2012): http://www.brooklynrail.org/2012/12/artseen/re-art-criticism-today-christian

[298] David Carrier discussed the mode of writing employed by Baudelaire in the *Salon of 1846*,

> The *bourgeois* are the majority, and so what they do is just. They are *"les amis naturels des arts,"* and any book not addressed to this majority is *"un sot livre."*

David Carrier. *Baudelaire and the Origins of Modernist Painting* (The Pennsylvania State University Press, 1996) 12.

[299] Entitled "Enlightenment for Children," Benjamin's broadcasts could be heard between 1929 and 1932. These broadcasts have been preserved and can be heard at the Internet Archive: http://archive.org/details/BenjaminOnTheRadio_420

[300] In his book on art criticism, which takes the "crisis" approach, Raphael Rubinstein remarked that art historians don't read art criticism, in other

words the historians ignore the very foundations that their descendants will use to discuss the art of their ancestors' time.
Raphael Rubinstein. *A Critical Mess: Art Critics on the State of their Practice* (Hard Press Editions, 2007)

[301] Critic, Noël Carroll would disagree with me. In his recent book he precisely stated that what distinguishes art criticism from other forms of writing is that it concerns itself with the object and evaluates the work of art.
Noël Carroll. *On Criticism. Thinking in Action* (Routledge, 2009)

[302] Charles Baudelaire. *The Painter of Modern Life and Other Essays.* Translated and edited by Jonathan Mayne (Phaidon Press): http://www.columbia.edu/itc/architecture/ockman/pdfs/dossier_4/Baudelaire.pdf

[303] David Carrier wrote of the anachronistic question of why Baudelaire wrote of Guys instead of Manet, considered today to be a major artist:

> And since there is precious little written evidence about Manet, art historians easily imagine connections between the men. Capable of generously receiving the greatness of Wagner and Delacroix, a passionate admirer of Poe, Baudelaire chose Guys, not Manet…how surprising that after in 1846 anticipating Manet's theme, painting of modern life, Baudelaire did not publicly admire his art.

Carrier then argues against T. J. Clark's attempt to link the contents of this essay to Manet's paintings. According to Carrier, the purpose of the essay is not to discuss Manet but to present modernism.

> …it is disappointing that he never discuses Manet's *La Musique aux Tuileries*, which depicts him…it is embarrassing that a great critic failed to see value of the work of a friend.

David Carrier. *High Art. Charles Baudelaire and the Origins of Modernist Painting* (The Pennsylvania State University Press, 1996) 51, 52.

[304] Roberto Calasso eloquently makes the argument that Baudelaire's choice of Constantine Guys was perverse and deliberate, done to make a

point about where a culture first expresses itself—among the crowd, not with artists.
Roberto Calasso. *La Folie Baudelaire* (Farrar, Straus, and Giroux, 2013)

[305] From the movie script, Rene Richard recites,

> Everybody wants to get on the Van Gogh boat. There's no trip so horrible that someone won't take it. The idea of the unrecognized genius slaving away in a garret is deliciously foolish one. We must credit the life of Vincent Van Gogh for really sending this myth into orbit. I mean, how many pictures did he sell, one? He couldn't give them away. He has to be the most modern artist, but everybody hated him. He was so ashamed of his life that the rest of our history will be contribution to Van Gogh's neglect. No one wants to be part of a generation that ignores another like Van Gogh. In this town, one is at the mercy of the recognition factor. One's public appearance is absolute. Part of the artist's job is to get the work where I will see it. I consider myself a metaphor on the public.

Lech Majewski and John Bowe, et. al. *Basquiat* (1996)

[306] Jeanne S. M. Willette. *The Writing of Cubism. The Construction of a Discourse, 1910-1914* (AHS Publishing, 2012)

[307] Beth S. Gersh-Nesic, Editor. *André Salmon on French Modern Art* (Cambridge, Cambridge University Press, 2005)

[308] My mentor during my student years was Edward Fry, who collected some of the early writings of the Cubist critics. After a distinguished career, he died young of a heart attack one year before I received my Ph.D. Roberta Smith. "Edward F. Fry, 56, A Historian Devoted to 20th Century Art." *The New York Times* (April 21, 1992):
http://www.nytimes.com/1992/04/21/arts/edward-f-fry-56-a-historian-devoted-to-20th-century-art.html

Edward Fry. *Cubism* (Oxford University Press, 1978)

[309] Any critic who ventures into a territory without shape and who attempts to construct it with the available tools must await the judgment of history on his or her efforts. With the benefit of hindsight, an

astonishing amount of ink has been spilled on analyzing Clement Greenberg and Harold Rosenberg. While the former lived long enough to have his words parsed as carefully as he parsed paintings decades earlier, the latter did not. The great Mieke Bal dissected Rosenberg and Greenberg in "Art History and its Theories." *The Art Bulletin* (Volume LXXVIII, Number 1, March 1996):
http://publications.ias.edu/sites/default/files/Lavin_CrisisArtHistory_1996.pdf

[310] Clement Greenberg. "Modernist Painting." *Forum Lectures* (Washington, D.C.: Voice of America), 1960; *Arts Yearbook* 4, 1961 (unrevised); *Art and Literature,* Spring 1965 (slightly revised); *The New Art: A Critical Anthology,* ed. Gregory Battcock, 1966; *Peinture-cahiers théoriques,* no. 8-9, 1974 (titled "La *peinture moderniste"); Esthetics Contemporary,* ed. Richard Kostelanetz, 1978; *Modern Art and Modernism: A Critical Anthology,* ed. Francis Frascina and Charles Harrison, 1982; *Clement Greenberg: The Collected Essays and Criticism vol. 4,* ed. John O'Brian, 1993:
http://cas.uchicago.edu/workshops/wittgenstein/files/2007/10/Greenbergmodpaint.pdf

[311] Clement Greenberg. "American Type Painting," 1955, 1958:
http://www.scribd.com/doc/54185848/Greenberg-American-Type-Painting-1955-58

[312] Harold Rosenberg. "American Action Painters." *ARTnews* (Volume 51, September 1952):
http://books.google.com/books?id=aD3azMow90MC&pg=PA55&lpg=PA55&dq=harold+rosenberg+the+american+action+painters&source=bl&ots=Q15_XPhajr&sig=g4OUVrfOtWnvuyzrEqxHn6G3y0s&hl=en&sa=X&ei=mNOjUdKCAcyoqwHAiYHADQ&ved=0CE4Q6AEwBQ#v=onepage&q=harold%20rosenberg%20the%20american%20action%20painters&f=false

[313] Critic James Panero wrote of Greenberg and Rosenberg whose writings were the basis of a 2008 exhibition at the Jewish Museum:

> The writers who defined the parameters of this criticism were Clement Greenberg (1909-1994) and Harold Rosenberg (1906-1978). Greenberg & Rosenberg were like Ali & Frazier. They made up the protagonists in art criticism's fight of the century—a Grapple in the Big Apple between personal and professional adversaries. It was also, undoubtedly, one of the few fights in art

criticism to make it into the record books. Yet as the passions of their engagement have dissipated, and the art world has moved on to largely financial concerns, the Greenberg-Rosenberg rivalry has, in hindsight, come to seem of a piece. I say this as someone who has always been more in the Greenberg camp. Greenberg and Rosenberg were diametrically opposed in their interpretations of Abstract Expressionism, but each interpretation was correct in its way. Their theories were not mutually exclusive, but instead opposite ends of a kind of dialectic. Through two forceful positions argued before the backdrop of Abstract Expressionism, in opposing language, together they laid out the full definition of modern art.

James Panero. "The Critical Moment. Abstract Expressionism's Dueling Duo." *Humanities* (Volume 29, Number 4, July/August 2008): http://www.neh.gov/humanities/2008/julyaugust/feature/the-critical-moment

[314] Critic Peter Schjeldahl wrote of the small art neighborhood that would be called The New York School:

> The hamlet-sized population, concentrated in the blocks northeast of Washington Square, already outnumbered the scene of the previous decade, when all the major styles of Abstract Expressionism coalesced—in a blur of eureka moments, studio by studio—amid poverty and obscurity, irradiated by passion. (For example, Franz Kline, a middling Greenwich Village Expressionist, leaped to a mighty style of frozen gestures in black and white.) As usually happens, the theories that supposedly informed the creative breakthroughs—set forth in Rosenberg's book "The Tradition of the New" (1959) and in Greenberg's "Art and Culture" (1961)—were worked out after the fact. Also predictably, commercial success, popular imagination, and the reactive originalities of new artists wrenched the movement from the critics' shepherding grasp. But the impact of Rosenberg and Greenberg in their heyday was as compelling as that of tribal shamans.

Peter Schjeldahl. "Action Figures." *The New Yorker* (May 26, 2008): http://www.newyorker.com/arts/critics/artworld/2008/05/26/080526craw_artworld_schjeldahl

[315] Art critics who seek these new opportunities need to be aware of the new responsibilities that writing on the Web brings. Decisions have to be made: do you want to be part of a virtual "staff" on an e-art publication? Do you want to be an editor who accepts submissions or the sole proprietor of your own Website? On one hand, the low cost of the Web makes it possible to fund your own work and to receive all the benefits but the Web makes incessant demands for which you must be prepared. The art writer must either be prepared to manage people or to manage him or herself.

[316] Explaining the demise of *Artnet Magazine*, Michael Pepi wrote,

> Anyone sensitive to the deterioration that has befallen the discipline of art criticism can examine *Artnet*'s history in an effort to understand the current shift in the critical landscape. Writing art criticism has for generations been a questionable career choice. There exists the constant pressure to write art news, which, may masquerade as criticism, though it is markedly different from the historically sensitive commentary produced in and around the academy. Increased competition via the internet, as well as the inherent fluidity of its publishing, has encouraged and rewarded many in the art writing field to migrate toward a content more befitting the medium. *Artnet*'s writing was a laboratory for the development of this trend. Even as the publication continued to advocate thoughtful writing, gossip and fetishistic auction price reporting held court under the glib umbrella of arts press. Like many of its peers in art criticism, *Artnet* failed to internalize the ways that digital content ecosystems, reader attention spans and perceptions of authority are eroding the notion of the professional, institutionalized critic. As the discourse in the visual arts has shifted, partially toward the agency of the curator, the notion of the paid critic—who "merely" writes—has for its only rational basis a given writer's scholarly knowledge and ability to contextualize the pluralistic contemporary art market, museum exhibitions, biennials and fair circuit. The new secondary art writer

that offers such contextualization and generic narrative in the journalistic mode need not be held in high academic esteem—in fact this is often a hindrance. These realities are, for the most part, outside *Artnet*'s control, though they are worth considering because they speak to larger issues that the crisis in criticism has faced *vis-à-vis* the web. If after *Artnet* we fully recognize our transitional phase in the production and reception of content through shifting media landscapes, then those assessing the crisis in criticism ought to consider the challenges posed by the Internet, as opposed to blindly assuming that it is a one-size-fits-all emancipatory force for good.

Michael Pepi. "The Demise of *Artnet Magazine* and the Crisis in Criticism." *Artwrit* (September 2012): http://www.artwrit.com/article/the-demise-of-artnet-magazine-and-the-crisis-in-criticism/

[317] Art critic Jerry Salz wrote of how the old local art world and its gallery shows is fading in the face of international art fairs. As Salz observed,

> ...the blood sport of taste is playing out in circles of hedge-fund billionaires and professional curators, many of whom claim to be anti-market. There used to be shared story lines of contemporary art: the way artists developed, exchanged ideas, caromed off each other's work, engaged with their critics. Now no one knows the narrative; the thread has been lost. Shows go up but don't seem to have consequences, other than sales or no sales. Nothing builds off much else. Art can't get traction. A jadedness appears in people who aren't jaded. Artists enjoying global-market success avoid showing in New York for fear any critical response will interfere with sales. (As if iffy international art stars could have their juggernauts stalled by a measly bad review or two. A critic can only dream.) Ask any artist: They're all starting to wonder what's going on.

Jerry Salz. "Salz on the Death of the Gallery Show." *New York Magazine* (April 8, 2013) reprinted on line on *Vulture*: http://www.vulture.com/2013/03/saltz-on-the-death-of-art-gallery-shows.html

[318] There is a very interesting 2010 series of videos on the decline of art criticism in print media, sponsored by 5Across: Art Criticism in the Digital Age. As Mark Glaser commented,

> As newspapers and magazines have cut staff in the shift to digital, arts critics find themselves with less sure footing when it comes to a full-time staff position. According to a recent article in the Australian, 65 full-time film critics have lost jobs on American newspapers and magazines since 2006. Can't local newspapers just use syndicated reviews for movies shown nationally? And isn't the Internet giving many more critics outside of traditional publications the chance to shine?

Mark Glaser. "5Across: Arts Criticism in the Digital Age." *Mediashift*. PBS: http://www.pbs.org/mediashift/2010/06/5across-arts-criticism-in-the-digital-age180

[319] The idea that only a few people should be allowed to publish is a rather narrow and provincial view of the intellects outside of the Ivory Tower. Literary critic Stephen Burns had a higher opinion of the educated public:

> …the commercialization of the Internet wove a network out of those minds, building a kind of massive neural web, a brain by turns conflicted, noisy, urgent. The Internet calls people out of their loneliness to create electronic selves perhaps more naked or strident than the fuzzy, compromised "I" that moves ghostlike through its everyday routines and disagreements. A solitary reader, brooding over an obscure contemporary novel, or slowly puzzling out a page of "Finnegans Wake," is suddenly not so solitary. Amid the network of networks there is always another reader, an improvised community into which she can merge and make visible her invented self.

Stephen Burns. "Why Criticism Matters. Beyond the Critic as Cultural Arbiter." *The New York Times* (December 31, 2010): http://www.nytimes.com/2011/01/02/books/review/Burn-t-web.html

[320] Like Website maintenance, the outgo of money is relatively minor but it is non-ending. If you have committed to write, your Website must work efficiently and be easy to use, the site needs to be cared for, and you must write---your readers are waiting and they are a fickle and demanding lot

and they will move on and abandon you if you let them down. In contrast to receiving occasional assignments or commissions, or writing a scholarly article and working on it for years, the art critic becomes an art writer and writers write. You go from writing occasionally to writing constantly. If the art critic makes the transition to art writer the stress shifts to "writer" and because of the incessant demands of the Web, writing improves. That's the good news; the bad news is that you will have no life.

[321] Jacques Ellul. *The Technological Society*. Translated by John Wilkinson (New York: Alfred A. Knopf, 1964) 14.

[322] Someone who has been writing on this topic for over twenty years is Carol Becker, who has written most recently *Thinking in Place: Art Action and Cultural Production* (Paradigm Publishers, 2009) and in her 2003 book, *Surpassing the Spectacle: Global Transformations and the Changing Politics*, she wrote eloquently of how artists could become public intellectuals,

> Artists have sensibilities that are distinctive and important to the well-being of society. Were artists taken seriously within U.S. society, were they sought out for their opinions and concerns and recognized as having rare skills, some of which are about how to see the world, they would enter their chosen profession with a much greater sense of confidence and self-esteem. Were society ready to accept them into its fold as fully participating citizens whose function, like that of intellectuals, is to remain on the margins asking the difficult questions, resisting assimilation and socialization in the traditional ways, refusing to accept the simplistic moral values that reflect the present political climate, there would be a great deal of psychic relief for artists.

Carol Becker. *Surpassing the Spectacle: Global Transformations and the Changing Politics* (Rowman & Littlefield Publishers, Inc. 2002) 13.
More recently Becker, the Deal of Columbia University School of the Arts gave a Seminar on "Artists as Public Intellectuals: Engaging Micro-Utopian Practice," part of a larger question, "How are Artists Redefining Their Role in the 21st Century?":
https://www.facebook.com/events/195783367213489/

[323] Among the thousands of TED talks, ten pages are tagged "art," but the few of these speakers are from the world of fine arts. They include Thelma Golden, Thomas B. Campbell, Tom Shannon, Olafur Eliasson, Maurizio

Seracini, Alwar Balasubramaniam, and so on. Surely there are more speakers on the fine arts but this is the extent of a search through TED talks: http://www.ted.com/talks/tags/name/art/page/1

[324] In 2006, Jodi Kushins wrote about artists as public intellectuals and recommended,

> My review of literature on public intellectualism in conjunction with analysis of socially-and politically-engaged artists revealed characteristics that should be cultivated by those invested in educating artists to "imagine themselves as citizens within the world - not only the art world" (Becker, 2000, p. 239). Many of these traits can be fostered through reforms of extant educational and artistic apparatuses. For example, art students should be encouraged to develop *interdisciplinary curiosity and a capacity to critically synthesize information from disparate sources within and outside the arts*. This might be fostered through explicit integration of studies in, and research practices derived from, the liberal arts and social sciences with projects conceived in the studio. Students and faculty alike cite disconnect between these, so-called, "creative" and "cognitive" areas (Mayer, 1994). Students should be provided with structured exposure to and discussion of works that demonstrate inter- and intra-disciplinary complexity. Likewise, art students need practice *communicating through visual, oral, and written media* and *identifying opportunities to interact with audiences*. During critiques, artists and art students should be encouraged to imagine and respond to their intended and likely audiences. They should contemplate and plan for how these individuals might engage with their work, in other words, they should consider how their work may or may not communicate to and through different viewers. This does not mean artists should attend to the lowest common denominator. Rather, they should consider building pathways into the work through its formal qualities or didactics like wall texts and artist's statements. Essays by Carol Becker, Henry Giroux, Maxine Greene, John Dewey and others who write about the pedagogical aspects of art can be incorporated into course assignments to encourage students to consider

the pedagogical functions of art in society. Ultimately, artists should consider how their artistic and discursive statements help or hinder viewer engagement and appreciation.

Jodi Kushins. "Recognizing Artists as Public Intellectuals: A Pedagogical Imperative." *CultureWork. A Periodic Broadside for Arts and Culture Workers* (Volume 10, Number 10, May 2006):
http://pages.uoregon.edu/culturwk/culturework34.html

[325] Simon Schama has his detractors, because he makes art accessible to the masses, and Simon Schama has his supporters, because he makes art accessible to the masses. As Ben Dowell wrote,

> Few people have summarised these criticisms better than the Sunday Times' Adrian Gill who took a swipe at Schama's 2006 series *Power of Art*: "The point of these authored, visually clotted documentaries is really to be infomercials for instant coffee table tomes". And yes, it is true that even Schama's premium brand of TV history cannot help skating over the deeper complexities of historical truth. But while it's always tempting to point a mocking finger at a man with a plum job as Columbia professor of art history and history, and lucrative TV contracts coming out of his ears, I love him and make a beeline for him every time. I'd go so far as to say he is easily Britain's best arts presenter.

Ben Dowell. "Simon Schama: TV Dumber-Down or Simply the Greatest?" *The Guardian* (June 28, 2012):
http://www.guardian.co.uk/culture/tvandradioblog/2012/jun/28/simon-schama-greatest-history-presentation

[326] One of the great public intellectuals, the late Edward Said, combined his erudition and his political passion in his lifetime cause as an anti-colonialist and as a pubic intellectual. Shortly before his death, Said wrote,

> All of us should therefore operate today with some notion of very probably reaching much larger audiences than any we could have conceived of even a decade ago, although the chances of retaining that audience are by the same token quite chancy. This is not simply a matter

> of optimism of the will; it is the very nature of writing today. This makes it very difficult for the writers to take common assumptions between them and their audiences for granted, or to assume that references and allusions are going to be understood immediately...But writing in this expanded new space strangely does have a further unusually risky consequence, which is to be encouraged to say things that are either completely opaque or completely transparent, and it one has any sense of the intellectual and political vocation...it should of course be the latter rather than the former. But then, transparent, simple, clear prose presents its own challenges, since the ever-present danger is that one call fall into the misleadingly simple neutrality of a journalistic Word-English idiom that is indistinguishable from CNN or USA-Today prose. The quandary is a real one, whether in the end to repel readers...or to win readers over in a style that perhaps resembles too closely the mind-set one is trying to expose and dismiss.

Edward Said. "The Public Role of Writers and Intellectuals." Edited Helen Small. *The Public Intellectual* (Oxford: Blackwell Publishing, 2002) 28.: http://cicac.tru.ca/readings/edward_said.pdf

[327] As a radical standpoint, perspective, position, 'the politics of location' necessarily calls those of us who would participate in the formation of counter-hegemonic cultural practice to identify the spaces where we begin the process of re-vision.

Later on hooks continued,

> For me this space of radical openness is a margin - a profound edge. Locating oneself there is difficult yet necessary. It is not a 'safe' place. One is always at risk. One needs a community of resistance.

bell hooks. "Choosing the Margin as a Space of Radical Openness." *Yearnings: Race, Gender and Cultural Politics* (South End Press, 1999) 203-209.

BIBLIOGRAPHY

Books

Allen, Graham. *Intertextuality* (New York: Routledge, 2000, 2011)

Roland Barthes (Routledge, 2003)

Anderson, Chris. *The Long Tail: Why the Future of Business is Selling Less of More* (New York: Hyperion. 2006)

Sapnar Ankerson, Megan. "Web Industries, Economies, Aesthetics: Mapping the Look of the Web in the Dot-Com Era." in Niels Brügger. *Web History* (New York: Peter Lang Publishing Company, 2010)

Araya, Daniel, Yana Breindl, Tessa J. Houghton. *Nexus: New Intersections in Internet Research* (New York, Peter Lang Publishing, Inc., 2011)

Bailey, Jr., Charles A. *Transforming Scholarly Publishing through Open Access: A Bibliography.* (Creative Commons, 2010)

Bardini, Thierry. *Bootstrapping: Douglas Engelbart, Coevolution, and the Origins of Personal Computing* (Stanford: Stanford University Press, 2000)

Barthes Roland. Roland Barthes. *Camera Lucida: Reflections on Photography*. Translated by Richard Howard (McMillian, 1982)

S/Z. Translated by Richard Miller (Farrar, Straus, and Giroux, Inc. 1974)

Jean Baudrillard. *Simulacra and Simulations*. Translated by Shelia Faria (University of Michigan Press, 1995):
http://www9.georgetown.edu/faculty/irvinem/theory/baudrillard-simulacra_and_simulation.pdf

Baudelaire, Charles. *The Painter of Modern Life and Other Essays*. Translated and edited by Jonathan Mayne (Phaidon Press):
http://www.columbia.edu/itc/architecture/ockman/pdfs/dossier_4/Baudelaire.pdf

Beck, Timo. *Web 2.0: User-Generated Content in Online Communities. A Theoretical and Empirical Investigation of its Determinants.* (Hamburg: Diplomica Verlag GmbH, 2007)

Becker, Carol. *Surpassing the Spectacle: Global Transformations and the Changing Politics* (Rowman & Littlefield Publishers, Inc. 2002)

"How are Artists Redefining Their Role in the 21st Century?": https://www.facebook.com/events/195783367213489/

Benkler, Yochai. "Designing Cooperative Systems for Knowledge Production: An Initial Synthesis from Experimental Economics" in *Making and Unmaking Intellectual Property: Creative Production in Legal and Cultural Perspective.* Edited by Mario Biagioli, Peter Jaszi, Martha Woodmansee (Chicago: University of Chicago Press, 2011)

The Wealth of Networks. How Social Production Transforms Markets and Freedom (Yale University Press, 2006)

Bentham, Jeremy. PANOPTICON; OR THE INSPECTION-HOUSE: CONTAINING THE IDEA OF A NEW PRINCIPLE OF CONSTRUCTION APPLICABLE TO ANY SORT OF ESTABLISHMENT, IN WHICH PERSONS OF ANY DESCRIPTION ARE TO BE KEPT UNDER INSPECTION; AND IN PARTICULAR TO PENITENTIARY-HOUSES, PRISONS, HOUSES OF INDUSTRY, WORK-HOUSES, POOR-HOUSES, LAZARETTOS, MANUFACTORIES, HOSPITALS, MAD-HOUSES, AND SCHOOLS: WITH A PLAN OF MANAGEMENT ADAPTED TO THE PRINCIPLE: IN A SERIES OF LETTERS, WRITTEN IN THE YEAR 1787, FROM CRECHEFF IN WHITE RUSSIA. TO A FRIEND IN ENGLAND *BY JEREMY BENTHAM, OF LINCOLN'S INN, ESQUIRE.* http://luci.ics.uci.edu/websiteContent/weAreLuci/biographies/faculty/djp3/LocalCopy/PANOPTICON.pdf

Bernstein, R. J. *The New Constellation: The Ethical-Political Horizons of Modernity/Postmodernity* (MIT Press. 1992)

Bishop, Ryan, Editor. *Baudrillard Now: Current Perspective in Baudrillard Studies* (New York: Polity Press, 2009)

Bollier, David. "Introduction." *Silent Theft. The Private Plunder of Our Common Weatlh.* (Routledge, 2003) 3-4.

Briggs, Asa and Peter Burke. *Social History of the Media: From Gutenberg to the Internet* (Polity Press, 2009)

Bruns, Alex. *Blogs, Wikipedia, Second Life, and Beyond. From Production to Produsage* (New York: Peter Lang Publishing, Include, 2008)

Bourdieu, Pierre. *Homo Academicus* (Stanford: Stanford University Press, 1984)
    "Outline of the Theory of Practice. Structures and the Habitus" reprinted in *Practicing History. New Directions in Historical Writing after the Linguistic Turn.* Edited by Gabrielle M. Spiegel (New York: Routledge, 2005)

    "The 'Berobed' and the Invention of the State" in *The State Nobility: Elite Schools in the Field of Power* (Stanford: Stanford University Press, 1989, 1996)

    "The Forms of Capital" in *Economic Sociology.* Edited by Nicole Woosley Biggart (Malden, Mass.: Blackwell Publishers Inc. 2002)

Calasso, Roberto. *La Folie Baudelaire* (Farrar, Straus, and Giroux, 2013)

Carrier, David. *Baudelaire and the Origins of Modernist Painting* (The Pennsylvania State University Press, 1996)

Cortese, Julianne. *Internet Learning and the Building of Knowledge* (Youngstown, New York: Cambria Press, 2007)

Culler, Jonathan. *Ferdinand De Saussure* (Ithaca: Cornell University, 1976, 1986)

Deleuze, Gilles and Félix Guattari. *A Thousand Plateaus: Capitalism and Schizophrenia* (New York: Continuum Publishing Company, 1987, 1988, 2004)

Derrida, Jacques. *Given Time. I: Counterfeit Money.* Translated by Peggy Kamuf (University of Chicago Press, 1994)

    "Structure Sign, and Play in the Discourse of the Human Sciences." Reprinted in *Writing and Difference*, trans. Alan Bass (London: Routledge, 1978)

Diaz, A. "Through the Google Goggles: Sociopolitical Bias in Search Engine Design" in *Web Search: Multidisciplinary Perspectives.* Edited by Amanda Spink and Michael T. Zimmer. (Berlin: Springer-Verlag Berlin Hedelberg, 2007)

Dilts, David A., Lawrence J. Haber and Donna Bailik. *Assessing What Professors Do: An Introduction to Academic Performance. An Introduction to Academic Performance Appraisal in Higher Education* (Westport, CT: Greenwood Press, 1994)

Dowell, Ben. "Simon Schama: TV Dumber-Down or Simply the Greatest?" *The Guardian* (June 28, 2012): http://www.guardian.co.uk/culture/tvandradioblog/2012/jun/28/simon-schama-greatest-history-presentation

Drucker, Johanna. "Humanistic Theory and Digital Scholarship." *Debates in the Digital Humanities.* Edited by Matthew K. Gold (University of Minnesota Press, 2012)

Elkins, James. *Our Beautiful, Dry, and Distant Texts: Art History as Writing. Art History as Writing* (New York: Routledge, 2000)

"What Happened to Art Criticism?" Pamphlet, 2004: http://criticaycontracritica.uniandes.edu.co/textossimposio/ElkinsWhathappened.pdf
The State of Art Criticism (Routledge, 2008)

Ellul, Jacques. *The Technological Society.* Translated by John Wilkinson (New York: Alfred A. Knopf, 1964)

Fitzpatrick, Kathleen. "Chapter 5. The University." *Planned Obsolescence: Publishing, Technology, and the Future of the Academy* (NYU Press: 2011)

Foucault, Michel. *Discipline and Punish.* Translated by Alan Sheridan (New York: Random House, 1977)

The Archaeology of Knowledge and the Discourse on Language. Translated by Rupert Swyer (Tavistock Publications, Ltd. 1969/1972)

Fry, Edward. *Cubism* (Oxford University Press, 1978)

Fuchs, Christian. *Foundations of Critical Media and Information Studies* (New York: Routledge, 2011)

Internet and Society: Social Theory in the Information Age (New York: Routledge, 2008)

Geiger, Roger L. *Knowledge and Money: Research Universities and the Paradox of the Marketplace* (Stanford University Press, 2004)

Gersh-Nesic, Beth S.,Editor. *André Salmon on French Modern Art* (Cambridge, Cambridge University Press, 2005)

Gladwell, Malcolm. *Outliers: The Story of Success* (Hachette Digital, Inc. 2008)

Gould, Thomas H. P. *Creating the Academic Commons: Guidelines for Learning, Teaching, and Research* (Plymouth, Scarecrow Press, 2011)

Greco, Albert N. *The State of Scholarly of Publishing: Challenges and Opportunities* (New Brunswick, N. J.: Transaction Publishers, 2009)

Griswold, Wendy. *Cultures and Societies in a Changing World* (Pine Forge Press, 2008)

Hermanowicz, Joseph C. "Chapter Eight. Anomie in the American Academic Profession." *The American Academic Profession: Transformation in Contemporary Higher Education* (Baltimore: The Johns Hopkins Press, 2011)

von Hippel, Eric. *Democratizing Innovation* (Creative Commons, 2005)

hooks, bell. "Choosing the Margin as a Space of Radical Openness." *Yearnings: Race, Gender and Cultural Politics* (South End Press, 1999)

Howard, V. A. *Gambling Up to Nowhere: Publishing and Perishing at Harvard* (Bloomington, Indiana: iUniverse, 2008)

Huyssen, Andreas. *Twilight Memories: Marking Time in a Culture of Amnesia* (New York: Routledge, 1995)

Issacson, Walter. *Steve Jobs* (Simon Schuster, 2011)

Jacobs, Ronald N. and Eleanor Townsley. *The Space of Opinion: Media Intellectuals and the Public Sphere* (New York: Oxford University Press, 2011)

Johnson, W. McAllister. *Art History: Its Use and Abuse.* (Toronto: University of Toronto Press: 1988, 1990)

Jarosinski, Eric. *The Hand of the Interpreter: Essays on Meaning After Theory* (Bern: Peter Lang AG, 2009)

Jenkins, Tim. "Derrida's Reading of Mauss." *Marcel Mauss: A Centenary Tribute.* Edited by Wendy James and N. J. Allen (Berghahn Books, 1998)

Kellner, Douglas. "Reflections on Modernity and Postmodernity in McLuhan and Baudrillard." *Transforming McLuhan: Cultural, Critical, and Postmodern Perspectives.* Edited by Paul Grosswiler (New York: Peter Lang Publishing, Inc., 2010)

Khonsary, Jeff. *Judgment and Contemporary Art Criticism: Folio Series A* (Fillip Editions/Artspeak, 2010)

Kirby, Alan. *Digimodernism: How New Technologies Dismantle the Postmodern and Reconfigure Our Culture* (New York: The Continuum International Publishing Group Inc., 2009)

"The Return of the Poisonous Grand Narrative." *Digimodernism: How New Technologies Dismantle the Postmodern and Reconfigure our Culture* (New York: The Continuum International Publishing Group Inc., 2009)

Kushins, Jodi. "Recognizing Artists as Public Intellectuals: A Pedagogical Imperative." *CultureWork. A Periodic Broadside for Arts and Culture Workers* (Volume 10, Number 10, May 2006):
http://pages.uoregon.edu/culturwk/culturework34.html

Jones, Sarah. "Scholarly Books." *Measuring Scholarly Metrics.* Edited by Gordon R. Mitchell (Lincoln, Nebraska: Oldfather Press, 2011)

Lamont, Michèle. *How Professors Think: Inside the Curious World of Academic Judgment* (Cambridge: President and Fellows of Harvard College, 2009)

Landow, George. *Hyptertext. Contemporary Critical Theory and Technology* (Baltimore: The Johns Hopkins University Press, 1992)

Hypertext 3.0: Critical Theory and New Media in an Age of Globalization (Baltimore: The Johns Hopkins University Press, 1992,1997, 2006)

Lane, Jeremy F. *Pierre Bourdieu: A Critical Introduction* (Sterling, Virginia: Pluto Press, 2000)

Lemert, Charles. *Durkheim's Ghosts: Cultural Logics and Social Things.* (Cambridge University Press, 2006)

Lessig, Lawrence. *The Future of Ideas: The Fate of the Commons in a Connected World* (Random House, 2001)

The Future of Ideas. The Fate of the Commons in a Connected World (New York: Random House, 2001)

Lloyd, Rosemary. *Mallarmé: The Poet and His Circle* (Cornell University Press, 1999)

Lyotard, Jean-François. *The Postmodern Condition.* Translated by Geoff Bennington and Brian Massumi (University Of Minnesota Press; 1st edition, June 21, 1984)

Majewski, Lech and John Bowe, Et. al. writers for *Basquiat* (1996)

Malpas, Simon. *Jean-François Lyotard* (New York: Routledge, 2003, 2005)

Markham, Annette N. and Nancy K. Baym, Editors. *Internet Inquiry: Conversations about Method* (Sage Publications, 2009)

Mauss, Marcel. "Conclusions." *The Gift. Forms and Functions of Exchange in Archaic Societies*. Translated by Ian Gunnison (W. Norton Library, 1967)

May, Todd. *The Philosophy of Foucault* (McGill-Queen's University Press, 2006)

Marshall McLuhan. "Chapter One." *Understanding Media: The Extensions of Man* (New York: McGraw Hill, 1964)

Mehta, Lyla. "The Scarce, Naturalization and Politicization of Scarcity." Lyla Mehta, Editor. *The Limits of Scarcity: Contesting the Politics of Allocation* (Routledge, 2013)

Miles, Sara. *Michel Foucault* (New York: Routledge, 2003)

Mitchell, Claudia. "The Damaged Mirror. Gérôme's Narrative Technique and the Fractures of French History." *Reconsidering Gérôme*. Edited by Scott Allan and Mary Morton (J. Paul Getty Trust, 2010)

Neumann, Anna. "Scholarly Learning and the Academic Profession in a Time of Change." Edited by Joseph C. Hermanowicz. *The American Academic Profession: Transformation in Contemporary Higher Education* (Baltimore: The Johns Hopkins Press, 2011)

The Oberlin Group, A Consortium of Liberal Arts College Libraries: http://www.oberlingroup.org/node/14078

Pearson, Roger. *Stéphane Mallarmé* (Reaktion Books Ltd, 2010)

Peer, Robin P., Gregory B. Newby, Maria Santos. *Scholarly Publishing: The Electronic Frontier* (Cambridge: MIT Press, 1996, 2000)

Plotnitsky, Arkady. "Un-Scriptible."*Writing the Image After Roland Barthes*. Edited by Jean-Michel Rabate (Philadelphia: University of Pennsylvania Press, 1997)

Posner, Richard. *Public Intellectuals: A Study in Decline* (Harvard University Press, 2001/2003, 2004)

Poster, Mark. *What's the Matter with the Internet?* (University of Minnesota, 2001)

    with David Savant *Deleuze and New Technology* (Edinburgh University Press, 2009)

    "Postmodern Virtualities." *The Second Media Age* (Blackwell, 1995): http://www.hnet.uci.edu/mposter/writings/internet.html

    "Lyotard and Computer Science." *The Mode of Information: Poststructuralism and the Social Context* (Chicago: The University of Chicago Press, 1990)

    Information Please: Culture and Politics in the Age of Digital Machines (Duke University Press, 2006)

Reber, Bernard and Claire Brossard, Editors. *Digital Cognitive Technologies: Epistemology and Knowledge Society.* "Chapter 10: Hypertext, an Intellectual Technology in the Era of Complexity." (Hoboken, N. J. John Wiley & Sons, 2010)

Revel, Judith. *Michel Foucault. Expériences de la pensée* (Paris: Bordas, 2005)

Rorty, Richard. *Philosophy and the Mirror of Nature* (Princeton, N. J.: Princeton University Press, 1979/2009)

Ryan, Johnny. *A History of the Internet and the Digital Future* (Wilshire: Anthony Rowe, 2010)

Said, Edward. "The Public Role of Writers and Intellectuals." Edited Helen Small. *The Public Intellectual* (Oxford: Blackwell Publishing, 2002): http://cicac.tru.ca/readings/edward_said.pdf

Sandbothe, Mike. "Media Philosophy and Media Education in the Age of the Internet." Geoffrey H. Satchell. *Physiology and Form of Fish Circulation* (Blackwell Publishers, Inc. 2000)

Savage, William W. "Scribble, Scribble, Toil and Trouble: Forced Productivity in the Modern University." *The State of Scholarly of Publishing: Challenges and Opportunities* (New Brunswick, N. J.: Transaction Publishers, 2009)

Schonfeld Roger C. *JSTOR. A History.* (Princeton University Press, 2003)

Shapiro, Andrew L. *The Control Revolution* (The Century Foundation, 1999)

Shantz, Jeff. *Constructive Anarchy: Building Infrastructures of Resistance* (Surrey: Ashgate Publishing Limited, 2010)

Shatz, David. *Peer Review: A Critical Inquiry* (Lanham, Maryland: The Rowman & Littlefield Publishing Group, Inc., 2004)

Shreyach, Michael. *The State of Art Criticism* (Routledge, 2008)

Spivak, Gayatri Chakravorty. *Outside the Teaching Machine* (New York: Routledge, 1993)

Summer, Jennifer. "Keeping the Commons in Academic Culture: Protecting the Knowledge Commons from the Enclosure of the Knowledge Economy." *The Exchange University: Corporations of Academic Culture* (The University of British Columbia Press, 2008)

Susen, Simon and Bryan S. Turner, Editors. *The Legacy of Pierre Bourdieu. Critical Essays* (London: Anthem Press, 2011)

Tartaglia, James. *Rorty and the Mirror of Nature* (London: Routledge, 2007)

Terranova, Tiziana. "Free Labor." in Trebor Scholz, Editor. *Digital Labor.The Internet as Playground and Factory.* (New York: Routledge, 2013)

Waters, Lindsay. *Enemies of Promise: Publishing, Perishing and the Eclipse of Scholarship* (Prickly Paradigm Press, 2004)

Network Culture: Politics for the Information Age (The University of Michigan: Pluto Press, 2004)

Thompson, John B. *Books in the Digital Age: The Transformation of Academic and Higher Education Publishing in Britain and the United States* (Polity, 2005)

Vandendorpe, Christian. *From Papyrus to Hypertext: Toward the Universal Library.* Translated by Phyllis Aronoff (University of Illinois Press, 1999, 2009)

Ward, Martha. *Pissarro, Neo-Impressionism, and the Spaces of the Avant-Garde* (Chicago: The University of Chicago Press, 1996)

Weller, Martin. *The Digital Scholar: How Technology is Transforming Scholarly Practice* (New York: Bloomsbury Academic, 2011)

Willette, Jeanne S. M. *The Writing of Cubism. The Construction of a Discourse, 1910-1914* (AHS Publishing, 2012)

Wilson, Morton. "Prospects for a Reevaluation of Academic Values." Edited by Joseph M. Moxley and Lagretta T. Lenker. *The Politics and Processes of Scholarship* (Westport, CT: Greenwood Press, 1995)

Wimmer, Roger D. and Joseph R. Dominick. *Mass Media Research: An Introduction* (Boston: Wadsworth, 2011)

Wood, Michael. *The Story of England.* Public Broadcasting System. July 2012: http://www.pbs.org/programs/michael-woods-story-england/

Ya'ir, Gad. *The Last Musketeer of the French Revolution* (Lanham, Maryland: The Rowman & Littlefield Publishing Group, Inc., 2009)

Yoo, Christopher. *The Dynamic Internet. How Technology, Users and Businesses are Transforming the Network* (Washington, D. C.: American Enterprise Institute, 2012)

Zittrain, Jonathan. *The Future of the Internet and How to Stop It* (New Haven: Yale University Press, 2008)

Articles

----"Intellectual Capital." *The Management Lab:* http://www.managementlab.org/files/u2/pdf/classic%20innovations/Intellectual_Capital.pdf

----"Trenddriver/Collapse of Conventions." *Trendwatching.com*. September 2010.
http://www.trendwatching.com/trends/maturialism/

Anderson, Chris. "The Long Tail." *Wired Magazine*. October 2004.
http://www.wired.com/wired/archive/12.10/tail.html

Interview with Chris Anderson. "Chris Anderson. The Long Tail." *Blogging Heroes:* http://www.longtail.com/bloggingheroes.pdf

Angus, Ian H. "Learning to Stop: A Critique of General Rhetoric." Ian H. Angus and Lenore Langsdorf, Editors. *The Critical Turn: Rhetoric and Philosophy in Postmodern Discourse* (Southern Illinois Press, 1993)

Auletta, Ken. "Publish or Perish." *The New Yorker*. April 26, 2010:
http://www.newyorker.com/reporting/2010/04/26/100426fa_fact_auletta#ixzz2DBNL7trm

Austin, Ann E. and Donald H. Wulff. "The Challenge to Prepare the Next Generation of Faculty." *Paths to the Professoriate: Strategies for Enriching the Preparation of Future Faculty* (Jossey-Bass, 2004):
http://media.johnwiley.com.au/product_data/excerpt/47/07879663/0787966347.pdf

Baca, Murtha and William Tronzo. "Art History and the Digital World." *Art Journal* (pp. 51-55): Stable URL: http://www.jstor.org/stable/20068498

Bal, Mieke. "Art History and its Theories." *The Art Bulletin* (Volume LXXVIII, Number 1, March 1996):
http://publications.ias.edu/sites/default/files/Lavin_CrisisArtHistory_1996.pdf

Barthes, Roland. "The Death of the Author." *Image, Music, Text* (1977):
http://evans-experientialism.freewebspace.com/barthes06.htm

Baudrillard, Jean. "Jean Baudrillard---Baudrillard on the New Technologies. An Interview with Claude Thibault," March 6, 1996. Translated by Suzanne Falcone. The European Graduate School. Graduate and Postgraduate Studies.
http://www.egs.edu/faculty/jean-baudrillard/articles/baudrillard-on-the-new-technologies-an-interview-with-claude-thibaut/

Bauerlein, Mark, Mohamed Gad-el-Hak, Wayne Grody, Bill McKelvey, and Stanley W. Trimble. *The Chronicle of Higher Education* (June 13, 2010): http://scholar.google.com/scholar?start=20&q=academic+culture%2Bpublish+or+perish&hl=en&as_sdt=0,5&as_vis=1

Benjamin, Walter. "The Author as Producer." *New Left Review*. 1/62, July-August, 1970: http://roundtable.kein.org/files/roundtable/Walter%20Benjamin_%20The%20Author%20as%20Producer.pdf

Benkler, Yochai. "The New Open-Source Economics." *Ted Talks* (2005): http://www.ted.com/talks/yochai_benkler_on_the_new_open_source_economics.html

Bennett, Tony. "Texts, Readers, Reading Formations." *The Bulleting of the Midwest Modern Language Association*. Volume 16, Number 1 (Spring, 1983)

"Texts in History: The Determinations of Readings and Their Texts." *The Journal of the Midwest Modern Language Association*. Volume 18, Number 1 (Spring, 1985)

Bernstein, R. J. "Serious Play. The Ethical-Political Horizon of Derrida." http://www.google.com/#hl=en&tbo=d&sclient=psy-ab&q=r.j.+bernstein%2Bserious+play&oq=r.j.+bernstein%2Bserious+play&gs_l=hp.3...807.8557.0.8941.27.27.0.0.0.1.346.3582.6j20j0j1.27.0.les%3Bcpsugrpq1..0.0...1.1.gWGWgrS25pY&pbx=1&bav=on.2,or.r_gc.r_pw.r_qf.&fp=488ae73babd585f2&bpcl=38897761&biw=1196&bih=702

Berkenkotter, Carol. "The Power and the Perils of Peer Review." *Rhetoric Review* (Volume 13, Number 2, Spring, 1995)

Berlin Declaration on Open Access to Knowledge in the Sciences and Humanities: http://www.zim.mpg.de/openaccess-berlin/berlin_declaration.pdf

Biagiloi, Mario. "From Book Censorship to Academic Peer Review." *Emergences* (Volume 12, Number 1, 2002): http://innovation.ucdavis.edu/people/publications/Biagioli%202008%20Censorship_review.pdf

Bollier, David. *Viral Spiral*: http://www.viralspiral.cc/sites/default/files/ViralSpiral.pdf

Bonham, Kevin. "Peerj—the Science Journal we Need and Deserve." *ScienceBlogs* (February 12, 2013):
http://scienceblogs.com/webeasties/2013/02/12/peerj-the-science-journal-we-need-and-deserve/

Bontis, Nick. "Managing Organizational Knowledge by Diagnosing Intellectual Capital." Daryl Morey, Mark Maybury, and Bhavani Thuraisingham, Editors. *Knowledge Management. Classic and Contemporary Works.* (MIT Press, 2000)

Dr. Jeff Borden. "The MOOC Heard Around the World." *WIRED* (May 13, 2013): http://www.wired.com/insights/2013/05/the-mooc-heard-around-the-world/

Bowser, Diane J. "Open Access Publishing in Philosophy." *thinkingshop.com* (October 3, 2009): http://www.thinkingshop.com/2009/10/03/open-access-publishing-in-philosophy/

Bourdieu, Pierre. "Social Space and Symbolic Power." *Sociological Theory*, Volume 7, umber 1 (Spring, 1989)

Boyle, James. "Foucault in Cyberspace. Surveillance, Sovereignty, and Hard-Wired Censors. *Duke University School of Law: http://law.duke.edu/boylesite/foucault.htm*

Bradsher, Keith. "China Toughens its Restrictions on the Use of the Internet." *The New York Times* (December 29, 2012):
http://topics.nytimes.com/topics/news/international/countriesandterritories/china/internet_censorship/index.html

Brantley, Peter. "Academic E-Books: innovation and Transition." *Publishers' Weekly*. February 3, 2012. http://www.publishersweekly.com/pw/by-topic/digital/content-and-e-books/article/50486-academic-e-books-innovation-and-transition.html

Bruns, Alex. "Produsage, Generation C, and Their Effects on the Democratic Process:" http://web.mit.edu/comm-forum/mit5/papers/Bruns.pdf

Buchanan, Ian. "Deleuze and the Internet." *Australian Humanities Review* (Issue 43, December 2007):

http://www.australianhumanitiesreview.org/archive/Issue-December-2007/Buchanan.html

Burns, Stephen. "Why Criticism Matters. Beyond the Critic as Cultural Arbiter." *The New York Times* (December 31, 2010):
http://www.nytimes.com/2011/01/02/books/review/Burn-t-web.html

Bush, Vannebar. "As We May Think." *The Atlantic Magazine.* July 1945.
http://www.theatlantic.com/magazine/archive/1945/07/as-we-may-think/303881/?single_page=true

Bustillos, Maria. "Was Aaron Swartz Stealing?" *The Awl* (August 3, 2011):
http://www.theawl.com/2011/08/was-aaron-swartz-stealing

Carr, Nicholas. "Is Google Making Us Stupid?" *The Atlantic.* July-August 2008.
http://www.theatlantic.com/magazine/archive/2008/07/is-google-making-us-stupid/306868/

Chiu, Dah Ming and Tom Z. J. Fu. "'Publish or Perish' in the Internet Age. A Study of Publication Statistics in Computer Networking Research" (2010):
http://home.ie.cuhk.edu.hk/~dmchiu/ccr_paper.pdf

Cohen, Patricia. "For Scholars, Web Changes Sacred Rite of Peer Review." *The New York Times* (August 23, 2010):
http://www.nytimes.com/2010/08/24/arts/24peer.html?pagewanted=all&_r=0

Cope, Bill and Mary Kalantzis. "Sighs of Disruption: Transformations in the Knowledge System of the Academic Journal." *First Monday* (Volume 14, Number 4, 6 April 2009):
http://firstmonday.org/htbin/cgiwrap/bin/ojs/index.php/fm/article/view/2309%3D/2163

Coulter, Gerry. "Launching (and Sustaining) a Scholarly Journal on the Internet: the International Journal of Baudrillard Studies" (Volume 13, Issue 1, Winter 2010):
http://quod.lib.umich.edu/j/jep/3336451.0013.104?rgn=main;view=fulltext

Crain, Caleb. "Twilight of the Books." *The New Yorker.* December 24, 2007.
http://www.newyorker.com/arts/critics/atlarge/2007/12/24/071224crat_atlarge_crain#ixzz2DBUAZ4nx

Creamer, Elizabeth G. "Addressing Faculty Publication Productivity: Issues of Equity. ERIC Digest:" http://www.ericdigests.org/1999-1/equity.html

Curry, Stephen. "The Inexorable Rise of Open Access Scientific Publishing." *The Guardian*. (22 October 2012): http://www.guardian.co.uk/science/occams-corner/2012/oct/22/inexorable-rise-open-access-scientific-publishing

van Dalen, Hendrik P. and Kène Henkers. "Intended or Unintended Consequences of a Publish-or-Perish Culture: A Worldwide Survey," *CentER Discussion Paper Series No. 2012-003* (January 11, 2012): http://papers.ssrn.com/sol3/papers.cfm?abstract_id=1983205

Davidson, Cathy. "Does Digital Publishing Need Peer Review?" HASTAC (July 20, 2011): http://hastac.org/blogs/cathy-davidson/does-digital-publishing-need-peer-review

Davis, Erik. "The Gift—Mauss, Bataille, Hyde and Derrida." *Imagining the Real World*. October 26, 2006: http://erikwdavis.wordpress.com/2006/10/26/the-gift-mauss-bataille-hyde-and-derrida/

Elberse, Anita and Felix Oberholzer-Gee. "Superstars and Underdogs: An Examination of the Long Tail Phenomenon in Video Sales." *Harvard Business School Working Paper Series, Nos. 07-015.* 2007: http://www.aeaweb.org/annual_mtg_papers/2007/0107_1015_1002.pdf

Epstein, Edward Jay. "The Diamond 'Overhang.'" *The New York Times* (December 3, 2009): http://www.nytimes.com/2009/02/23/opinion/23iht-edepstein.1.20368819.html?_r=0

Esposito, Joseph J. "The Wisdom of Oz: The Role of the University Press in Scholarly Communications." *The Journal of Electronic Publishing.* Volume 10, Issue 1, Winter 2007: http://quod.lib.umich.edu/cgi/t/text/text-idx?c=jep;cc=jep;view=text;rgn=main;idno=3336451.0010.103

Eubanks, Philip and John D. Schaeffer. "A Kind Word for Bullshit: The Problem of Academic Writing." *College Composition and Communication* (Volume 59, Number 3, February 2008)

The Faculty Advisory Council. "Faculty Advisory Council Memorandum on Journal Pricing." April 17, 2012:

http://isites.harvard.edu/icb/icb.do?keyword=k77982&tabgroupid=icb.tabgroup143448

Feldman, Edmund Burke. "A Socialist Critique of Art History." *Leonardo.* Volume 11, No. 1 (Winter 1978)

Fish, Stanley. "Can Postmodernists Condemn Terrorism? Don't Blame Relativism.:" http://www.gwu.edu/~ccps/rcq/Fish.pdf

Fisher, M.D., Julian. "Read This Academic Journal Article, but Prepare to Pay." *The Atlantic* (February 222, 2011):
http://www.theatlantic.com/national/archive/2011/02/read-this-academic-journal-article-but-prepare-to-pay/71536/

Fitzpatrick, Kathleen. "Giving it Away: Sharing and the Future of Scholarly Education." *Planned Obsolescence* (January 2012):
http://www.plannedobsolescence.net/blog/giving-it-away/

"From Crisis to Commons." *Cinema Journal* (Volume 44, Number 3, Spring, 2005)

"Peer-to-Peer Review and the Future of Scholarly Authority. *Cinema Journal* (Volume 48, Number 2, Winter, 209)

Frost, Charlotte. "Is Art History too Bookish?" *Arts Future Book*:
http://www.gylphi.co.uk/artsfuturebook/

Fuchs, Christian. "Towards Marxist Internet Studies." *Triple C* (10(2): 2012 ISSN 1726-670X http://www.triple-c.at)

"Critical Theory in the Age of the Internet, Part One:"
http://www.youtube.com/watch?v=qPr8qof8YtQ
and "Part Two:" http://www.youtube.com/watch?v=LQ6xyJYdFKY

Garfield, Eugene. "What is the Primordial Reference for The Phrase 'Publish or Perish'?" *The Scientist* (Volume 10, Number 12, June 10, 1996):
http://www.garfield.library.upenn.edu/commentaries/tsv10(12)p11y19960610.pdf

Glance, David. "The Long Tail of Academic Publishing and Why it isn't Such a Bad Thing." *The London School of Economics and Political Science.* August 22, 2012.
http://blogs.lse.ac.uk/impactofsocialsciences/2012/08/22/the-long-tail-of-academic-publishing-and-why-that-isnt-a-bad-thing/

and also in "The Long Tail of Academic Publishing and Why it isn't a Bad Thing." *The Conversation* (July 8, 2012):
http://theconversation.com/the-long-tail-of-academic-publishing-and-why-it-isnt-a-bad-thing-8126

Glaser, Mark. "5Across: Arts Criticism in the Digital Age." *Mediashift. PBS:* http://www.pbs.org/mediashift/2010/06/5across-arts-criticism-in-the-digital-age180

Gongloff, Mark. "Influential Reinhart-Rogoff Pro-Austerity Research Riddled with Errors: Study." *Huffington Post Business* (04/16/2013):
http://www.huffingtonpost.com/2013/04/16/reinhart-rogoff-austerity-research-errors_n_3094015.html

Grabowicz, Paul. "The Transition to Digital Journalism." *Knight Digital Media Center.* Updated November 2012.
http://multimedia.journalism.berkeley.edu/tutorials/digital-transform/Websites/

Greenberg, Clement. "Modernist Painting." *Forum Lectures* (Washington, D.C.: Voice of America), 1960; *Arts Yearbook* 4, 1961 (unrevised); *Art and Literature,* Spring 1965 (slightly revised); *The New Art: A Critical Anthology,* ed. Gregory Battcock, 1966; *Peinture-cahiers théoriques,* no. 8-9, 1974 (titled "La *peinture moderniste"); Esthetics Contemporary,* ed. Richard Kostelanetz, 1978; *Modern Art and Modernism: A Critical Anthology,* ed. Francis Frascina and Charles Harrison, 1982; *Clement Greenberg: The Collected Essays and Criticism vol. 4,* ed. John O'Brian, 1993:
http://cas.uchicago.edu/workshops/wittgenstein/files/2007/10/Greenbergmodpaint.pdf

"American Type Painting," 1955, 1958:
http://www.scribd.com/doc/54185848/Greenberg-American-Type-Painting-1955-58

Greer, Mike. "Has the Internet allowed Derrida's 'impossible gift' to Become an Everyday Occurrence?" *Media and Culture* (This is an abstract, available on the Web as a PDF, with no date or other references.)

Grimes, William. "Art Critics are Critical of Each Other's Criticism." *The New York Times* (May 18, 1996):
http://www.nytimes.com/1996/05/18/arts/art-critics-are-critical-of-each-other-s-criticism.html

Gowers, Timothy. "Cost of Knowledge Petition":
http://gowers.files.wordpress.com/2012/02/elsevierstatementfinal.pdf

Guédon, Jean-Claude. "The Credibility of Electronic Publishing: A Report to the Humanities and Social Sciences Federation of Canada." (2001)
http://web.viu.ca/hssfc/final/credibility.htm

Gusterson, Hugh. "Want to Change Academic Publishing? Just Say No." *The Chronicle of Higher Education.* September 23, 2012.
http://chronicle.com/article/Want-to-Change-Academic/134546/

Martin Halbert. *Performitivity, Cultural Capital, & The Internet.* "Lyotard: Postmodern Condition." See also "Performitivity & Paralogy." *First Year ILA Research Paper* (15 April 1998):
http://userwww.service.emory.edu/~mhalber/Research/Paper/pci-internet.html

"Bourdieu. *Home Academicus.*" Performity, Cultural Capital, and the Internet. Emory University:
http://userwww.service.emory.edu/~mhalber/Research/Paper/pci-internet.html

Hamman, Robin B. "Rhizome @Internet. Using the Internet as an Example of Deleuze and Guattari's 'Rhizome.'" *Cybersociology Magazine.* (1996):
http://www.socio.demon.co.uk/rhizome.html

Hartley, John. "Digital Scholarship and Pedagogy, the Next Step: Cultural Science." *Cinema Journal* (Volume 48, Number 2, Winter 2009):
http://muse.jhu.edu/login?auth=0&type=summary&url=/journals/cinema_journal/v048/48.2.hartley.pdf

von Hippel, Eric. "Democratizing Innovation and Norms-based Intellectual Property Rights:" http://www.youtube.com/watch?v=m6RttLCiKxI

Ho, Mae-Wan. "What is Schrödinger's Negentropy?" Institute of Science in Society. *Modern Trends in BioThermoKinetics* (Number 3, 1994) 50-61:
http://www.i-sis.org.uk/negentr.php

Hofmokl, Justyna. "The Internet Commons" Towards an Electric Theoretical Framework." *International Journal of the Commons* (Volume 4, Number 1, 2010)
http://www.thecommonsjournal.org/index.php/ijc/article/view/111/106

Holly, Michael Ann. Et. al. "Art History and Its Publishers" *Art Journal* (pp. 41-50): Stable URL: http://www.jstor.org/stable/20068497

Holtorf, Cornelius. "A Comment on Hybrid Fields and Academic Gate-Keeping." *Public Archaeology: Archaeological Entnographies* (Volume 8, Number 2-3, 2009): http://www.google.com/#hl=en&gs_rn=12&gs_ri=psy-ab&gs_mss=academi%20gatekeeping&pq=pamela%20shoemaker%20gatekeeping&cp=8&gs_id=2v&xhr=t&q=academic+gatekeeping&es_nrs=true&pf=p&sclient=psy-ab&oq=academic+gatekeeping&gs_l=&pbx=1&bav=on.2,or.r_qf.&bvm=bv.46471029,d.dmQ&fp=3aad8e69494a147&biw=1196&bih=664

Horn Denise. "Academic Publishing. This is not a Dissertation." *The Guardian* (30 January 2012): http://www.guardian.co.uk/higher-education-network/blog/2012/jan/30/academic-publishing-not-dissertation

Ingram, Matthew. "Why do we need Academic Journals in the First Place?" *Gigaom* (Feburary 22, 2012): http://gigaom.com/2012/02/22/why-do-we-need-academic-journals-in-the-first-place/

Jacob, A. J. "Two Courses for Web U!" *The New York Times* (April 20, 2013): http://www.nytimes.com/2013/04/21/opinion/sunday/grading-the-mooc-university.html?pagewanted=all&_r=0

Jaschik, Scott. "Hope on Ph.D. Attrition Rates---Except in the Humanities." *Inside Higher Ed* (December 7, 2007): http://www.insidehighered.com/news/2007/12/07/doctoral

Jauregui, Andreas. "Academics Tweet Tribute to Aaron Swartz, Share Research with Internet in Honor of Activist." *The Huffington Post*. January 15, 2013: http://www.huffingtonpost.com/2013/01/13/academics-tweet-tribute-aaron-swartz_n_2468272.html

Joseph, Heather. "The Impact of Open Access on Research and Scholarship. Reflections on the Berlin 9 Open Access Conference." *College & Research Libraries News*. 2012. http://crln.acrl.org/content/73/2/83.full

Julesz, Bela. "Texton Gradients: The Texton Theory Revisited." *Biological Cybernetics* (Volume 54, 1986): http://link.springer.com/article/10.1007/BF00318420#page-1

Kaiser, Michael. "The Death of Criticism or Everyone is a Critic." *Huffpost Arts & Culture* (November 14, 2011):

http://www.huffingtonpost.com/michael-kaiser/the-death-of-criticism-or_b_1092125.html

Karr, Rick. "Trouble for Elsevier, the Leading Academic Publisher." *NPR* broadcast posted on [BLOG] Alex Goldman. "Harvard Library: Subscribing to Academic Periodicals is Too Expensive" (April 24, 2012): http://www.onthemedia.org/blogs/on-the-media/2012/apr/24/harvard-library-subscribing-academic-periodicals-too-expensive/?utm_source=/2012/feb/17/trouble-elsevier-leading-academic-publisher/&utm_medium=treatment&utm_campaign=morelikethis

Kendzior, Sarah. "Academic Paywalls Mean Publish or Perish." *Aljazeera* (October 2012): http://www.aljazeera.com/indepth/opinion/2012/10/20121017558785551.html

Kirby, Alan. "The Death of Postmodernism and Beyond." *Philosophy Now. A Magazine of Ideas* (January/February 2013): http://philosophynow.org/issues/58/The_Death_of_Postmodernism_And_Beyond

Kristeva, Julia. "Word, Dialogue and Novel." *The Kristeva Reader*. Edited by Toril Moi (New York: Columbia University Press, 1986)

Krugman, Paul. "The Excel Depression." *The New York Times* (April 18, 2013): http://www.nytimes.com/2013/04/19/opinion/krugman-the-excel-depression.html

Kunzru, Hari. "Postmodernism. From the Cutting Edge to the Museum." *The Guardian* (Thursday, 15 September 2011): http://www.guardian.co.uk/artanddesign/2011/sep/15/postmodernism-cutting-edge-to-museum

Laermans, Rudi and Pascal Gielen. "The Archive of the Digital Non-Archive." *Image [&] Narrative*, Issue 17, "The Digital Archive." April 2007 http://www.imageandnarrative.be/inarchive/digital_archive/laermans_gielen.htm

Landow, George P.. "The Definition of Hypertext and its History as a Concept."
http://www.cyberartsweb.org/cpace/ht/jhup/history.html

Lavoie, Joanie and Dominique Bérubé. "Crisis in Academic Publishing." *Phys.Org*. June 2012: http://phys.org/news/2012-06-crisis-academic-publishing.html#jCp

Lawley, Elizabeth Lane. "The Sociology of Culture in Computer-Mediated Communication: An Initial Exploration:"
http://www.itcs.com/elawley/bourdieu.html

Lessig, Lawrence. "Interview with Lawrence Lessig." *WPO Magazine.* February 2011:
http://www.wipo.int/wipo_magazine/en/2011/01/article_0002.html

Leszczynski, Daniel. "Opinion: Scientific Peer Review in Crisis." *The Scientist Magazine* (February 25, 2013): http://www.the-scientist.com/?articles.view/articleNo/34518/title/Opinion--Scientific-Peer-Review-in-Crisis/

Lewandowski, Dirk and Philipp Mayr. "Exploring the Academic Invisible Web:" http://arxiv.org/pdf/cs/0702103.pdf

Martin, William. "Re-Programming Lyotard: From the Postmodern to the Posthuman Condition." *Parrhesia* (Number 8, 2009) 60-75.

McGuigan, Glenn S. and Robert D. Russell. "The Business of Academic Publishing: A Strategic Analysis of the Academic Journal Publishing Industry and its Impact Upon the Future of Scholarly Publishing." *Electronic Journal of Academic and Special Librarianship.* Volume 3, Number 3 (Winter 2008):
http://southernlibrarianship.icaap.org/content/v09n03/mcguigan_g01.html

McKenna, Laura. "Locked in the Ivory Tower: Why JSTOR Imprisons Academic Research." *The Atlantic* (January 20, 2012):
http://www.theatlantic.com/business/archive/2012/01/locked-in-the-ivory-tower-why-jstor-imprisons-academic-research/251649/

Mead, Walter Russell. "Publish or Perish or Pay Through the Nose."*The American Interest* (April 28, 2012): http://blogs.the-american-interest.com/wrm/2012/04/28/publish-rubbish-or-perish-and-pay-through-the-nose/

Midgette, Anne. "Ai Weiwei: Separating the Dissident from the Artist." *The Washington Post.* October 2012.
http://www.washingtonpost.com/entertainment/museums/separating-the-dissident-from-the-artist/2012/10/04/4165e77c-0caa-11e2-bd1a-b868e65d57eb_story.html

Miller, Ruth. "Insurgency in Academic Publishing." *Berkeley Planning Journal*. 25(1)(2012) http://ced.berkeley.edu/bpj/2012/05/insurgency-in-academic-publishing/

Monblot, George. "Academic Publishers Make Murdoch Look Like a Socialist." *The Guardian*. 29 August 2011. http://m.guardian.co.uk/commentisfree/2011/aug/29/academic-publishers-murdoch-socialist?cat=commentisfree&type=article

Noughton, John. "Academic Publishing Doesn't Add Up." *The Guardian* (April 21, 2012): http://www.guardian.co.uk/technology/2012/apr/22/academic-publishing-monopoly-challenged

Olsen, Robert. "China's Shifting Censorship Regime Puts Squeeze on Internet Giants." *Forbes* (March 12, 2013): http://www.forbes.com/sites/robertolsen/2013/03/12/chinas-shifting-censorship-regime-puts-squeeze-on-internet-giants/

Oosthuizen, Susan. "Medieval Field Systems and Settlement Nucleation: Common or Separate Origins?" *Academia.edu*: http://www.academia.edu/1561621/Medieval_field_systems_and_settlement_nucleation_Common_or_separate_origins

Opal, Puneet. "Don't Forget the Dream of Open Access Journals Die." *The Atlantic* (March 26, 2013): http://www.theatlantic.com/health/archive/2013/03/dont-let-the-dream-of-open-access-journals-die/274371/

Owens, Simon. "Is the Academic Publishing industry on the Verge of Disruption?" *U.S. News Weekly*. July 23, 2012. http://www.usnews.com/news/articles/2012/07/23/is-the-academic-publishing-industry-on-the-verge-of-disruption

Panero, James. "The Critical Moment. Abstract Expressionism's Dueling Duo." *Humanities* (Volume 29, Number 4, July/August 2008): http://www.neh.gov/humanities/2008/julyaugust/feature/the-critical-moment

Pauling, Linus. "Schrödinger's Contribution to Chemistry and Biology." in *Schrödinger: Centenary Celebration of a Polymath*. C. W. Kilmister, editor (Cambridge University Press, 1989) 225-223.

Poster, Jamie. "Code Orange: Career Fear and Publishing." *Cinema Journal*

(Volume 44, Number 3, Spring 2005)

Priest, Eric. "Copyright and the Harvard Open Access Mandate." *Northwestern Journal of Technology & Intellectual Property.* Social Science Research Network (August 1, 2012):
http://papers.ssrn.com/sol3/papers.cfm?abstract_id=1890467

Prof Hacker. "Creating Your Web Presence: A Primer for Academics." *The Chronicle of Higher Education.* February 11, 2012:
http://chronicle.com/blogs/profhacker/creating-your-web-presence-a-primer-for-academics/30458

Ramadhan, Areif, Dana Indra Asesuse, Aniati Murni Arymurthy. "Postmodernism in e-Government." *International Journal of Computer Science Issues* (Volume 8, Issue 4, Number 1, July 2011):
http://ijcsi.org/papers/IJCSI-8-4-1-623-629.pdf

Reinhart, Carmen and Kenneth Rogoff. "Debt, Growth, and the Austerity Debate." *The New York Times* (April 25, 2013):
http://www.nytimes.com/2013/04/26/opinion/debt-growth-and-the-austerity-debate.html?pagewanted=all

Ritchie, Euan and Joern Fischer. "Cracks in the Ivory Tower: Is Academic's Culture Sustainable?" *The Conversation* (August 23, 2012):

Ritzer, George. *Contemporary Sociological Theory and its Classical Roots: The Basics* (McGraw-Hill, Incorporated, 2009)
        Postmodern Social Theory (McGraw-Hill, 1997)

Roberts, Peter. "Rereading Lyotard: Knowledge, Commodification and Higher Education." *Electronic Journal of Sociology* (1998)
http://www.sociology.org/content/vol003.003/roberts.html

Rond, Mark de and Alan N. Miller. "Publish or Perish. Bane or Boon of Academic Life? *Journal of Management Inquiry* (Volume 14, Number 4, December 2005): http://laisumedu.org/DESIN_Ibarra/salon/2007p/UAMX-teoria/Rond-01.pdf

Rosen, Jay. "The People Formerly Known as the Audience." *PressThink.Ghost of Democracy in the Media Machine:*
http://archive.pressthink.org/2006/06/27/ppl_frmr.html

Rosenberg, Harold. "American Action Painters." *ARTnews* (Volume 51, September 1952):

http://books.google.com/books?id=aD3azMow90MC&pg=PA55&lpg=PA55&dq=harold+rosenberg+the+american+action+painters&source=bl&ots=Q15_XPhajr&sig=g4OUVrfOtWnvuyzrEqxHn6G3y0s&hl=en&sa=X&ei=mNOjUdKCAcyoqwHAiYHADQ&ved=0CE4Q6AEwBQ#v=onepage&q=harold%20rosenberg%20the%20american%20action%20painters&f=false

Rosenzweig, Roy. "Can History be Open Source? Wikipedia and the Future of the Past" from "Essay on History and New Media." Also printed in *The Journal of American History* Volume 93, Number 1 (June, 2006): 117-46 http://chnm.gmu.edu/essays-on-history-new-media/essays/?essayid=42

Rowland, Fytton. "The Peer Review Process. A Report to the JISC Scholarly Communications Group" http://www.jisc.ac.uk/uploaded_documents/rowland.pdf

Sayre, Woodrow Wilson. "It's Publish or Perish." *Life* (January 29, 1965)

Schjeldahl, Peter. "Action Figures." *The New Yorker* (May 26, 2008): http://www.newyorker.com/arts/critics/artworld/2008/05/26/080526craw_artworld_schjeldahl

Schultz, William. "J. F. Lyotard. The Ambivalence of our Postmodern Condition. Lyotrad's Diagnosis and Prognosis."
http://www.costis.org/x/lyotard/schultz.htm
Raymond Siemens. "The Credibility of Electronic Publishing. Introduction and Overview:" http://web.viu.ca/hssfc/final/Overview.htm

Sims, Nancy. "Academic Publishing is Full of Problems; Let's Get Them Right," disagreeing with the details if not the main points of McKenna's article:
http://blog.lib.umn.edu/copyrightlibn/2012/01/factcheckingtheatlantic.html

Singer, Peter and Agata Sagan. ""The Death of Aaron Swartz." *The New York Review of Books*. January 18, 2013:
http://www.nybooks.com/blogs/nyrblog/2013/jan/18/death-aaron-swartz/

Smith, Dinitia. "Hoping the Web Will Rescue Young Professors; In the Publish-or-Perish World, Can They Live on the Internet?" *The New York Times* (June 12, 1999): http://www.nytimes.com/1999/06/12/arts/hoping-web-will-rescue-young-professors-publish-perish-world-can-they-live.html?pagewanted=all&src=pm

Smith, Roberta. "Edward F. Fry, 56, A Historian Devoted to 20th Century Art." *The New York Times* (April 21, 1992): http://www.nytimes.com/1992/04/21/arts/edward-f-fry-56-a-historian-devoted-to-20th-century-art.html

"The Cross-Dressing of Art and Couture. Impressionism, Fashion and Modernity at the Met." (February 21, 2013)*The New York Times* (February 21, 2013): http://www.nytimes.com/2013/02/22/arts/design/impressionism-fashion-and-modernity-at-the-met.html?pagewanted=all

Soussloff, Catherine M.. "Publishing Paradigms in Art History." *Art Journal* (pp. 36-40): Stable URL: http://www.jstor.org/stable/20068496

Spivak, Cary. "The Fact-Checking Explosion." *American Journalism Review*. (December/January 2011): http://www.ajr.org/article.asp?id=4980

Steele, Colin. "Scholarly Monograph Publishing in the 21st century: The Future More Than Ever Should be an Open Book." *The Journal of Electronic Publishing* (Volume 11, Issue 2, Spring, 2008): http://quod.lib.umich.edu/cgi/t/text/text-idx?c=jep;cc=jep;rgn=main;view=text;idno=3336451.0011.201

Stephanson, Anders and Frederic Jameson. "Regarding Postmodernism---A Conversation with Frederic Jameson." *Social Text. Universal Abandon? The Politics of Postmodernism* (No. 21, Duke University Press: 1989): http://postcolonial.net/@Backfile/_entries/3/file-pdf.pdf

Sterling, Bruce. "As Art Critics Face Sudden Planetary Extinction." *Beyond the Beyond* (November 18, 2009): http://www.wired.com/beyond_the_beyond/2009/11/as-art-critics-face-sudden-planetary-extinction/

Street, Steve, Maria Maisto, Esther Merves, and Gary Rhoades. "Who is Professor 'Staff' and How can this Person Teach so Many Classes?" *Center for Higher Education Policy Report #2* (August 23, 2012): http://www.insidehighered.com/sites/default/server_files/files/profstaff(2).pdf

Suber, Peter. "Open Access Overview:" http://www.earlham.edu/~peters/fos/overview.htm
His book *Open Access* was published by MIT Press in June of 2012 but became OA by June 2013.

Suskind, Ron. "Faith, Certainty, and the Presidency of George W. Bush." *The New York Times Magazine.* October 17, 2004. http://www.nytimes.com/2004/10/17/magazine/17BUSH.html?ex=1255665600&en=890a96189e162076&ei=5090&partner=rssuserland

Tadween Editors. "Despite New Program Promising Open Access, JSTOR Prices Remain a Concern. *Tadween Publishing* (January 22, 2013): http://tadweenpublishing.com/blogs/news/7215458-despite-new-program-promising-open-access-jstor-prices-remain-a-concern

Taibbi, Matt. "The Mad Science of the National Debt." *Rolling Stone* (May 22, 2013): http://www.rollingstone.com/politics/news/the-mad-science-of-the-national-debt-20130522

Taylor, Mike. "The Future of Academic Publishing." *The Independent.* 9 February 2012. http://blogs.independent.co.uk/2012/02/09/the-future-of-academic-publishing/

"Opinion: Academic Opinion is Broken." *The Scientist.* March 19, 2012. http://www.the-scientist.com/?articles.view/articleNo/31858/title/Opinion--Academic-Publishing-Is-Broken-/

Teske, Doris. "Beyond Postmodernist Thirdspace?---The Internet in a Post-Modern World." *Beyond Postmodernism: Reassessments in Literature, Theory, and Culture* edited by Kalus Stierstorfer (Berlin: Walter de Gruyter gmbH & Co., 2003)

Trefis Team. "Facebook Earnings: Revenue Growth and Mobile Monetization in Focus." *Forbes* (January 29, 2013): http://www.forbes.com/sites/greatspeculations/2013/01/29/facebook-earnings-revenue-growth-and-mobile-monetization-in-focus/

Vidokle, Anton. "Art without Market, Art without Education: Political Economy of Art." *e-flux* (2013): http://www.e-flux.com/journal/art-without-market-art-without-education-political-economy-of-art/

The Vly House. "The iTunes Business Model and its Widespread Effects." *Culture and Society.* January 28, 2011 http://www.thevlyhouse.com/2011/01/the-itunes-business-model-and-its-widespread-effects/

Wallace, K. A.. "Who Profits When You Publish?" *WWW. AAUP.org* (July-August 2008): http://www.kathwallace.com/whoprofitswallace.pdf

Warnick, Barbara. "Rhetorical Criticism of Public Discourse on the Internet: Theoretical Implications." *RSQ: Rhetoric Society Quarterly* (Volume 28, Number 4, Fall 1998)

Welsch, Wolfgang. "Richard Rorty: Philosophy beyond Argument and Truth?" from the home page of the *Institut für Philosophie*. Friedrich-Schiller-Universität Jena (22 January 1999): http://www.ifp.uni-jena.de

White, Brian. "Why Academic Jargon Thrives." Published as "Secret Passwords at the Gate of Knowledge." *The Australian* (September 23, 1992) 16: http://www.bmartin.cc/pubs/92aust09.html

Whitworth, Brian. "Reinventing Academic Publishing Online Part I: Rigor, Relevance and Practice" and "Part II: A Socio-Technical Vision." *First Monday* (Volume 14, Number 8, 3 August 2009) and (Volume 14, Number 9, September 2009)
"Full Access and Review: Applying Socio-technical Practice to Academia." http://brianwhitworth.com/Fullaccess-review-2008.pdf

with Rob Friedman. "The Challenge of Modern Academic Knowledge Exchange." SIGITE Newsletter (Volume 5, Number 2, 2008): http://brianwhitworth.com/Rigor-SIGITEJune2008.pdf

Willinsky, John. "Proposing a Knowledge Exchange Model for Scholarly Publishing." *Current Issues in Education* (Volume 3, Number 6, 2000): http://cie.asu.edu/volume3/number6/

"The Nine Flavours of Open Access Scholarly Publishing."*Journal of Postgraduate Medicine* (Volume 49, Issue 3, 2003)

Wilson, Robin. "The Hard Numbers Behind Scholarly Publishing's Gender Gap." *The Chronicle of Higher Education*. October 22, 2012: http://chronicle.com/article/The-Hard-Numbers-Behind/135236/

Worstall, Tom. "The Coming Collapse of the Academic Publishing Model." http://www.forbes.com/sites/timworstall/2012/04/10/the-coming-collapse-of-the-academic-publishing-model/

Yeats, William Butler. "The Second Coming." Published in *Michael Robartes and the Dancer* (Churchtown, Dundrum, Ireland: The Chuala Press, 1920)

Zeitlyn, David. "Research Note. Gift Economics in the Development of Open Source Software: Anthropological Reflections." *Research Policy* 32

(2003):
http://www.idi.ntnu.no/grupper/su/bibliography/pdf/newoyvh/zeitlyn2003.pdf

Zemsky, Robert, Senior Editor. "To Publish and Perish." *Policy Perspectives* (Special Issue, Volume 7, Number 4, March 1998):
http://www.arl.org/storage/documents/publications/to-publish-and-perish-mar98.pdf

www.ingramcontent.com/pod-product-compliance
Lightning Source LLC
Chambersburg PA
CBHW051801170526
45167CB00005B/1829